Your Child's Success Begins with You

Your Child's Success Begins with You

Getting It Right from Birth to Age Five

~~~

Jack Raskin, M.D.

Marmot Publishing

Endicott, Wash.

Your Child's Success Begins with You:
Getting It Right from Birth to Age Five
by
Jack Raskin, M.D.

Published by

4652 Union Flat Creek Road
Endicott, WA 99125
www.marmotpublishing.com
sales@marmotpublishing.com

Copyright © 2005 by Jack Raskin, M.D.

First printing, October 2005

All rights reserved. No part of this book may be reproduced, translated, stored in a retrieval system, or transmitted, in any form or by any means, electronic or mechanical, including photocopying, microfilming, or recording, without permission in writing from the publisher.

ISBN 0-9641263-2-X

Library of Congress Control Number: 2005929503

Printed in the United States of America

About the Author

Doctor Jack Raskin received his medical degree from Albert Einstein College of Medicine and has been a child psychiatrist for nearly forty years. Although he has worked with people of all ages, his special interest has been in children from birth to age five. He served a low-income community in New York City and was in charge of an intake clinic at one of the largest centers in the region. He encountered an entirely different population when, as a lieutenant colonel in the U.S. Army, he became the director of child services at Madigan Army Medical Center in Tacoma, Washington.

After completing his time in the army, he became associate director of behavioral sciences, and then director of clinical services, at Children's Hospital in Seattle. In those roles he provided psychiatric services to children in the community as well as those stricken with various physical illnesses. He was in charge of many programs, including those for child abuse, autism, and the screening of all children entering into the behavioral sciences department of Children's Hospital. He was also a consultant to a variety of other programs.

As an associate professor of psychiatry and pediatrics at the University of Washington he played an integral part in the teaching programs of young doctors, nurses, and other professionals who were involved with children. Throughout the years he has presented numerous seminars about children's issues and has participated in panel discussions. Doctor Raskin has appeared on radio and television programs in the Seattle area and has written several articles for magazines and newspapers. He resides with his family in Washington state.

CONTENTS

PREFACE	Thinking Ahead – The Key to Good Parenting	xix
ABOUT THIS BOOK		xxiii

PART ONE

BASIC CONCEPTS

CHAPTER 1	The Importance of Parenting During the First Five Years	3
CHAPTER 2	The Meaning of Personality, or Character, and Its Early Foundation	5
CHAPTER 3	The Common Denominator of Good Parenting – Supplying Children with the Essential Ingredients – Love and Reasonable Care	9
CHAPTER 4	The Concept of Developmental Hurdles	12
CHAPTER 5	Emotional Blisters and the Second Time Around	18
CHAPTER 6	Perceptual Distortion – A Concept Needed to Understand the Meaning of Children's Behavior	23
CHAPTER 7	Making Sense of Children's Behavior	27
CHAPTER 8	The Real Meaning of Discipline	29

CHAPTER 9   The Important Link Between the Correction of Distorted Perceptions and Effective Discipline   31

CHAPTER 10 The Many Forms of Love – The Meaning of Indulgence   34

CHAPTER 11 Summary   40

PART TWO

LEARNING TO BE A PERSON – THE FIRST LOVE

BIRTH TO EIGHT MONTHS

SECTION ONE – Learning to Be a Person – The Task and Its Importance

CHAPTER 1   The Importance of the First Love   46

CHAPTER 2   The Infant as a Teacher   49

SECTION TWO – Understanding What Needs to Be Done

CHAPTER 3   Supplying the Essential Ingredients   54

CHAPTER 4   A Daily Reminder of the Importance of Love   56

CHAPTER 5   Impaired Bonding – A Deficiency of Early Love   58

SECTION THREE – Understanding the Meaning of Children's Behavior During the First Developmental Phase and Its Management

CHAPTER 6   Crying During Infancy – Its Meaning and Management   62

Warning! Watch Out for Emotional Blisters

Concerns about Spoiling During Infancy
The Danger of "Crying It Out"
Crying That Does Not Stop
A Parent Who Loved Crying, but Hated Crying That Did Not Stop

CHAPTER 7 Pacifiers of All Kinds – Their Meaning and Management   70
What Are Pacifiers?
The Ideal Pacifier for Infants – Loving Parents
Feeding – Man Does Not Live by Bread Alone
Pacifiers – The Inert Variety
A Brief Review of the Steps Required for Good Parenting – Pacifier Use
An Example of Good Decision Making – Abe and the Pacifier
An Example of a Parenting Decision Made with Little Understanding of Their Child's Developmental Needs – Elliot and the Pacifier

CHAPTER 8 Each Child Is Unique – Inborn Differences   78
Is There Something Wrong with My Child?
The Fear of a Defect Causes a Defect – Is There Something Wrong with Nancy?

CHAPTER 9 Giving a Helping Hand – The Role of the Other Parent   84
Coping with Emotional Blisters – A Brief Review

CHAPTER 10 Depression – A Common Emotional Blister   88

CHAPTER 11 Early Separations – Vacations and Other Times Away from the Child – The First Six Months   91
Guidelines for Separations During Infancy

CHAPTER 12 An Early Return to Work?   95
    The One-Mother Rule
    Understanding the Child's Point of View
    Substitute Care – Weighing the Alternatives
    The Least-Bad Alternative
    What about Larger Child Care Settings?
    Three Strikes and You're Out
    Sound Decisions Are Based on Knowledge and Reason
    The Hidden Message Transmitted in an Early Return to Work
    A Job Worth Doing Well
    Guidelines for Working Parents

CHAPTER 13 Summary – Bonding – The Foundation of a Stable Personality   108

PART THREE

LEARNING TO BE A SEPARATE PERSON – BASIC TRUST

ONE YEAR TO THREE YEARS

SECTION ONE – Learning to Be a Separate Person – The Task and Its Importance

CHAPTER 1   In the Still of the Night – The Terror of Being Alone   114

CHAPTER 2   Learning to Be Alone – The Task and Its Importance   116

CHAPTER 3   Understanding What Needs to Be Done   119

SECTION TWO – Understanding the Meaning of Children's Behavior During This Period

Chapter 4 Separation Anxiety – Facing Being Alone for the First Time ... 124
   The First Loss

Chapter 5 Identifying the Signs of Separation Anxiety ... 126
   Nighttime Awakening
   Stranger Anxiety
   Changes in Appetite or Feeding Times
   Changes of Mood or Disposition

Chapter 6 The Absence of Separation Anxiety ... 130

SECTION THREE – Getting the Job Done

Chapter 7 Learning That Out of Sight Does Not Mean Gone Forever ... 134

Chapter 8 Beginning on the Path Towards Secure Trust ... 135

Chapter 9 Finding the Best Balance Between Frustration and Gratification ... 137
   Separation Anxiety and Emotional Blisters

Chapter 10 Strategies for Nighttime Awakening ... 144
   Preparations for Sleep
   The Nighttime Bottle
   Settling Down
   The Cry In the Middle of the Night – Guidelines

Chapter 11 Manipulation? ... 152

Chapter 12 Nighttime Awakening and Other Signs of Separation in Older Children ... 154

CHAPTER 13 Daytime Strategies That Help to Master Separation Anxiety   156

CHAPTER 14 A Brief Review of Parenting   162

CHAPTER 15 Pacifiers and Separation Anxiety – Thumb Sucking and Security Blankets   163

   Thumb Sucking and the Concept of a Longitudinal Assessment of Our Child's Progress

   Security Blankets and Other Soft Fuzzy Things

CHAPTER 16 Separations of All Kinds   172

   Baby-Sitters and Other Types of Substitute Care

   The Child's Clock Is Not the Same as Ours

CHAPTER 17 A Return to Work?   177

   Understanding – A Requirement for Making Good Parenting Decisions

   When Substitute Care Is a Must

   Substitute Child Care after Age Three

CHAPTER 18 Divorce   185

   The Child's Perception of Divorce

   Guidelines to Mute the Damage of Divorce

   Decisions – Decisions – Decisions

   Dividing Children's Loyalties

   Telling the Truth

   Continuing Dialogue – A Prescription for Better Communication

   Distorting the Child's Role

CHAPTER 19 Summary – Building Trust – Learning to Be Alone   206

PART FOUR

LEARNING TO BE A PERSON CAPABLE OF REASONABLE BEHAVIOR – THE THIRD DEVELOPMENTAL HURDLE

ONE-AND-ONE-HALF YEARS TO FOUR YEARS

SECTION ONE – Learning to Be a Person Capable of Reasonable Behavior – The Task and Its Importance

CHAPTER 1 The Terrible Twos   212

SECTION TWO – Understanding the Meaning of Children's Behavior During This Developmental Phase – Learning to Get Along When You Don't Get Your Way

CHAPTER 2 Making Sense of This Period of Development   218
Avoiding Stereotyping

CHAPTER 3 The Two Themes of the Third Developmental Hurdle – Impulse Gratification and Perception Distortion   220
Impulse Gratification – The First Theme
Perception Distortion – The Section Theme

SECTION THREE – Understanding the Goals of the Third Developmental Hurdle – Learning to Get Along When You Don't Get Your Way

CHAPTER 4 Maturity versus Obedience   224
CHAPTER 5 Clarification of Important Concepts   225
Discipline

The Difference Between Surface Behavior and
Character Formation

The Difference Between Discipline and Punishment

Self-Esteem

Goals – The Third Developmental Hurdle

SECTION FOUR – Getting the Job Done – The Mastery of the Third Developmental Hurdle – Learning to Get Along When You Don't Get Your Way

CHAPTER 6   Assessing and Accepting Age-Appropriate Behavior   236

Children's Responses to Frustration

CHAPTER 7   Behavior That Is Not Age-Appropriate   239

What Does It Mean and What Should Be Done?

CHAPTER 8   The Basic Concepts Underlying All Effective Discipline   241

Learning to Tolerate Frustration

Emotional Blisters – The Enemy of Reason and Love

CHAPTER 9   Parental Attitudes, Feelings, and Values   251

A Key Element in the Successful Negotiation of This Development Hurdle

CHAPTER 10   A Developmental Review of the Progression Leading to Mature Self-Control   256

The Role of Approval and Disapproval in the Acquisition of Mature Self-Control

Consistency – Not Always a Formula for Successful Parenting

CHAPTER 11   The Little Details about Discipline That Parents Always Want to Know – Answering the "What Do I Do Now?" Questions   262

Keeping Confrontations to a Minimum

Sometimes It Is "Necessary"

Substitution and Distraction – Another Approach for Younger Children

"When Then" – A Reasonable Way to Encourage Compliance

Learning to Do Nothing Constructively – Another Technique to Avoid Confrontations

The Difference Between Removal and Isolation

What about Spanking?

CHAPTER 12 Summary   285

Learning to Get Along When You Don't Get Your Way – Self-Control

PART FIVE

BECOMING AN AUTONOMOUSLY FUNCTIONING PERSON

ONE-AND-ONE-HALF YEARS TO FOUR YEARS

SECTION ONE – Becoming an Autonomously Functioning Person – The Task and Its Importance

CHAPTER 1   A Battle of Wills   290

CHAPTER 2   Becoming a Self – What Does This Really Mean?   293

SECTION TWO – Understanding the Meaning of Children's Behavior During Their Struggle for Autonomy and Its Management

CHAPTER 3   The Difference Between Being Appropriately Assertive and Being "Strong Willed"   298

CHAPTER 4 The Two Tasks of Parenting – Caring and Letting Go 300

CHAPTER 5 Surrendering Ownership of Our Child's Mobility 303
   Making Sense of the Mobility of the Two-Year-Old
   Protective Facilitation versus Constrictive Protection
   Whose Play? The Child's or the Parents'?
   Constructive Supervision

CHAPTER 6 Surrendering Ownership of Our Children's Bodies 312
   Battle for the Ownership of Our Child's Tummy
   Avoiding the Battle over Toilet Training

CHAPTER 7 Surrendering Ownership of Our Children's
   Thoughts and Feelings 323
   Naughty Language
   The Expression of Anger
   Moving Up the Developmental Ladder – Encouraging
      More Mature Methods of Expression

CHAPTER 8 Summary – The Development of Autonomy 335

PART SIX

LEARNING TO BE A PERSON IN THE OUTSIDE WORLD
OF PEOPLE – ACQUIRING A SOCIAL IDENTITY

THREE YEARS TO FIVE YEARS

SECTION ONE – Acquiring a Social Identity – New Rules – The Task and Its Importance

CHAPTER 1   Entry into the World Outside the Home 340

SECTION TWO – Understanding the Meaning of Children's Behavior During This Period

Boundaries – Learning to Think about Others and about What Others Think of Us 343

CHAPTER 2   A Review of Earlier Boundaries 345

CHAPTER 3   New Boundaries – When and How 347

CHAPTER 4   Accepting the Changing Packaging of Love Another Boundary 351

CHAPTER 5   Boundaries, Structure, and Self-Control 355

SECTION THREE – Getting the Job Done

CHAPTER 6   Becoming Little Boys and Girls – Sexual Identity 362
Sex Education
Talking to Our Children
Sexual Behavior – Its Meaning and Management

CHAPTER 7	Responsibilities – New Roles to Learn	375
CHAPTER 8	The Management of Fighting and Wild Play	379
CHAPTER 9	Getting Ready in the Morning – Adapting to Schedules	387
CHAPTER 10	Getting a Head Start for Entry into School	391
CHAPTER 11	The Role of Play	398
CHAPTER 12	Imaginary Fears – New Roles Are Often Accompanied by New Problems	404
CHAPTER 13	Learning Values Lying – Stealing – Cheating	411
CHAPTER 14	Television and Little Children	416
CHAPTER 15	Summary – Acquiring a Social Identity – Moving Forward	421

Preface

THINKING AHEAD – THE KEY TO GOOD PARENTING

I have always enjoyed being with children. Many of my moments of greatest joy have been those spent with children, my own and those that I have had the privilege of meeting during my forty-year career as a child psychiatrist. Most parents agree that children are often a source of joy. Too often, however, they disagree with my next comments. **Children are easy. Children are easy to understand, easy to be with, and easy to help.** There is no reason that our precious little ones should ever be a source of stress to us. But I have heard repeatedly from parents in my office and from friends, that they often find parenting very difficult.

What accounts for this disparity? In every facet of life, mastery and finally pleasure and grace of performance require the acquisition of knowledge. Every thing is hard until we know what is needed for success. Children are easy for me because there is nothing they do that requires more than a small fraction of the effort or mental acumen that I must expend on most other endeavors. Unfortunately, most parents are not armed with the knowledge about children and parenting that makes the task easy and nearly always pleasurable.

The purpose of this book is to provide you with that foundation of knowledge. It will help you to understand the bewildering and too often stress-producing array of behavior that kids show as they move from one growing-up problem to another. Most material about children focuses on what parents need to do. This book will help you to understand what is happening in your children's minds as they progress from one developmental stage to another. It will help to free you from misconceptions and the accompanying emotional responses that are jarring to you and harmful to your children.

The information is not aimed at giving you a cookbook recipe for parenting. Indeed, there is none. Its purpose is to give you knowledge that will free you to be more in harmony with the inevitable upheavals that are a part of every child's life. The book was written to help you to tap into your own wisdom and creativity so that you will be more adept at finding your own sensible and loving solutions to the everyday stuff that being with our kids is all about. We all want to raise children who will have the tools and values needed for them to function successfully as adults. Armed with the knowledge contained in this book, that path will be easier to follow.

An often-repeated cliché is that we don't get any training for parenthood until it's too late. I have found in my own life, and in my work with parents and children, that an understanding of our children's unfolding development helps us to get it right the first time. The moments in our children's lives pass so quickly and are forever gone. As important as they may be, we are not able to relive them with the benefit of the knowledge accrued from the mistakes made during that first and only run. When an activity is important enough to get right the first time, it deserves some serious thought before it is undertaken and while it is unfolding. Is there any activity that we will tackle in our lives that is more important than raising our children so that they will be sound, happy, and well functioning adults? A better understanding of what the task entails provides us with needed skills, a higher comfort level, and a greater capacity to appreciate and enjoy the journey.

The best approach to parenting problems should always begin with a question that is rarely asked by most parents. Faced with any of the usual daily confrontations with their kids, the typical question parents always ask themselves as well as others is, "What do I do?" An important goal of this book is to suggest another question that needs to be asked first. That question is, "What does it mean?" Asking this question allows us to pause for a moment and consider what is happening within our precious little children's minds when they make noises and engage in behaviors that are bewildering and frustrating. In all endeavors it is essential to know *what* before we can decide *how*. Unless we know the meaning of what we are observing any attempt to fix it will likely be flawed. Parents use this reasoned approach in most facets of their lives but will often discard it for a shoot-first-and-think-later response with their children. The parents I have counseled nearly always feel an urgent need to "know what to do." Without an understanding of the meaning of their child's behavior, and of their short and long term goals, they lack the flexibility and confidence that successful and stress-free parenting requires.

I have always been very pleased when parents have been far-thinking enough to express concerns about what may lie ahead for their very young child. I tell them how fortunate it is that they have asked that question when it counts – during the first years of their child's life. This is the time when they have it within their power to guarantee a favorable outcome. Waiting just a few more years is often too late, and by adolescence it may be beyond remedy.

I was motivated to write this book because of the dramatic and gratifying changes I saw in families when they began to make sense of their child's behavior. Every day, I encountered stressed and confused parents responding inappropriately to behavior that was a normal part of development. Understanding the behavior made quite a difference, and parents would return confidently reporting that the problem that had knocked them off balance was on the mend. These gains were rapid because the problems encountered during this early period were nearly always transient and a by-product of normal developmental stresses. When the parents were better informed, they were able to provide a home setting that fostered progress. I have been particularly interested in children in their first five years and have rarely seen kids in that age group who I thought had serious problems. The serious problems gradually emerged when confused parents became part of the problem rather than its solution.

I sometimes hear glowing stories from parents who had been pessimistic about their child's future when they entered my office for the first time. The moment I heard that their child was in the under-five-years age range I smiled silently, very optimistic about a favorable outcome. Timely information made all the difference. This book supplies that information. With it, parents will be much more adept at responding with confidence and comfort to any of the issues that arise during the first five years of life.

Following the introduction, I have used a fictitious family comprised of Dan, his mother Sally, and father Bob, to illustrate important concepts and principles of good parenting. The problems they face and solve as they progress from birth until Dan begins his first day at school are real and typical of those of the many parents I encountered daily in my office. Sally, Dan's mother is exceptionally insightful, but of course she has the benefit of me standing behind her and whispering advice. She usually achieves a level of wisdom and goodness that can never be entirely emulated in real life. I have told parents that it is useful to attempt to paint a picture of the ideal since it is our best guide to good parenting. I also emphasize that our children do not need us to be up to the standards achieved by Dan's mother Sally. They only need parents who love them and try to use understanding to guide to their actions. This book provides that understanding.

About This Book

Part One of *Your Child's Success Begins with You* contains a series of chapters describing the essential concepts that are used repeatedly throughout the book. These are concepts that delineate the important principles of parenting.

The rest of the book is divided into an additional five sections that correspond to the sequence of developmental problems that children face from birth to age five. Helping their kids to master these tasks is the most important goal of parenting. As children struggle with these requirements for growing up, behavior is generated that parents find confusing and stressful. Each part of the book addresses one of these problems and corresponds to a typical span of time. The parts are divided into sections in a sequence that coincides with the steps parents should take to be confident of a good outcome. Knowledge of the task that provides an understanding of the meaning of their child's behavior comes first, followed by a description of the typical patterns of behavior generated by each task, and ending with the strategies parents need to know to get the job done successfully.

PART ONE

BASIC CONCEPTS

Your Child's Success Begins with You

Chapter 1

THE IMPORTANCE OF PARENTING DURING THE FIRST FIVE YEARS

Question – I have just given birth to our first child. How can we really make a difference? How can I best ensure that my child will function well as an adult, that he will like himself, and be happy?

It would be wonderful if all parents asked this question prior to the birth of their children. If I could, I would recommend that the question, in written form, be slipped into the blanket of each new baby when the parents greet the child for the first time. In the midst of the hectic daily lives of most families, the important goals of parenting are nearly always overlooked. The primary goal is the gradual creation of a mature, content, and well-functioning adult. There are many things that are unclear in this world, but the formation of a stable and mature person is not one of them. **The foundation of character is built in the daily interactions between parents and their children during the first years of life.**

Without an understanding of their long-term goals, parents generally respond to their children spontaneously and with little thought. Many children are resilient and survive, even thrive, despite parenting that does not even begin to address their needs. Many parents have the knack or maturity to be on their child's wavelength. Large numbers of children are not so fortunate. The culmination of hurts they experience with parents who are out of tune with them may have undesirable long-term consequences.

The things that go wrong in later childhood, adolescence, and adulthood are not created out of the blue. Parents scratch their heads in bewilderment when they discover that their kids are not paying attention in school at age ten, and skipping school and using drugs at age fourteen. In these families, the parents' approach of "doing what came naturally," during their child's early years too often missed the target. When things go desperately wrong we like to attribute this to external factors, and there are certainly many things in the outside world that need to be addressed. In the final analysis, however, our kids' successful progress through the pains of growing up and their eventual happiness and sound functioning will depend on the stability and strength of their character.

Points to Remember

- The real goal of parenting is the creation of mature, well-functioning adults.
- The foundation for later maturity is set by the quality of parental care.
- This foundation building begins at birth.

Chapter 2

THE MEANING OF PERSONALITY, OR CHARACTER, AND ITS EARLY FOUNDATION

Question – I now appreciate the importance of the early years, when the foundation for our child's character is laid in place. Can you more clearly define the personality characteristics we are hoping to gradually instill in our child so I can keep them in mind during these busy days?

Whether we are aware of it or not, we each have a core set of values that underlies our motivations and shapes the personality characteristics that define who we are. To a large degree, these values determine the choices we will make in life. These, as well as the basic level of self-esteem that we will carry with us, are forged in the crucible of early family life. Yet this vital, irretrievable time with our young children flies by so quickly and we find ourselves suddenly faced with our once-little kids who have become people of their own. Too late we think and wonder about what might have been, we remember opportunities missed and ponder the wisdom of past attitudes and decisions.

This book addresses, in detail, the parenting required at each stage of development to build a strong character foundation. But, I emphasize repeatedly that at each step on that path it is crucial to understand the final destination. Parents must never overlook their ultimate goals. All thinking persons know intuitively what these are, but they are rarely spelled out. They are the array of characteristics evident in people we hold in highest regard. We should maintain an awareness of these goals since they are too easily forgotten or cast aside. When my children were young, I posted a list of these characteristics on the refrigerator. **This list of**

mature character values included goodness, kindness, respectfulness, wisdom, generosity, thoughtfulness, love, gratitude, usefulness, responsibility, honesty, compassion, and many others. The list grew longer as the children attained the capacity to think beyond the usual immediate concerns that preoccupied their lives and they were able to add some of their own values.

A strong foundation established during the first five years is a requirement for the later assimilation of these and other important values and attributes.

Parents cannot avoid focusing on the immediate concerns and issues that dominate their daily lives. Two important perspectives need to be added. First, parents need a vision of the future. That vision is the emergence of an individual who has incorporated basic values. Second, parents must understand the sequence of steps that will lead to the fruition of that vision. Reminding ourselves of these goals each day as we are interacting with our kids helps to avoid many missteps. It is so easy to brush them aside for the sake of the quick fix.

Question – The values you have mentioned are so obviously important to all of us. Why do we have problems teaching them to our children and making them a part of our own lives?

If it were a simple matter for intelligent and loving parents to integrate these values into their kids, there would be no reason to write this book. It turns out to be more complicated since values can't be learned the way we might, for example, learn to use the computer. The seeds that will later blossom into values require fertile soil for them to root. This is the basic foundation for character that is built very early in life. Absent that foundation, attempts to teach these important values are generally unsuccessful. During much of the time that these vital building blocks are being put into place, children are preverbal, or have just acquired language. The values that we cherish most highly are far beyond their ability to grasp, let alone begin to integrate into their character. Parents also discover, with dismay, that these values cannot be pasted on later if the foundation needed for them to adhere has not been soundly constructed. The later appreciation of good literature requires a lengthy, early educational grounding. Similarly, the later appreciation and acquisition of good values needs a solid early-developmental foundation.

This book is about that foundation. I have found that when a stable foundation has been erected, good character and mature values will nearly always follow. Children possessing that solid foundation will assimilate values as they are taught and modeled by their parents. This might have been expected. The outcome for those children who have mastered early developmental hurdles is even more favorable. These children will usually have the capacity to develop those wonderful traits of human nature, even when their parents have made no conscious effort to teach them. On the other hand, efforts to teach values at a later time will not be successful if early development has gone astray during the first five-year period.

The mastery of the sequence of developmental hurdles that this book addresses leads to a solid, stable personality foundation. The concept of such a foundation was very real to me as I observed and worked with children on a daily basis. I realize that this idea may seem nebulous to the reader. An analogy to computers may be helpful. It is clear that everything we think, every motivation and feeling we have, is taking place in the brain. At birth, there is a great deal of important hardware in place, but most of what determines how we live our lives is learned after birth. Every new bit of information that becomes a part of our thinking means that a change has taking place in the actual substance of the brain. Like the computer, the brain is being downloaded with important programs during the formative years. Unlike the computer, these programs can't be erased. They remain with us for the rest of our lives. Minor changes can be made, but these are difficult to accomplish and limited in scope.

Modern research about the brain supports this important concept. It is clear now that any new learning entails a growth of new brain connections. Genetic influences account for less than eight percent of our feelings, thoughts, and actions. Where does the rest come from? It is learned. Personality and character derives from the foundation of learning transmitted by our parents, and much of it occurs early and is nonverbal. The actual shape of the brain is changing and growing as we learn. Doesn't it make sense to get it into the best shape possible the first time around, rather than to spend a lifetime suffering or trying to fine-tune a poorly done job? Parents are helping their children get it right the first time by understanding the building blocks of maturity that need to be set into place at each stage in the developmental process. That understanding acts as a compass, helping them to use their judgment wisely at each turn in the path.

Question – You are suggesting that our parenting must be flexible and continually adjusted so that we can be in tune with the flow of our child's development? Is this why parenting so often seems confusing?

Parenting does not lend itself to simple, how-to solutions. There may be only one way to fix a car and one way to solve a mathematical problem, but there seems to be an infinite variety of ways to bring up children. Even the experts contradict one another. One expert says, "Be firm, and they will learn," another, "Show love, they need security," a third, "Help them understand." If there were only one correct way to parent, the task would be easy and the results always pleasing. Those who used the correct method would turn out great kids and the others would flop. Regardless of the method used, some children turn out well and others do not. Even more puzzling is that many of the children whose parents haven't particularly tried to learn anything about parenting do extremely well. It will be important to define the characteristics that effective parents have in common.

Points to Remember

- Our personalities are defined by our values.

- Strong values require a solid foundation, which is built during the first five years of life.

- The strength of the foundation depends upon the quality of parenting.

Chapter 3

THE COMMON DENOMINATOR OF GOOD PARENTING – SUPPLYING CHILDREN WITH THE ESSENTIAL INGREDIENTS – LOVE AND REASONABLE CARE

A common denominator can be found in parenting when the process is successful and leads to the formation of mature character traits. Parents who have learned very little about the subject often turn out good kids for a very simple reason. They have provided the essential ingredients of effective parenting: **love and reasonable care.** There are other parents who have learned a great deal, but nevertheless are deficient in this regard. Constructing a sound building requires a stable foundation so it will function well when completed. The stable foundation that needs to be instilled into children for them to do well as adults is constructed with the basic ingredients supplied to them by their parents. These ingredients remain the same at each stage of development, but their packaging must change as development progresses.

Question – Can you clarify the basic ingredients that parents need to incorporate at each stage of development and explain why they are often neglected?

I have had many friends who have questioned the need to write another book about parenting. They have repeatedly told me of their conviction that kids will do fine if parents are reasonable and loving. **They are right; love and reason are the basic ingredients of good parenting.** Parents who are sure that they are reasonable and loving with their children have no need to read on, but based upon my experience with families and with people generally, I am dubious about the capacity of most parents to achieve this goal. In fact, I have found that parents are often far less reasonable and loving with their little ones than with others in their lives. What does being reasonable and loving really mean? Is it possible to be loving and reasonable with loved ones if we are unaware of their thought processes and needs? Confusion leads to stress, which is the enemy of reason and love.

The devil is in the doing. Good intentions may suffice in some facets of life, but they frequently fall short in parenting for two reasons. First, it is never a simple matter to define "reasonable" with young children whose responses are often so unreasonable. **Reasonable from our adult point of view may be completely unreasonable when used as a guide for parenting strategies to meet the needs of very young kids.** Without an understanding of early development it is often extremely difficult to define what is reasonable.

Second, life would be more blissful if we were able to love on demand. Sadly, even many loving people often find themselves being very unloving. **Young children are especially adept at engendering unloving responses from the people who love them the most.** There are many reasons that individuals who are loving and reasonable find it difficult to be loving and reasonable with the people they may cherish most, their children. We cannot legislate being loving. The thesis of this book is that knowledge about children's ever-changing development helps to diminish the stress and confusion that mutes their capacity for love. In the chapters that follow, a fuller picture of reasonable love will emerge, often using Dan, and his parents Sally and Bob, to illustrate important principles.

POINTS TO REMEMBER

- All children need love and care.
- In spite of good intentions, many parents fall short for two reasons:
    a. Inadequate knowledge about their children's needs early in their lives
    b. The emotional unrest and confusion often engendered in them by their young children
- This book supplies the knowledge and methods needed to reduce the stress of parenting.

Chapter 4

THE CONCEPT OF DEVELOPMENTAL HURDLES

Question – Children are often hard to understand and frustrating to be with. Everyone seems to have a different theory about parenting. How am I to find my way?

Understanding the developmental process that accounts for their children's behavior allows parents to respond appropriately. Parents are then able to shift their approach so that it coincides with their child's continuously changing needs.

In all endeavors, our skill level increases as we acquire more knowledge. I have found that the body of knowledge that is most essential for parenting is the series of developmental hurdles that each child encounters as he moves from infancy to adulthood. These are not terribly complicated or difficult to learn. Knowledge of the specific phases of your children's development will allow you to make sense of the array of behavior they display as they struggle with each hurdle. It will help you to give them the basic ingredients needed at each step to master these problems. This information is widely known, but has not been disseminated to the people who need it most – parents. Too often, parents are told what to do without any explanation or rationale based on an understanding of the underlying developmental problem. This is like a physician prescribing medication without first accurately diagnosing the illness.

Understanding development is essential since our children's lives are not static. Children change from day to day and each child is unique. In addition, the problems they are tackling shift with increasing age, as do the skills they bring to these problems. Parents are often advised to "just be consistent," but if they are incorrect in their approaches and they are consistent, they will be consistently wrong.

Knowledge about children removes much of the confusion and stress from parenting, making it manageable and far less hectic. There are a series of developmental hurdles that all children face as they progress towards maturity. These are reliable signposts that can guide parents more accurately than the cookbook strategies that are geared to superficial manifestations of behavior.

Without this information about development and children's changing needs, parents frequently hang on to their favorite parenting ploys after they are no longer applicable when their child has moved on to another developmental problem. Holding or placating a crying one-year-old may make sense, but may be counterproductive for the three-year-old. An understanding of the series of developmental problems children face, and the typical behavior that these elicit, allow parents to shift approaches to dovetail with their children's changing needs. Details about these developmental phases that must be successfully negotiated to achieve maturity will be described in the following chapters.

Question – What does the mastery of developmental problems have to do with what my child will be like later in life?

The process that unfolds as children struggle with a series of developmental hurdles will determine the personality skills and other attributes that define character. A brief description of one developmental problem may shed light on how this happens.

A common form of malaise and discontent is the feeling of being alone. Often this feeling evolves into, "if onlys." "If only" I got more approval and attention, then my feelings of emptiness and loneliness would evaporate and I would finally feel better about myself. "If only" I was more attractive and successful, "if only" my wife loved me more, and on and on. The endless fantasy of "if onlys" is generated by the belief that their fulfillment offers the cure for the terrible feeling of being alone that haunts the lives of so many adults. They are sadly mistaken about this.

Feelings of being alone are not confined to people who lack the attention, approval, love, and other emotional and material things that most people covet. They can be found in the most popular and attractive as well as the least, and in the richest as well as the poorest. Even those who seem to have more than an ample share of approval and love from others fall prey to this malady.

This type of suffering is not born anew into the life of an adult. It can usually be easily traced back to developmental hurdles not successfully mastered early in life. Being separated from loved ones is a fact of life that all children are compelled to confront during the first two years of their lives. Children who get the basic ingredients they need from their parents are able to negotiate this hurdle, and gradually learn to cope with being alone.

This is never easy. As children face the problem of being alone for the first few times, they feel tremendous fear and helplessness and show this in a variety of ways. Resisting separation (especially at bedtime), nighttime awakening, demanding immediate attention, and a heightened intolerance of unfamiliar faces are symptoms that they are struggling with this universal problem. To a large degree, the mastery of this developmental hurdle will depend upon the quality of the parents' daily interactions with their children during this time.

Unfortunately, too often the outcome of this important process is less than ideal. There are many adults who perceive and react to separation and being alone as they did when they were dependent and helpless children. The years have passed. They are now grown up and may have developed many skills and abilities. But in this one important area of their lives, they are crippled. They continue to experience a problem that should have been solved when they were very young. In addition, the very infantile, often pathetic methods they used to deal with being alone when they were age one or two are the only ones available to them as adults. They continue to long for the satisfaction of the "if onlys" that will free them from their misery.

Ellen, for example, at twenty-two, withdraws, remaining in her home and wanting to sleep whenever she experiences disapproval or when she interprets a friend's behavior as a rebuff or rejection. Home alone, she thinks, "If only people really liked me."

Another example is a man who finds it hard to control his anger and on a number of occasions has physically abused his wife, because he feels excluded and unloved when she "spends too much time" talking to her friends on the phone. "If only she loved me more," he says to himself as his anger mounts.

We are all familiar with many of the other maladaptive patterns of behavior that are set into motion by the fear of being alone. These behavior patterns begin in childhood and continue into adulthood. We have seen them in family members as well as in friends. If we look, we will always see at least a bit of them in ourselves. Those who are more profoundly affected by this unresolved problem are often extremely unhappy, some are severely depressed. Often, they seek relief in drugs or alcohol. They long for praise and adoration and their image of themselves is overwhelmingly steered by the perceived opinions of others. They are at the mercy of even subtle rejections, and their lives become a roller coaster of emotional upheavals. **These problems all have their roots in an early developmental hurdle that was not successfully mastered.**

There are three undesirable consequences of our children's inadequate solution of the problem of being alone, and the other developmental hurdles that they will face as they grow up. First, the problem continues to be a source of discomfort, long past the point in the child's life when the problem should have been solved. For example, he may be plagued by loneliness into adulthood. Second, the child, unable to master the problem will resort to maladaptive ways of coping and these become part of his personality. For example, childlike patterns of clinging and a need for reassurance persist in individuals who have carried their fear of being alone into adulthood. Lastly, when a developmental hurdle is not successfully negotiated, it becomes more difficult for children to master subsequent hurdles. It should now be apparent why early problems are more damaging than later ones. They have a greater cumulative effect.

Question – I can now better appreciate the link between early development and the acquisition of personality skills and attributes. But how will this information about the early developmental hurdles that children must face actually help me with my own kids?

Without this knowledge, we are far more likely to miss opportunities to help our kids master developmental hurdles. I have found in my practice of child psychiatry, and in my personal life, that understanding the meaning of our kids' behavior is usually helpful and at times crucial. Knowledge helps because it is always easier to figure out what to do when we know what we are trying to accomplish. This is true in all of our activities, but of even more importance when we are involved with our children. Imagine trying to fix a car, knowing nothing about how the engine works, or a physician tackling a surgical procedure without any real understanding of what he is going to do. We would not be reassured if their response to our query about what they were trying to accomplish was, "I don't really know what's going on, but I sure want to fix it." That's often our mind set when we are facing our kids' problems.

There is no way to avoid or wish away the provocative and irritating behavior that children display. **The behavior means that they are struggling with a developmental problem.** To the harassed parent, it may seem more like a cunning plot devised to drive them crazy. At these times, a bit of knowledge about what the little guy is up to can save the day. Redirecting and even accepting the exuberant, boisterous behavior of a two-year-old, instead of restraining or spanking, may be time consuming and frustrating. But if this type of investment enhances self-esteem and a stronger sense of autonomy, it is well worth making.

Being prepared for what lies ahead is essential when your three-year-old has been able to make you feel that in the battle of wills, he will come out the winner. I might remind the reader of how high the stakes are in possessing the know-how to get it right, by pointing out the long-term consequences of repeatedly missing the target with this three-year-old. Years pass and the developmental problems, as well as resulting behaviors, remain unchanged. As unattractive as it is to face a three-year-old venting anger and hate, the picture of your kid, now age fourteen and as big as you, doing the same is even scarier.

POINTS TO REMEMBER

- Children's behavior is often confusing and stressful to parents.
- At each age, children struggle with specific problems that account for their behavior.
- Parents who understand these problems and the typical behavior engendered by them, and those who apply appropriate parenting techniques, will be more likely to be successful.

Chapter 5

EMOTIONAL BLISTERS AND THE SECOND TIME AROUND

Making sense of the stress of parenting

Question – Why does my child's behavior make me so stressed and what can I do about this? Why is it that I can tackle complicated tasks and remain cool, but my very sweet little girl is able to set me off?

Parents are often stressed by their children's behavior. They experience a variety of uncomfortable feelings, including anger, anxiety, frustration, and guilt that erode their capacity to love and interfere with effective parenting. I will be using the term *emotional blisters* to designate these feelings. An example will clarify what they are and how they operate.

There was a look of fatigue and fear in the facial expression of one young mother who began talking about her child. "I'm becoming afraid of him. I feel that he rules me. There is nothing I can do to control him and I've tried everything. I'm exhausted and ready to give up. Do you have a drug for him?"

As I listened to this parents' words, I visualized a hulking, weightlifting sixteen-year-old who was terrorizing the family. That image was corrected when there was a knock on the door and a cute little three-year-old boy, pulling his blanket behind him, walked into my office to be with his mother because he was afraid of being alone. This mother had become overwhelmed, angry, and out of control because her three-year-old had irritated her emotional blisters. I will be addressing parental emotional blisters repeatedly, since they are one of the main obstacles to effective parenting.

Question – Why are we able to cope well in situations that are far more difficult to manage than this, but confused and upset so quickly when we are with the people we love most? What causes our emotional blisters?

Children, through their behavior, are communicating extremely upsetting emotional messages: *I'm afraid of being alone, of being helpless. I'm afraid that I will never see you again; I hate you.* These messages can have an enormous impact and bring to the surface our own fears of being alone and helpless and make us angry. In addition, many parents are frustrated when their children repeatedly refuse to comply with their wishes.

As adults, we have all grown up in years, but continue to carry with us some of the feelings, sensitivities, and responses that we had during our first time around – our own childhood. The reason for this is that none of us completely resolved the developmental problems we faced during that early time. Our children's behavior makes us feel uncomfortable because it brings to the surface those old feelings. They are stomping on our emotional blisters.

It should not be a surprise that delightful little kids are routinely described by their parents with adjectives including, "overwhelming, exhausting, monstrous, malicious demons," and even, "he is out to get me." There is nothing inherently nightmarish about the crying, whining, or bickering of our little kids. In theory, the efforts needed to respond wisely and calmly are no greater than those made successfully by parents in many other facets of their lives on a daily basis. **The element that makes the noises and behavior of their kids so disconcerting to parents is that it brings to the surface an echo of earlier pain and hurt.** Whining, screaming, rage, and refusing to quiet down are so stressful to us because of those painful emotional blisters.

Painful emotional blisters end up causing more lasting pain for the kids than their parents. This is because they often generate responses by parents that stand in the way of children getting the basic ingredients they need to master developmental hurdles. **It is hard to be loving and reasonable when you are stressed or very angry.** The myriad of emotional messages received by children from their parents on a daily basis are what mold character. Painful emotional blisters cause a deterioration of the quality of the messages. They prod parents to act impulsively to stop the hurt. The messages transmitted to their kids when parents act impulsively may communicate something such as this dramatized version: "I need you to change and not cry anymore. When the crying goes on and on, it makes me feel the way I did during my first time around; it makes me feel unloved, worthless, and helpless. Change, stop crying, I need you to be happy so that I will feel better and be able to love you again. If you don't and my blisters continue to ache, I will hate you and do whatever is necessary to stop your noise." These types of messages can be devastating when conveyed over and over again to a very young child. On a very powerful emotional level, they are saying that, "there is something very bad and unlovable about you that has made me suffer and hate you." When these messages become the child's image, the result is ominous.

If parents have these old blisters under control, or if they are mild, the stress level may be manageable and not interfere too much with adequate parenting. When kids' behavior strike more sensitive emotional blisters, the stress and confusion may drastically interfere with adequate parenting. **The cause of serious child abuse should now be clear – exquisitely painful emotional blisters.** It should also now be clear how good intentions to be loving and reasonable might become diverted by the power of painful emotional blisters.

Laura was a twenty-six-year-old woman who had been physically abusive to her eight-month-old child. Laura had been unhappy most of her life. She longed for closeness with others, but experienced a sense of futility about this. She had a pleasant demeanor, but was sure that there was something grotesque and utterly unlikable about her that would repulse others. Many people liked her at first, but she was always certain that this would not last. Minor disappointments would support her conviction that she was disliked and she would withdraw in anger. Her fears of being disliked and abandoned became a self-fulfilling prophesy.

When she became pregnant with her little girl, Sarah, she was delighted, believing that she would finally have someone to love and who would love her. She did fine when Sarah responded favorably to her care and adoration. But like all children, Sarah would often cry and be hard to console. Laura's painful blisters made these times intolerable. She felt desperate and then angry that her own child had joined the ranks of all the others that had cast her aside. Laura sometimes tried to stop the crying in any way she could. This included the infliction of both emotional and physical pain on Sarah. The painful emotional blisters were causing Laura to suffer. They were also causing her to destroy her daughter's life.

Emotional blisters are the primary cause of stress during parenting and the most significant obstacle to good parenting. Emotional blisters lead to discomfort and confusion that are the enemies of sound functioning.

The rule of comfort – The reduction of stress

The greatest threat to good parenting is the distress from emotional blisters. Parents who are comfortable with their kids are nearly always able to provide the basic ingredients of love and reasonable care. Theoretically, it should not be hard to be happy, calm, and content when we are with our children. Parenting is, after all, an act of love given to those who are most precious to us. Being with our children, watching and helping them develop, should be the moments in our lives that we most cherish. In many families this is the exception rather than the rule. As children struggle with their developmental problems, they invariably stomp on our emotional blisters. Is there any way of keeping our emotional blisters under control?

I have found that the most effective method of dispelling the stress and chaos of parenting is the acquisition of knowledge about the meaning of our child's distress as well as our own. Understanding can be a powerful ally, clarifying what needs to be done, helping to restore confidence, and reducing stress. It is always easier to respond comfortably to loved ones when we understand what is actually on their minds, rather than having confusion rule our feelings.

We function well when we feel comfortable with what we are doing. The star quarterback begins to falter and the adept salesperson loses his touch when their confidence and comfort begin to ebb. There is a correlation between the effectiveness of parents and their comfort in this role.

POINTS TO REMEMBER

- The basic principles of parenting are simple – be loving and reasonable.

- It's hard to be loving and reasonable when stressed or angry, and kids are very good at making their parents stressed or angry.

- The best remedy is to understand the meaning of children's behavior and know what needs to be done.

- Confidence in parenting principles will lead to comfort in their application.

Chapter 6

PERCEPTUAL DISTORTION – A CONCEPT NEEDED TO UNDERSTAND THE MEANING OF CHILDREN'S BEHAVIOR

Question – Why do young children continually do and say things that don't make sense?

You will often be mistaken if you assume that your children's perceptions of daily events are the same as yours. Many of the problems we have with our children, and with other adults as well, are caused by our tendency to believe that others think as we do. Your children's perceptions and thoughts are dramatically distorted by their immaturity, the particular developmental hurdles with which they are struggling, and the powerful feelings that are unleashed by this struggle. Unless you are cognizant of this and attempt to understand the tenor of their thinking, your ability to influence them constructively will be dramatically impeded.

An important goal of successful parenting is to help children overcome developmental hurdles so that they can gradually perceive the world more realistically. When you put your children to sleep, you are not abandoning them. When you don't provide them with immediate gratification, it does not actually mean that you are being evil and deserve to be punished. These common misperceptions need to be corrected. Here is where emotional blisters enter the picture. You will not be able to help your kids to learn to correct their distorted perceptions of your behavior if you are continually misperceiving and distorting the meaning of theirs. Understanding the real meaning of our children's behavior helps to free us from the impact of emotional blisters, making it easier to respond constructively.

John was a ten-year-old boy who didn't want to go to school. This confused and irritated his parents since he was a bright, capable lad who liked other kids. The explanation was simple and based on his distorted perceptions. He was able to confide in me that when he was away from home, he was afraid that there could be a war or a fire and he would never see his parents again. Many young children, when tucked into bed, refuse to comply with a gentle request for them to stay in their bed, close their eyes, and go to sleep. Parents become confused and impatient when their children's protests become louder and more insistent. From the parents' perspective, the kid is being "manipulative and trying to get away with something." If the parents could read their children's actual thoughts they would realize that the children were terrified at the thought of being separated from their parents for what to them seems like an eternity. If the parents understood the meaning of their children's behavior at this point in their lives, they would realize that they are struggling with the problem of being alone. This knowledge would make them better equipped and prepared to help. It would also offer some protection from the mischievous influence of their emotional blisters.

We would not be able to fix a broken car if we could not clearly see the nature of the problem. Our efforts would be far from successful if we became upset when the engine did not start and we wagged an angry finger at it asking, "What right do you have to make me so miserable?" Or if we said, "Just you watch, my mother-in-law has been telling me that the best thing in the world for you is to give you a swift kick in the transmission." Our possessions, such as cars and houses, are valuable to us and we take the time and care to clearly understand a problem before we pick up a hammer or screwdriver. Are our children of less value?

Often the pain from emotional blisters, rather then a sound understanding of the problem, dictates our responses to our children. A vicious cycle unfolds. The child misperceives a situation because of his immaturity. He overreacts and his behavior is disruptive. His parents misperceive the meaning of his disruptive behavior and they overreact. Misperceptions become the order of the day and become more deeply ingrained into our child's thinking. As a result, the child doesn't obtain the ingredients he needs, developmental hurdles are not mastered, and movement towards a stable character structure is impeded.

Another example may help to clarify this important concept. A verbal ten-year-old once told me why his reaction was agitated and violent when his mother asked him to stop playing outside and come into the house for dinner. Heated confrontations at these times would sometimes require the strength of both parents to subdue this husky lad's attempts to destroy part of the house or attack a parent. His reply to my questions about his thoughts following his mother's request for him to terminate his play went something like this. "It made me feel that she hated me so much, that it was like she was throwing me off a cliff into the ocean and watching as I was eaten by sharks, and there would be nothing left but bones."

I knew the mother quite well and she was a kind and caring person. Her request that he come in for dinner obviously did not mean that she hated him. His angry outbursts were inexplicable, and upsetting to her.

We cannot make sense of his behavior and comments unless we understand how he was distorting his perception of his parents. In fact, many of his conclusions about the world and himself were influenced in a similar manner. Needless to say the behavior resulting from these distorted perceptions did not help him to win friends and adjust in school.

Another child, Jenny, age six, said, "When my mommy talks on the phone and won't answer me, it makes me feel like I'm a slobby pig. Sometimes it makes me feel that she does not see me and I'm not there anymore and I get scared."

Jenny was a frightened little girl who needed a great deal of reassurance that she was loved. Her perceptions of herself and her mother became dramatically distorted when her mother's attention was elsewhere. Jenny needed help to master the developmental hurdle that caused her problem. Unfortunately, Jenny's mother had very painful emotional blisters. They made her fall into the same trap as her child, and she distorted the meaning of Jenny's behavior. As far as she was concerned, Jenny had become a hassle and a bother to her and she often wished that Jenny would disappear so that she could enjoy her phone conversations without the frequent interruptions. The mother's distorted view of Jenny had become the same as Jenny's own view of herself. Jenny's fear that her mother's attention to the phone meant that Jenny was unwanted was being realized, and this fear was becoming indelibly etched in her mind. Her image of herself, with her mother's help, was that she was "a slobby pig that was in the way."

Exaggerated distortions of perceptions based on feelings precipitated by developmental hurdles are characteristic of the way young children think. Most young children will believe that they are hated when they do not receive the gratification that they demand. They are certain that their own anger and desire for retribution at these times are entirely justified. Parents who are able to decode this behavior will be less confused and more competent is their parenting role.

Points to Remember

- The immature thinking and powerful feelings of young children distort their perceptions and interpretations of the world.

- This distortion accounts for their puzzling behavior.

- Parents who understand how their children think are less prone to become stressed, and are better equipped to target their children's needs.

Chapter 7

MAKING SENSE OF CHILDREN'S BEHAVIOR

Question – I understand now why so much of what my kids do is confusing to me. They are at the mercy of their distorted perceptions. Is there some way for us to be better equipped to understand their thinking so we can make more accurate assessments of the meaning of their behavior?

In order to help another person we must have some understanding about what they are thinking. The adults in our lives sometimes make this endeavor easier when they put their fears and needs into words. Preverbal children are obviously not able to do this. Parents will be disappointed if they anticipate that the development of speech will remedy this handicap. A common complaint from parents is that even their older kids won't talk about their feelings and thoughts; they often won't even answer simple questions about their behavior. This is the rule rather than the exception, and it is entirely normal. Children are too sensitive and cannot distance themselves sufficiently to converse about the things that cause them pain. Loving parents who are genuinely interested are perplexed when their queries fail to elicit meaningful information. Their confusion may deteriorate into frustration when they repeatedly face a youngster whose answer to their questions is a shrug of the shoulders, a blank stare and, "I don't know."

But children do communicate with their parents, and parents can gain a good impression about what's troubling them. This can't be done by questioning the children directly, or by attempting to converse with them as if they were another adult. Children cannot hide their inner world and it is constantly emerging in the form of behavior, words, and play. Their language is rich with meaning for the parent who has learned to listen and understand. **The key to unlocking this meaning is an understanding of the developmental hurdle that fuels the behavior.** So much of our behavior is the surface manifestation of our inner fears and desires. For example, knowing that an adult friend was preoccupied with concerns about the serious illness of a parent might allow us to have a better understanding of uncharacteristic behavior.

Children are constantly at the mercy of powerful feelings engendered by their struggles with developmental problems. The behavior that is often so inexplicable to parents is a byproduct of these struggles. **Parents will generally have little problem making sense of what is on their kid's mind when they are armed with knowledge about developmental hurdles and a willingness to think about how these powerful motivators are being played out in the form of behavior.** When confused about their child's behavior, the right question for parents to ask is, What does it mean? Or, What is the developmental problem that accounts for the behavior? The results are far less favorable when they ask the wrong question – What should I do? – and take action without understanding what the behavior means.

Points to Remember

- In their haste to "do something" parents often miss the first essential step of good parenting – understanding the problem.

- Making sense of their children's behavior and the motivations for that behavior allow parents to respond with confidence that their remedy will be effective.

Chapter 8

THE REAL MEANING OF DISCIPLINE

Question – What does discipline really mean and how can I use it successfully?

Effective discipline is aimed at helping our children to master developmental hurdles. Our role is one of a catalyst participating in a process that builds a strong personality foundation leading towards adult maturity. The purpose of discipline is the same as the goals of parenting: To provide the ingredients needed for the development of mature, effective coping mechanisms, and other personality characteristics that lead to happy and successful functioning later in life.

There is a great deal of confusion about discipline. In the minds of many, discipline means getting their children to do the right thing, or getting them to obey or be respectful. Parents are usually satisfied with themselves if they have an obedient child. This is certainly important, but is it enough?

We want our children to be good, but also to be independent. We want them to listen, but also to think for themselves and not be easily intimidated. It is apparent that there are goals of discipline beyond the usual immediate focus of most parents. Unless disciplinary efforts assist children in their mastery of developmental problems, the outcome is unlikely to be completely favorable.

The concept of discipline begins to make sense only when two questions are posed and answered: Discipline for whom? and Discipline to what end? When it is discipline solely to enforce the will of the parent, then its aim is simple and not too difficult to accomplish. We usually have the wherewithal to compel our young children to behave in accord with our expectations, and be pleased for the moment. We are, after all, very powerful and our young children are weak and completely dependent upon us. This is a somewhat accurate analysis of the parent/child status when our children are very young, but this changes quickly.

The ultimate outcome may be far less pleasing if our children's motivation for compliance continues to be the fear of disapproval or punishment. We would not be very happy if our children reached adolescence still making decisions based mainly upon their fear of punishment or the disapproval of others. Obedience based on the fear of our disapproval turns nightmarish when we find her at fourteen, discarding the use of her own capable judgment and common sense in favor of maintaining the approval of friends. We need to be reminded that the power we have over our children's decisions, which we often mistakenly label as effective discipline, disappears very quickly with the passage of a few years.

Effective discipline must be aimed at helping our children to master developmental hurdles. The mastery of these tasks is a prerequisite for later effective functioning.

Points to Remember

- Parents know that there are many times when it is essential for their children to comply with their requests.

- Most parents overlook their primary mission and the real meaning of discipline – to act as catalysts in a process that enables their children to acquire the many attributes and skills they will need later in life.

- This requires influencing children's thinking, not merely obtaining compliance.

CHAPTER 9

THE IMPORTANT LINK BETWEEN THE CORRECTION OF DISTORTED PERCEPTIONS AND EFFECTIVE DISCIPLINE

Question – What does it mean when my child knows better but still misbehaves? I just can't explain some of the things he says and does.

As children grow older they develop higher levels of intelligence and a variety of skills. This process is important and should be encouraged by parents, but it is not enough. There is another important component to their unreasonable behavior that can not be canceled out solely by intelligence. An extremely significant characteristic of the very young is the tendency to respond to the world based on infantile feelings and perceptions, instead of seeing the world realistically. This tendency continues to be pronounced throughout childhood. This is why children who seem so intelligent and reasonable may suddenly do or say things that are unreasonable, confusing, or irritating. They are being prodded by distorted perceptions. When this pattern of distorted thinking persists significantly into adulthood, it accounts for the emotional immaturity that becomes evident in the individual. If these adults have children of their own, their persistent distorted perceptions will nearly always make their presence known in the form of severe emotional blisters.

Question – How can parents discern the distorted perceptions that account for their child's behavior?

The developmental hurdle with which their child is struggling causes most of the behavior that is stressful and confusing to parents. In the following chapters, I will address the series of hurdles and the resulting distorted perceptions. Each stage has its typical themes. For example, one common theme is the tendency of two- to four-year-olds to interpret not getting what they want as a mean, hateful act that justifies their rage and desire for revenge. Children are really very easy to understand once we have identified the developmental struggle that accounts for their behavior.

Although no one can be sure of what the four-month-old baby's thinking is like, it would not be hard to imagine the perceptions that are fueling his feelings and behavior.

Joe is four weeks old and at this moment is very hungry. If his thoughts could somehow be translated into speech they might sound something like this, "Grr, I need milk. Grr, I need it now, and I need it to go into my mouth where it feels so good." Joe's mother is on the phone and the milk is not immediately available. She is a capable mom and quickly spots the telltale signs of Joe's mounting hunger and says, "Sorry old chap, nothing ready now, and it will take a few moments to get ready. Why don't you pass the time by looking at the light streaming through the window, I have noticed you find that interesting."

Joe, of course, has no understanding of this. Even if he did, it would have little influence on his subsequent thinking or behavior. His perceptions, felt in his body as well as his mind, are completely dominated by the painful ache of his hunger. At that moment his interpretation of his world, comprised of his empty belly, a mouth longing to suck in the sweet white fluid, and his mother, is that they are all bad, hurting, and confusing. He is enraged and shows it. The words I am using to describe his perceptions of not getting his way do not do justice to the disorganizing pain he actually feels during that very early time in his life. Are his perceptions correct? Of course not! They are based on the immature level of his emotional and cognitive development. Sadly, there are adults whose thoughts sometimes resemble little baby Joe's. They are called addicts.

I hope that you are beginning to appreciate that the concept of effective discipline is much more profound than merely stopping behavior that displeases us and encouraging behavior that we desire. The goal of effective discipline is to influence thinking. We are accomplishing very little unless we are helping our youngster to replace distorted perceptions with ones that are more in accord with the real world.

Distorted perceptions account for behavior that is labeled by parents as "needs discipline." Good discipline may take many forms. They all have one thing in common that makes them effective. They help children to substitute realistic perceptions for the distorted variety that prevails early in life.

Little baby Joe has been fortunate. His mother has used effective discipline. As a consequence his perceptions and interpretations of the things happening to him have become more realistic. Although it rarely happens in real life, the hope springs eternal within all that by the time little Joe has reached sixteen years of age, he has acquired the ability to size up events more realistically. He bounds into the kitchen at 6:00 P.M. after basketball practice. He is 6 feet 2 inches tall, weighs 175 pounds and has become the most efficient eating machine on earth. "Food ready Mom?" "Sorry, I haven't started," she replies. With a smile in his heart, he says, "no problem, why don't you rest this time and I'll make dinner." Of course this is more than maturity. This is utopia!

Points to Remember

- The unreasonable things that young children do are fueled by their infantile feelings and perceptions.

- Good parenting, which is synonymous with good discipline, helps children to substitute realistic perceptions for the distorted ones that were characteristic of early life.

- For example, children need to realize that not getting a cookie does not mean that they are hated.

Chapter 10

THE MANY FORMS OF LOVE – THE MEANING OF INDULGENCE

Question – Everyone takes it for granted that children need our love. But love can mean so many different things and can be given in a multitude of different ways. How can we know which is best?

There is a great deal of truth to the adage "love cures all," especially as far as young children are concerned. For those few parents who are able to consistently love their children, there is no need to read this or any book. I am convinced that these parents will turn out great kids no matter what child-rearing methods they use. The problem is in the definition of love. Nearly all parents are sure they love their children and believe that they know when their actions are manifestations of love. Most of them are often wrong in their assessment.

Parents who abuse their kids are as sure that they love them, as are parents who indulge their children. Both believe that they are telling the truth, but both are actually in error. In the name of love many parents have crippled their children emotionally and some even physically. How are we to distinguish love that is authentic from the endless varieties of false substitutes? Some of the concepts already addressed may provide some help. Each of the remaining chapters of this book will fill in the details with basic principles, guidelines, and examples.

Loving responses begin with an acceptance of our children just the way they are. Added to this are parenting strategies aimed at helping them to master the problems with which they are struggling. Its ultimate goal is the participation in a wonderful journey leading to the creation of a well functioning, confident adult.

The opposite of love is not hate, it is selfishness. Too often our responses to our kids are predicated upon our preoccupation with what we want, rather than an understanding of what they need from us so that they can master developmental hurdles and make their way on the path towards maturity. Loving responses are less likely to occur when our own needs, feelings, and agendas are placed ahead of our children's. I am not implying that we are being remiss when we find that reality requires that we attend to our own business at the expense of attention to our kids. I am saying that all activities, these as well, can be accomplished lovingly and can incorporate the guidelines of effective parenting.

None of us will do this all the time. Our children don't need us to do it all the time. Only the very good players in the major leagues are hitting over .300. We are doing well with most kids if we can do the same. Some kids can handle a lower average; some that are much more vulnerable may need a much higher one. A decent average for parents requires two attributes: a love that remains consistent and a reasonably accurate perception of their children and the meaning of their behavior. We won't see the ball if we don't know what we are looking at. When we are able to see our kids accurately we will understand what needs to be done enough of the time to do a good job. Knowledge about child development is the key tool in this endeavor.

The greatest impediments to a decent parental batting average are painful emotional blisters. The stress and distorted perceptions these engender preclude concentrating on the ball well enough to hit it. At this point, motivated by our own feelings, we are flailing about wildly and deserve putting ourselves on the bench for awhile until we can sort out our feelings and figure out what needs to be done. Taking another turn at bat when we are overwhelmed by our own discomfort is the way to lose the game.

Real love of children does cure. It cures because it is synonymous with good parenting. It provides children with what they need from us to master developmental hurdles and develop a strong, stable personality.

The meaning of indulgence

Question – Aren't we showing love when we satisfy and please our kids?

Indulgence is a variety of parenting often mistaken as love. An observer, for example a relative or neighbor, can usually discern the difference quite easily. The parents themselves can almost never distinguish one from the other. Nor are they able to see the untoward consequences of their brand of love, even when this is clearly pointed out to them. Their perceptions have been commandeered by the power of their emotional blisters.

There is a time in our children's lives that the care they need swings dramatically in the direction of providing pleasure on the terms demanded by them. This is during the earliest months. The parents' intense interest in providing pleasure and care might have the appearance of indulgence, but it is based on an accurate perception of their child and his real needs

Providing care, attention, and pleasure is always an important part of the love children need. During infancy it is the overwhelmingly dominant part. But even during this early time, and increasingly as the months pass, another component must be added for the love to be optimally packaged. Children need to learn to cope with frustration. The gradual addition of this component is essential for children to move to the next plateau of development. Without appropriate doses of frustration our children never learn that they are loved when the love is not immediately available. Children always feel good when they are getting the attention, gratification, and love they demand. We all do. An essential requirement for maturity is the capacity to feel loved and be able to manage during the many moments when attention is absent. **Indulgence is love supplied in a form that impedes that transition.**

Being loved and gratified by another is wonderful, but there is a fact of life that can not be denied. There will be many times, eventually most of the time, when this component of love will not be available. Helping our children to know that they are loved when they are not obtaining any concrete evidence of this is one of the most crucial tasks of parenting. Infants have no way of knowing this during most of their first year. If they have not begun to appreciate it by their fifth year, they will encounter many problems. And if it has still not been mastered by adulthood, the road ahead for them will be extremely rocky. Parental love that does not teach this lesson is indulgence, not love.

Johnny, age six, comes down for breakfast with a tear in his eye. His mother who loves him very much notices this and asks him what's wrong. He says, "If you love me and want me to be happy, never send me to that horrible school. If you do, I will hate you forever." His mother has the power to keep him happy, but they both will pay a high price for this act of indulgence if it reflects a repeated trend.

The goal of meaningful parental love must include much more than pleasing and gratification. A love that neglects the mastery of developmental hurdles is not a love at all. Love aimed excessively at making everyone feel good is indulging and often called spoiling. It destines the child and parent to an endless menu of the pain that it was implemented to avoid. This is true because indulgence may produce fleeting moments of pleasure, but it fosters helplessness, dependency, and future bondage to external gratification.

In contrast, children who have been helped to be less dependent upon reassurance, caring, and gratification from others will have gained needed skills and self-esteem. Their inner sense of worth will become less dependent upon the words and actions of others. In addition, these new tools will lead ultimately to the development of a very special human attribute, the capacity to love others.

At each step of your child's life, love is synonymous with good parenting. This packaging of love is the kind that will nudge your child's development towards maturity. Sometimes this desirable package of love also provides pleasure. Often, however, it does not. It is often not "feel good" love, but aspires always to be reasonable love.

The balance of love and reasonable frustration needed at each step will be addressed in detail in later chapters.

Question – Some members of my husband's family have told me that I am spoiling my son because I enjoy getting him playthings. Is it a mistake to provide children with too many toys?

Parents are often confused and concerned about the possible harmful effects of material affluence upon their children. They have observed that many children from affluent families grow up unable to accept frustration. These children are demanding and lack the discipline needed to apply themselves in school. Later they become vulnerable to drug use and other serious problems. These parents question whether children surrounded by material affluence can avoid being spoiled. Other parents have the opposite concern. They believe that their children will be adversely affected if they do not have the material wealth to supply them with the array of clothing and other products now available in our society.

The simple linkage of material gratifications with indulgence in the minds of many parents reveals an essential misunderstanding of child developmental and the actual cause of spoiling. The quality or quantity of material gratification supplied to a child does not define spoiling. It is rather a function of the child's response to not getting his way. Many children can be given a great deal and be surrounded by the material benefits of wealth and do fine. They may enjoy receiving material gratifications, but they have attained the ability to cope when what they desire is not available. Others in the same environment become spoiled. **Spoiling occurs when parents have been unable to help their children negotiate a crucial developmental hurdle – learning to know that they are loved when they are not getting the immediate attention or gratification they demand.** The diagnosis of spoiled is made by observing a child's response to discrepancies between what he wants and what he gets. It is not based upon a measurement of the amount of goodies that he might possess. Children who have been overindulged continue to equate "getting" with being loved, and "not getting" with personal rejection. The spoiled or indulged child does not merely like to be gratified; he needs to be gratified. Like the drug addict who has not had his fix, he feels overwhelmed, helpless, and angry when his want is not immediately satisfied.

POINTS TO REMEMBER

- Love comes in many forms, not all of them are desirable.
- The form of love needed by children is aimed at helping them to develop the skills needed to live flourishing lives.
- Children need a tremendous amount of gratification from their parents, but as they get older gratification must be balanced with appropriate doses of frustration.
- Love that impedes developmental progress deserves to be called spoiling rather than love.

Chapter 11

SUMMARY

We are all aware that there are skills and attributes our children will need to function effectively and happily. These abilities are acquired gradually as children progress from birth to adulthood. They are acquired through a process of confronting and mastering a series of developmental problems. At each age, our children display characteristic forms of behavior that are a by-product of their struggle with these developmental hurdles. Often these are the patterns of behavior that we feel require discipline. They are also the patterns of behavior that are particularly troublesome because of the uncomfortable feelings they generate in us.

Each child will find his own way to solve these developmental problems. There is a great deal at stake in the outcome of this process, since it will determine the roots of the character structure that our kids will carry with them for the remainder of their lives. The most important factor regarding outcome is the quality of our love and our responses to the endless array of daily interactions that shape our lives together. The quality will be significantly enhanced if our perceptions of our children and their needs are accurate. Knowledge about development is the best tool to help us stay on target.

By helping our children towards optimal solutions to these problems, they become stronger and better equipped to handle the challenge of the next developmental hurdle. We are helping them to move forward on the path leading to maturity. If a problem is not solved, it remains a source of trouble throughout adulthood. The maladaptive methods our children finally use to cope with the problem will become imbedded into their character, creating a foundation that is unstable.

The first time around is the early years in a child's life. This is the time when the basic building blocks of personality are laid in place. It is far easier to get it right the first time around than to go back at a later time to make adjustments. A poor golf swing can be improved, but the process is often difficult and the outcome variable. A youngster who has been fortunate enough to learn to swing correctly the first time is well on his way towards the development of sound technique. Personality characteristics are infinitely more difficult to modify, even after the passage of very little time.

The purpose of this book is to help parents get it right the first time. In the following chapters, each developmental stage will be addressed in detail. The basic concepts that have been presented in this chapter will be expanded and applied to each stage. Good parenting is a fluid phenomenon that needs to be continually molded to the ever-changing problems, skills levels, and array of behaviors our special and unique child will present to us as we move with him through time. Information that clarifies this process can help us do the job more effectively and also allow us to better appreciate the beauty of the journey. Armed with this knowledge, parents will be able to get it right the first time around. Is there any endeavor as important?

Additional Points for Consideration

We are all aware that there are skills and attributes our children will need to function effectively and happily. These abilities are acquired gradually as children progress from birth to adulthood. They are acquired through a process of confronting and mastering a series of developmental problems. At each age, our children display characteristic forms of behavior that are a by-product of their struggle with these developmental hurdles. Often these are the patterns of behavior that we feel require discipline. They are also the patterns of behavior that are particularly troublesome because of the uncomfortable feelings they generate in us.

PART TWO

LEARNING TO BE A PERSON – THE FIRST LOVE

BIRTH TO EIGHT MONTHS

PART TWO

SECTION ONE

LEARNING TO BE A PERSON – THE TASK AND ITS IMPORTANCE

Question – I will soon give birth to my first child. What does he need most from me?

The most precious gift you can provide him, right from birth, is the daily love and care that forges strong bonds of love between the two of you. These bonds will form the bedrock of his emerging personality. Many of the later strengths he develops will hinge upon the quality of these early bonds.

Chapter 1

THE IMPORTANCE OF THE FIRST LOVE

Dan is just three-weeks-old. He is Sally's and Bob's first child and they were overjoyed when he arrived. Sally is gazing intently at him as he feeds in the very early morning light. She is still in awe of this perfect little person who is hers. A feeling of peace and contentment fills her during this quiet time they have together. She is enjoying the feeding process and has found that she does not even mind the cleaning and other chores that his presence requires. As she watches him, a thought crosses her mind. She thinks, *My Dan is more than a new human being. He is a person with a conscious awareness even at this early time in his life. I wonder what he's thinking. What is he thinking of me? I wonder how that thinking evolves and how I will influence that change that will gradually transform this precious child into a wonderful adult.*

I wish that before, or soon after, the birth of their child parents would ask these kinds of questions. If they did, my answer would sound something like this. There is something precious that you can give to your tiny newborn infant that will have more influence on his future happiness and success than anything else you or others can ever give him. It will determine the stability of the basic foundation of his personality. This gift is the meaningful love and responsive care that he needs from you every day, so that he can begin taking confident steps on the path of learning to become a person.

Your love and care are what awakens his mind and heart to you, and through you, to the rest of the world. This gift creates bonds that tie the two of you together with love. The quality and security of these bonds of love are what will color his earliest perceptions of himself and others. If they are solid and this first developmental hurdle is mastered, you will have helped him to establish a stable foundation for his emerging personality. This is a prerequisite for the latter development of good self-esteem, maturity, and ultimately the variety of other attributes and values needed for a happy, successful life.

Making sure that he is well fed, giving him material benefits, and helping him to be a better student, all pale in comparison with the significance of this gift that he must receive from you primarily during the first months of his life. Its impact is far reaching, and the consequences of its absence often devastating. In spite of its importance, it has an elusive quality and can easily pass unnoticed by both the giver and the receiver. The salutary effects of this gift of love become diminished if there is a delay of even days or weeks until it is provided. As the delay lengthens, so do the destructive effects and too soon the time is reached that the damage of its absence cannot be reversed.

The deprivation of love and responsiveness during this developmental stage weakens bonding and ultimately is the cause of the most serious types of human problems and suffering. Our entire personality is built on an inner core. This might be best described as the conviction that our existence, or who we are, has intrinsic validity, is real, and substantial rather than something fleeting or inconsequential. This inner core of strength may be hard to define in words since it is formed early in life and is experienced mainly in nonverbal terms. Although we rarely think about this core of our personalities, we know it when we see it and are aware of its absence. Its presence is conveyed by a sense of being grounded, showing an inner contentment that is less easily eroded by others, and a capacity to roll with the punches of life that we all must inevitably face.

I have heard so many people with a variety of serious maladies echoing the same refrain, "Somehow I feel that I am nothing, and it is very frightening. I have spent my life searching for something that will relieve this dreadful feeling and halt this sense of impending dissolution that I carry with me. More approval, drugs, hiding from the world, I'll try anything, but nothing seems to work."

These individuals lack that inner core of strength, the bedrock on which a stable personality is constructed. Its stability derives from the bonds of love forged during the first months of a child's life.

Points to Remember

- Children thrive on love and contact, and need these from the first moments of their lives.

Chapter 2

THE INFANT AS A TEACHER

Question – I want to make good use of this precious time. How can I more fully appreciate what is actually happening within my child during the times that we are together?

We have learned a great deal about children from children. A vast amount of data about early infancy sheds light on the basic ingredients our children need from us. Parents of newborns are usually preoccupied and concerned about the amount of food they can get into the little ones' tummies. Our babies crave another ingredient just as strongly as they do food. If this ingredient is not in adequate supply, it will cause a state of deprivation leading to life-long disabilities. Few, if any babies have problems later in life because they were underfed. But there are untold numbers of adults who suffer because they missed an adequate feeding of the most important gift of all – the gift of love.

For a long time, experts in the field of early childhood development believed that the infant's gradual attachment to his parents was entirely due to the holding, touching, feeding, and love given by his parents. They viewed the child as the more passive partner in this process. Children actually show their own innate longing for that gift of love right from the time they are born. They have built-in mechanisms that help them to pull the love and attention they need from their parents.

Question – How are infants capable of accomplishing this?

Detailed observations of newborn babies reveal a clear distinction between their reactions to inanimate objects, such as toys, and their responses to people. With inanimate objects, they reach out abruptly and then move back. Their movements are staccato in form. When a human face moves towards the infant, their responses are quite different. There is a smoother movement of facial expressions and of extremities towards the parent, followed by a smooth phase of withdrawal, completing the cycle. To the observer, it is as though the child is engaging the parent in a choreographed ballet. This is gratifying to watch and nearly always a source of intense satisfaction to the participants. There is a powerful seductive quality to the child's facial expressions and movements that tend to gently coerce loving adults into this pleasant interplay. We have all experienced this in the presence of small babies when they somehow tempt us to say "goo goo" and make other ridiculous babbling sounds. As we are drawn closer to the baby, we let out a squeal of delight when our efforts elicit a smile or other pleasing response.

The importance of this interplay far transcends the immediate pleasure it affords the parents. Our infants are actively beckoning us to provide the emotional feeding they need to master the first developmental hurdle on their climb towards maturity. It is through the synchronous interplay of love occurring over and over again, in an endless array of different situations during this early time, that bonding occurs. Our child is taking his first steps towards becoming a person.

Question – How do infants respond if they are not able to elicit the desired attention they seem to innately crave?

There is another lesson to be learned by the observations of early parent-infant interactions. If the parent does not heed the child's request to become a partner in that beautiful ballet of love, the sequence of events that follow is extremely disquieting. The frustration of the infant's built-in longing for a loving exchange leads to his visible irritation. For example, if he is presented with a still or unresponsive face, instead of one that is smiling, his movements soon become jerky. He averts his face and makes additional but less smooth attempts to once again elicit the desired pattern. If this also fails, the infant finally withdraws into an attitude described by observers as one of helplessness, resignation, and apathy. His face turns away and his body curls up and becomes motionless.

How easy it is in the busy lives of most families to overlook this emotional feeding and how dire are the consequences. Experiencing this repeatedly, it becomes a source of considerable emotional, and probably physical, pain to our vulnerable infants who have virtually no way to protect themselves. This pain also has more serious implications. It is not a one-time-and-it-is-over kind of pain. This pain is a sign that means that the bonds of love that tie our babies to us are not being strongly forged. Failure to master this first developmental hurdle has an adverse effect upon the infant's later image of himself and others.

Taking the time to observe our babies helps us to understand their nonverbal language and more fully appreciate the importance of the gift of love.

Question – I am beginning to appreciate the importance of my love during this early time in my child's life, but I find it hard to conceptualize his thinking and how this is influenced by the quality of my care. Can you explain how this happens?

Most thought requires conceptualizations that depend upon verbal skills, and these are absent at birth. At birth, consciousness might best be described as a continuous stream of lights, shapes, colors, sounds, and other sensations and feelings, devoid of any meaning apart from a visceral distinction between pleasure and pain. Out of this panoply of sights, sounds, smells, and tastes, a particular image begins to stand out from the rest because it is so continuously associated with pleasure and the reduction of tension. This is the mental picture of the infant's mother, who repeatedly assesses his needs and responds appropriately. The infant is taking the first step towards becoming a person. It is a very tentative step, and he cannot yet discern the difference between the image of his actual mother and the memory of her that he begins to retain when she is absent.

The distinction between the mental picture of his mother and the real thing emerges gradually as he becomes cognizant of the essential difference between the two. The real person, his mother, is associated with loving care and its resultant reduction of tension is in stark contrast to the imagined image that provides no actual relief. The infant is taking his first mental steps into the world of people. It should be apparent that the quality and trustworthiness of the love and care he obtains will dramatically influence these first steps, leaving an indelible impression that will become the foundation of his personality.

Imagine both the immediate as well as the long term effects if he experiences inconsistencies and prolonged periods of heightened tension, instead of reliable love and care. We would understand this child's reluctance to move into the world of people and instead turn inwards for relief. Any outward movements he did make would be dramatically tainted by this traumatic early experience.

Points to Remember

- The quality care of parental care during infancy is the basic building block for later self-esteem.

- Quality care conveys a feeling of being loved and valued.

- Quality care requires taking the time to observe, to understand, and to be in tune with an infant's nonverbal language.

PART TWO

SECTION TWO

UNDERSTANDING WHAT NEEDS TO BE DONE

Chapter 3

SUPPLYING THE ESSENTIAL INGREDIENTS

Question – I now understand what bonding is and its importance. What can I learn that will assist me in helping my newborn to accomplish this goal?

Simply stated, during the first months of life, children need an optimum amount of parental love.

It is not possible to describe what this should be like for each child. We generally know it when we see it, and we know it when we are not seeing it. If we have been fortunate enough to have been the recipients of love in our own lives, we also have an impression of what it is like to be on the receiving end. Describing that experience from the perspective of the infant who we have magically endowed with the capacity to translate very primitive feelings into clear words, might sound something like this. "When you are looking at me and I am looking at you, at your face and into your eyes, I know that I am totally accepted and cherished. This instills in me a wonderful feeling of confidence that I am precious, special, and perfect just the way I am. My whole body and all of me overflow with a feeling of well-being and contentment."

Compare that feeling of being loved with the one a child might experience if over and over his longing for love was frustrated and instead parental expressions communicated something like this. "What a nuisance and bother you are. Your noise and demands take me away from what I want to do. Sometimes I wish you were not here, or that someone else was around to take care of you. Your presence in my life makes me depressed and there are times that I don't even want to look at you." You may be wondering why parents would communicate this type of ugly message to their very vulnerable infant. Yet, these are exactly the sentiments I have heard repeatedly from many parents.

Points to Remember

- The first months are crucial for a successful outcome.
- This first building block for later success is set during the first eight months.

Chapter 4

A DAILY REMINDER OF THE IMPORTANCE OF LOVE

Hint – On the mirror you use upon awakening, write a reminder of the importance of love.

The importance of love during this early time in our children's lives needs to be emphasized because it is often overlooked. Nearly all parents love their children and have the capacity to demonstrate that love during this crucial stage of development. Often they are just not aware of the importance of the gift of love and inadvertently err on the side of providing it in less than optimum quantities. In their busy schedules they find it easier to prop bottles, use mechanical rockers, push the pacifier, and find other ways for their little ones to "entertain themselves."

A reminder of the importance of putting "love" on the top of our list of priorities at a time in our lives when we are being pulled in many directions can make a dramatic difference.

Parents are beset by an endless array of demands and pressures from within the family. In addition, in our culture today they find themselves pulled by a variety of groups, each advocating its own theories about parenting. Issues such as going back to work, substitute care, the question of multiple caretakers, and the search for personal fulfillment, add to the complexity of parenting. Most of these will be addressed later. The focus of this book is not to mandate the one right way; there is none. There is, however, a right parent. **The right parent is one who is guided by an accurate reading of his child's special needs. Knowledge about the particular developmental hurdle that is being negotiated is a prerequisite for doing this successfully.** Good parenting follows from an understanding of the child. It cannot be found in the ideology of a political or social group, with a special parenting strategy, or in our own whims.

There is no recipe for meaningful love, but we all can tap into it if we are aware of its importance and are willing to place it first on our list of priorities. The importance of doing this during early infancy must not be underestimated. If bonds are damaged beyond repair the infant becomes incapable of successfully negotiating later developmental hurdles. The weakening of this first building block of a stable personality leads to the most serious types of emotional problems.

Points to Remember

- During infancy, providing quality care must be the parents' highest priority.
- The first eight months are when children most need the most precious gift parents will ever provide – an abundance of love.

Chapter 5

IMPAIRED BONDING – A DEFICIENCY OF EARLY LOVE

Question – I am aware now of the importance of strong bonding, but what are the consequences of this being neglected?

Impaired bonding means that infants have been diverted from the first developmental task – earning to be a person. If the impairment is pronounced, their ties to others will remain meager at best. These children often appear somber and apathetic. They lack the range of emotional responses that most children display as they learn to interact with their parents. If they were capable of speech, their description of what they might be experiencing on a very primitive level may sound something like this. "I have given up. There is nothing I can hope for in the world of people. I have been disappointed too many times to try again. I'll turn away, turn inward, and tune out people who have caused me so much pain."

This trend is manifested in varying degrees of intensity depending upon the extent of the early deprivation. More severely deprived children can sometimes be observed rocking rhythmically with a glazed, far-away expression, oblivious of people and objects around them. This more profound withdrawal is entirely different from the occasional tuning out and daydreaming manifested by most kids. Normal kids are involved with others in their daydreams and they readily return to a rich repertoire of responses to others as soon as the opportunity is offered. The outcome for children who use withdrawal as one of their primary methods of coping with a painful world is much more ominous. As this trend of turning away becomes established, they miss the interplay with loved ones that is so necessary for later learning and emotional growth.

Points to Remember

- The damage done by poor-quality care during infancy is easily overlooked – infants can't complain and the damage is usually not evident until later childhood.

PART TWO

Section Three

UNDERSTANDING THE MEANING OF CHILDREN'S BEHAVIOR DURING THE FIRST DEVELOPMENTAL PHASE AND ITS MANAGEMENT

Infants have an extremely limited repertoire of behavior. When they are not sleeping, their hours are passed by protests of distress vacillating with periods of calm. Both of these periods present opportunities for parents to help their children successfully negotiate their first developmental hurdle.

In the remainder of this chapter, I address the typical patterns of behavior and the principles and guidelines for their effective management.

Chapter 6

CRYING DURING INFANCY – ITS MEANING AND MANAGEMENT

Each day parents make an endless array of decisions about their children. During infancy, many of these decisions revolve around how to respond to their child's crying. An understanding of the importance of bonding and how this is achieved will help them make these decisions more accurately and with greater confidence.

Question – What can I learn about crying during infancy that will enable me to use these times as opportunities to help my child bond successfully and master the first developmental hurdle? I have always wondered why my child's screams are so disconcerting to me. This discomfort adds to the uncertainty I have about my parenting techniques.

WARNING! WATCH OUT FOR EMOTIONAL BLISTERS

The prescription for good bonding is simple. Bonds are forged from the love and care provided by parents. It is not hard for most parents to love a smiling, responsive infant. It's a great deal more difficult when our kid's behavior is less endearing. Crying during this early time leads the list of things that infants do that make their parents uncomfortable. **Parents need to be forewarned and to understand the source of the stress and confusion they are likely to feel as they attempt to respond to their crying infant. An understanding of these emotional blisters can help parents to be less diverted from their important task.**

Many parents would not be proud of videos taken of them responding to their crying infant. There is a good reason for this. Words fall short in attempting to describe the feelings of helplessness and bewilderment rekindled in us at those times. Raising children compels us to experience all over again the hurts and insecurities we felt during our first time around, when we were infants ourselves. These feelings often sabotage our ability to provide our infants with the special love and care they need. Our own discomfort diverts us from this task and instead prods us towards another goal – quieting the source of the discomfort, our baby. Even if it were possible to be successful in this endeavor, its long-term consequences are extremely unpleasant. As a result, our children would receive deficient supplies of love when they need it most, bonding would be weakened, and developmental progress stalled.

Question – What can I do to minimize the impact of these disturbing feelings?

Acknowledging and understanding these feelings are your best allies. The feelings can be muted, but can rarely be entirely eliminated. On the baseball field I can imagine pitching only strikes, but in real life this is impossible. The same is true about a resolve to be an ideal parent to a newborn. We need to be reminded that with our children, as in baseball, we do not have to throw strikes all of the time. On the other hand, flinging the ball aimlessly is a prescription for failure.

An understanding of bonding, the meaning of crying, and a general impression of what needs to be done helps us to be considerably closer to the target. This type of knowledge also serves to sooth those painful emotional blisters and eliminate some of the distorted perceptions that would otherwise get in the way.

Concerns about Spoiling During Infancy

Question – You are suggesting that we give our babies as much love and attention as we can. But isn't it possible to go overboard and shower our kids with so much love and attention that our responses to crying will spoil them?

Children always need a balance between the two components of love: providing pleasure and helping them to cope with frustration. In order to create strong bonds during this developmental phase, this

balance should swing fairly dramatically in the direction of love, pleasure, and gratification.

Parents may already believe, or have been told by older and presumably wiser relatives, that they should "let their infants cry it out" to avoid spoiling. This is only one of the many mistaken beliefs about children. These beliefs have one thing in common. They all are in conflict with the most important principle of good parenting. **Good parenting requires that we address the special developmental needs of our special child, rather than adopting one-plan-fits-all schemes.** There should now be no question about what our children need most from us during infancy – love and responsive care. If the foundation created by that love is strong, we will have ample opportunity to wean them from the fairly continuous infusion of love and gratification they demand, and must have, during this early period. This is not the time to do that. After all, the infant has, at best, a very primitive internal apparatus to quell mounting tensions on his own. This is the time that it is appropriate to err on the side of indulgence. It is hard to imagine an infant being damaged because he obtained too much pleasure from love, cuddling, holding, soothing, and rocking during his first months of life.

If the parents of a two-month-old asked, "What can I do now to minimize discipline problems at age six or fourteen?" my answer would be, **"Love him very much so that that basic building block of bonding can be firmly set in place."** If this is solidly accomplished, the later efforts towards self-esteem and good functioning will be much easier for him to achieve. On the other hand, if bonding is poor, the best-laid plans for the inculcation of discipline at age two or four are likely to go astray.

Even if parents lean excessively towards providing love and attention during the first months, there is really little danger of infants not experiencing enough frustration. The countless little things that happen in every home make it impossible for parents to respond quickly to each demand made of them. God made parents with two arms, not eight.

The months roll by swiftly and soon enough our children will have developed a variety of skills, allowing them to profit from increasing doses of the second component of love – appropriate frustration. Even at four and five months, that process is unfolding. If the foundation of strong bonds has been made secure, they will be able to profit from the second component of love—learning to feel loved when it is not immediately available. The strong bonds that our love has forged are the precursors to the gradual emergence of confidence in facing and coping with frustration. On the other hand, if time passes and bonds are not being forged, the chances of a satisfactory outcome diminish rapidly. The longer the gift of love is withheld from a child the harder it becomes for the child to accept love when it is offered.

The Danger of "Crying it Out"

Question – I have been told that it is sometimes useful to allow infants to cry until they stop on their own. Is this accurate?

Repeated episodes of crying for a long period without any intervention by the parent can only serve to weaken bonding during these early months.

The child left to cry until exhaustion finally brings it to an end can't say to himself, "Gee it looks like my mom is not coming this time. I've just got to suck it up, settle down, and learn to handle this on my own." There are many adults who can't do this. If we could use words to describe the baby's feelings, it might sound like this. "My whole world, everything that is good, my parents, my body, is exploding into unrelenting pain and nothingness." The experience of a two-month-old left to cry it out might be analogous to the terror of a vulnerable person convinced that he and his loved ones will meet imminent horrible destruction. Of course, there is a great deal of variability among children. Some children can tolerate frequent episodes of this type of emotional turmoil and still maintain strong ties and bonds to their parents. Others can tolerate very little. But for all children, if the deprivation is sufficiently repeated, the bonds begin to fray and the damage becomes irreparable.

Crying That Does Not Stop

Question – I do my best to provide love and sooth my crying infant but sometimes this is to no avail. What should I do? I realize now that it is best not to ignore this and let him "cry it out."

When infants continue to cry, despite our efforts to please them, the vital gift they need remains the same. They need us to continue to love them.

If we define "doing" as trying to find some means to quell our child's tension and stop the crying, there may be nothing we can do. Infants do not always stop crying when they are appropriately loved, held, fed, and cared for by their parents. Loving does not always mean pleasing. Even motivated and responsive attempts to sooth a tense, crying infant are often not successful. We can't always achieve our immediate goal, the cessation of crying, but we can always help our child to achieve his goal, the mastery of his current developmental hurdle. This is accomplished by doing the only constructive thing we can at this point, continuing to love him.

This seems simple. What could be easier than to remain calm and loving? After all, getting frustrated, angry, or tense is very unpleasant and serves no useful purpose. Yet many parents find it extremely difficult to attend to an inconsolable little baby. The reader is now well aware of the reason for this apparent contradiction. The crying has irritated emotional blisters.

The danger for our children is never the crying. Crying is what all infants do, some more than others. The danger is the emotional transformation occurring in parents who have become irritated. Children are unlikely to feel love from irritated parents. Parents need to be reminded that their babies are developing the basic foundation for their self-image. To a great extent this is built from the emotional messages transmitted to them by their parents. There can be little ambiguity about the meanings of the messages received from an angry, irritated, or withdrawn parent. Even as adults, these messages are read loud and clear and, in spite of our superior adult armor, still hurt. They do considerably more damage, often lasting damage, in our susceptible babies. The core of our child's personality is being programmed by these messages.

Let's review how this happens. The child's crying causes the parents' pain. As a reaction to this, their image of their child has been suddenly transformed from that of a precious, loved child to an unwanted, devalued object. The infant's first budding thoughts about himself are mainly influenced by his parents' image of him. These negative images, if repeated often enough, become his own.

When children are crying, their perceptions of the world around them, and especially of others, is distorted. They are sure that they are hated and that somehow this means that there is something bad about them. What hope is there for these distorted images to be corrected if unloving and angry parents confirm them? I am not advocating that parents give their infants unending attention or always find a way to sooth their child. This is impossible and would convey an unrealistic message. **I am emphasizing that parents remain loving when their attempts to placate their crying child have been unsuccessful.** Parents who continue loving when their child's distress is unabated help the child learn that he is loved, even during those many times when he is not being pleased by his parents and he is not pleasing them.

This becomes the foundation for the later development of stable self-esteem. The child is being helped to take his first steps towards learning to see the flaw in the equation, "love equals getting what you want and being pleased." This is an enormously important developmental hurdle that few negotiate completely, and will be addressed in more detail in later chapters. Knowing that we have intrinsic value when this is not being confirmed by others is the basic building block of self-esteem and, as we can see, it begins to be set in place during this very early time in our children's lives. **Crying, even crying that does not stop, need not have the power to erode our love.**

A Parent Who Loved Crying, but Hated Crying That Did Not Stop

Laura was a college-educated woman of twenty-five. She had wanted to have a child and was delighted when she gave birth to a healthy and easygoing baby. He ate well, was easily pleased, and slept for lengthy periods of time. Many parents not blessed with such a child would have been very satisfied. But things did not work out so well in Laura's household.

Laura found herself feeling frustrated and unhappy. She sought help when she was no longer able to control her impulse to pinch or slap Tony while he was sleeping until he awoke and began crying. Why would something like this happen?

Laura needed to be needed. Although she was extremely intelligent, her emotional blisters began to win out in her struggle with self-control. Her perception of Tony's periods of contentment had become dramatically distorted. Even though in one part of her mind she knew better, his contentment disturbed her because it made her feel unneeded and rejected by him. She wanted him to cry so that she could comfort him and feel needed again. Since he was a very contented child, she felt compelled to pinch and slap him to elicit crying.

Points to Remember

- Infants are not able to manage for long without their parents' involvement, and they become overwhelmed by their rapidly escalating discomfort.

- Early bonding may be impaired if parents consistently fail to tune in to their infant's needs for comfort.

- During the first six months, err on the side of extra attention and love rather than risk the consequences of demanding too much too soon.

- There will be ample time after infancy for parents to help their children become more independent.

- Infants should not be allowed to "cry it out" or cry to the point that they fall into an exhausted sleep.

- It is common for parents to be disturbed by their infant's crying, especially crying that they are unable to soothe.

- This reaction may make it difficult for parents to tune in to their infant's need for love and care.

- Sometimes there is nothing parents can do to quell their child's crying.
- Remaining loving, calm, and attentive is the best course of action. This nonverbal message builds strong bonds.

Chapter 7

PACIFIERS OF ALL KINDS – THEIR MEANING AND MANAGEMENT

Infants spend their days eating and crying, with seemingly brief periods of quiescence in between. Parents spend their days attending to their crying infants. There are a variety of ways that parents soothe and pacify their children. They need to be aware of the possible long-term implications of their choices.

Question – Do pacifiers help or hinder the mastery of this developmental hurdle? I am uncertain about their use.

What Are Pacifiers?

The types of pacifiers, both animate and inanimate, and their use may vary widely, but for all, children as well as adults, the motivation for their use is the same. Nearly all young children, and most adults, experience stress and a variety of other unpleasant emotions when the world and the people in it conspire to frustrate their wishes. At these times they respond in many ways, some more adaptive and some less. One of the things they do is resort to some form of pacifier for relief.

Nearly everyone uses one type of pacifier or another. The particular one chosen and its manner of use reveals a great deal about the user. The adult varieties come in a wide assortment of shapes, sizes, forms, and categories. The pacifiers that adults use include food, drugs, alcohol, and may sometimes extend to work, friends, and even ideals and causes. When fanatic idealists begin to pursue objectives that fly in the face of common sense, there should be the suspicion that they are using the activity as a pacifier.

THE IDEAL PACIFIER FOR INFANTS – LOVING PARENTS

Question – Is it wise to allow or even encourage the use of pacifiers during infancy?

Answering this question requires a change in the way we ordinarily think about parenting decisions. We need to shift from our tendency to focus on the immediate problem, e.g. crying that does not stop, to an understanding of a more important goal: **The mastery of the developmental hurdle that accounts for the crying.**

A better way, therefore, to pose the question about pacifiers is to ask if and how they can be used to support the mastery of developmental hurdles.

During the first six months of life, the developmental task is the creation of bonds of love. The mastery of that task leads to the construction of a personality core that is stable and will become a solid foundation for all later development. **It follows that the most appropriate pacifier is the one that best helps to achieve this important goal. During this phase, the shape of the ideal pacifier is very clear – parents, lovingly providing the comfort and care their infants need to quiet their distress.**

This may seem a bit disconcerting to parents as they picture themselves functioning endlessly as a giant pacifier. Carried to its ultimate conclusion, they would need to be available for their little ones when they were no longer little. Instead of giving the bride away or bidding farewell to the groom, at least one of them would need to become one of the wedding gifts in order to continue in their role of the giant pacifier.

We can breathe more easily about this frightening vision when we are reminded that it is only during this first phase of development that we need to lean so heavily on the side of being our child's primary pacifier. If this is done successfully and strong bonds have developed, the process of weaning will unfold smoothly. As they move from childhood to adolescence they will be able to feel, if not actually think, the following: "Mom and Dad, the love and many other things that you gave to me and continue to give to me are wonderful and I am grateful. I love you now and will always love you. But now, thanks to your love, I can get along on my own. I can easily manage the long periods of time that I am alone or without the infusions of your love and care I so desperately needed when I was very little. Thank you for loving me in a way that has given me these strengths." In stark contrast, the child who received deficient supplies of love during his first time around will continue to need excessive gratification and reassurance. And saddest of all, this child will be destined to discover that the level of love and gratification received will never be enough to fill the emptiness.

Question – How much parental pacifying is best and how soon should it be provided?

Based on what we know about infancy – More is great! Sooner is better!

Parents' love and care are the most important, but not the sole factors, that determine the strength of bonding. Other extremely important variables enter into this equation. These include the parents' moods, their perceptions of their child, and their sensitivity to his needs. In-born characteristics of our children also affect the outcome. Among these are the child's ease of soothing, level of irritability, and reaction to stimuli.

Some of these are beyond our capacity to control. But there is one that we do control, and it turns out to be first on the list. Based on an understanding of this developmental hurdle we can elect to give our infants the time, attention, and love they need. The dividends that accrue from such a decision become apparent very quickly. For example, observers have found that infants whose mothers make an effort to have more loving contact with them are ahead of others in the bonding process. This difference can be observed very early. When one-week-old children who have had this advantage are observed interacting with their mothers, they are more easily comforted than children who have not had this experience.

The strong bonds that lead to a solid, stable personality core are less likely to be forged if non-parental pacifiers are used too often as substitutes for the large doses of parental love and attention needed by infants.

Feeding – Man Does Not Live by Bread Alone

Feeding is a central part of the lives of infants and their parents. This setting, therefore, provides an opportunity to supply our children with another kind of feeding, an emotional one, that rivals the nutritional one in importance. The pleasurable stimulus of feeding, when combined with the sight and touch of a loving parent, provides an impetus to the bonding process.

While there are many types of interactions that foster bonding, there is one type that definitely does not. A child cannot become bonded to a parent who is absent.

A propped bottle is an absent parent. And although physically present, parents are emotionally absent when they are depressed, withdrawn, or distracted. Parents are literally absent if a substitute caretaker or a series of caretakers perform the bulk of the feedings. The timing of substitute care and its dangers will be addressed in detail later.

If the deprivation of love and attention is extremely severe and sustained, very young infants are affected physically as well as emotionally. They stop feeding properly and fail to assimilate the food they do ingest. These children may lose weight, fail to thrive physically, and may even die. Food, without the love that must accompany it, is not enough. "Man does not live by bread alone" may be symbolically applicable to the lives of adults, but is a more literally accurate statement about infants.

Pacifiers – The Inert Variety

Question – I understand that pacifiers given to infants to suck should not be used as a substitute for parental love and care. Is there any appropriate use for them?

One of the goals of this book is to help parents understand the thinking process that leads to accurate caregiving guidelines. A cookbook approach does not provide parents with the flexibility and confidence necessary to face the ever-changing problems that they will encounter. There are some simple steps that will help them get closer to the target. Parents will find that these can be used to develop helpful approaches to many of the other issues that they will face.

A Brief Review of the Steps Required for Good Parenting – Pacifier Use

Step 1 – Understanding the issue

Children lack the skills needed for more adaptive methods of discharge. They will therefore search for pacifiers on their own, or use the ones we offer.

The high level of intolerance of very young children to tension leads them to quickly turn to parts of their own body, or anything else that will do the job. Early on this will be sucking the thumb, rocking, or rhythmical head banging. Later they may touch their hair or other parts of their body, or use the nipple of the bottle for this purpose. Still later they may adopt a special blanket.

Step 2 – Understanding the goal

The primary goal during infancy is to build strong bonds of love. Therefore, whether we view the use of a pacifier as favorable or not will depend on the effect it has on the mastery of this developmental hurdle.

If we are careful not to use pacifiers as a substitute for adequate doses of loving attention, their use during this period of early infancy may sometimes be appropriate.

Step 3 – Making a decision

The introduction of a pacifier during early infancy may be appropriate for periods of extreme fussiness that parents are not able to quell. It is important that this practice does not persist beyond this period. By five to six months of age, infants can be expected to have acquired sufficient coping mechanisms of their own to handle elevated tension. **There is no developmentally sound reason for children to be provided with pacifiers after six months of age.** Doing so hinders their acquisition of more effective mechanisms for the relief of tension.

An Example of Good Decision Making – Abe and the Pacifier

Abe is three-weeks-old. His parents love him very much, but they are often not able to get him settled down. Even after their best efforts, he remains cranky and irritable. He is an extremely active child who consumes nourishment vigorously. He seems to enjoy being held, but is squirmy and active. He is dissimilar to his older sister who would often fall into a blissful sleep after consuming her quota of milk. After feeding, Abe often continues to be fussy. His parents found that he was not amenable to any of the usual remedies for soothing and his continued fussing led to spitting up. After discussing this problem, Abe's parents decided to introduce a pacifier for these excessively irritable episodes.

Infants Abe's age have few options available to channel elevated feelings of tension. They can't jog around the block, watch television, sit quietly and reason it out, get grumpy with their wife, or do any of the myriad things that require skills they do not have. In fact, the only methods they can use are crying, sucking, and tuning out.

Feeding has been completed and is not an option. His parents have been unable to sooth him due to his high energy level. They are aware of the pitfall of allowing this irritable child to cry until he tunes out in apathetic exhaustion. Bonds would be in danger of being weakened. They decided that the best alternative for these episodes was to give Abe a pacifier to help him discharge his fussiness by sucking.

The pacifier is not being used as a substitute for the love he needs from his parents. They know the importance of that love and attention and are eager to supply it whenever possible. Allowing him to discharge his excess tension by sucking, instead of continuing to cry, is also helpful to them. Although they try to avoid allowing his crying to irritate their emotional blisters, they are not always successful and find that sometimes his continued crying makes them uncomfortable. Having the pacifier available increases their confidence and this, in turn is good for Abe, who is extremely sensitive to their feelings.

As his development moves forward, they will encourage his use of more mature methods of dealing with stress. By the time he reaches six months of age he will have that potential, and they plan to discontinue the pacifier. He will be less fragile, more advanced developmentally, and better equipped to cope with higher levels of frustration.

An Example of a Parenting Decision Made with Little Understanding of Their Child's Developmental Needs – Elliot and the Pacifier

From the beginning of his life, neither Elliot nor his parents found it easy to handle his stress. Elliot was stressed most of his waking hours and the sounds he made disturbed and confused his parents. They devised a mutually agreed upon solution that helped them all feel much better. They give him a pacifier that they put into his mouth any time he became irritable. This dramatically reduced the frequency of those unpleasant episodes. It had an additional advantage for the parents, who used it so that they did not have to interrupt their own activities. The months passed, but since this method of quelling his distress seemed to work so well, it remained the option of choice.

Now Elliot is three-years-old. His pacifier dangles from a necklace he wears for most of the day. His parents have its use down to a science. The moment he begins to register discomfort, he or someone else pushes the pacifier into his mouth. This satisfies everyone, but something very important is being overlooked. Elliot is not mastering his developmental hurdles. If his parents took the time to observe him more carefully, they would see that he is more like a typical two-year-old.

His bonds are not strong and he is not building the skills needed to handle stress. There was no need for him to learn coping mechanisms, since his parents supplied him with an easy way out. The road for him is destined to become increasingly difficult as he confronts new and more difficult problems, such as entry into school. Within a year or so he will begrudgingly give up the pacifier that had dangled around his neck. But by this time he will have fallen behind and will continue to need pacifiers of one kind or the other. His parents may not be very pleased by his choices as he approaches adolescence.

Points to Remember

- During the first eight months, children often cannot cope with tension, and it is normal for them to resort to the use of pacifiers for relief.

- Since parental love and contact is essential during this time, the best pacifier is the parents' loving involvement.

- It is sensible as well as inevitable that during this period there will be many moments when children are left to their own resources.

- It is normal for some infants to find their thumbs, the blanket, or other objects they can use to release their built-up tension.

- The use of an artificial pacifier may be appropriate during periods of fussiness that continue in spite of parental attempts at soothing.

- By six months, children should be developing better coping mechanisms and the pacifier can be gradually eliminated.

- The continued use of the pacifier into the second year will impede the acquisition of better coping mechanisms.

Chapter 8

EACH CHILD IS UNIQUE – INBORN DIFFERENCES

Strong bonding derives from love. Love means the appreciation and total acceptance of another. I have often heard parents say that their child is hard to love. Parents are sometimes disappointed and disturbed by the discrepancy between the smiling, contented child they imagined they would have and the one they find in their care. Their feelings of frustration can easily erode the quality of their love during this crucial time.

Question – I sometimes envy my friends. Their babies are so cuddly and smile all the time. Mine has seemed to resist and fight me right from birth. What accounts for this? Could there be something that is physically wrong, or is it something that I did?

Right from birth, children are dramatically different from each other. Some love to be loved, sleep well, and gobble up their feedings. Others are hard to soothe, cry a lot, and eat poorly. Both groups can do well if they are helped by their parents to master developmental hurdles. **There are two reasons that parenting may fall short – misinformation about their child and his developmental needs, and their own painful emotional blisters.**

I am stating the obvious when I say that there are wide differences between individuals. This needs to be said repeatedly because all of us tend to go through life with expectations of how others should behave. We are especially dismayed when our little kids, our own flesh and blood, fail to conform to our expectations. Many parents are derailed right from the start because of this frustration. The first weeks of our children's lives require many new adjustments. Sometimes, one of the most difficult of these is an acceptance of their hard to sooth, irritable baby.

Some kids, it always seems like the ones next door, appear like little angels. They may even allow their parents to get a reasonable amount of sleep at night. In contrast, the one upstairs is cranky, irritable, and worst of all does not love being loved. These more irritable babies seem to provide little return for the excessive demands, both physical and emotional, they place upon their parents. Love not returned in its hoped for form is one of the more hurtful experiences we encounter. We all love to love babies and many feel confused and dismayed when our best attempts are met with scowls and howls. This frustration and fatigue account for the often heard, half-humorous comments made by parents about these very little babies, "What did I do to deserve this?" "Can I trade him in?" or "You take care of him until he gets old enough to be pleasant." Information about the wide spectrum of normal behavior helps reduce the impact of potential painful emotional blisters.

IS THERE SOMETHING WRONG WITH MY CHILD?

Question – Do irritability and crankiness indicate some kind of physical malady?

One of the most common flaws in reasoning follows from the enormous attraction to simple and emotionally appealing answers to life's problems. This is why parents and even many professionals may quickly attribute children's unpleasant behavior to a physical cause, such as a food allergy, or minimal brain damage. It is certainly important to detect and treat the extremely few real physical problems sometimes present at birth. The very rare disorder that needs to be treated is easily detected. Most of the physical explanations for disturbing behavior are completely unfounded. The behavior patterns of newborn babies vary as much as will their heights and weights when they are full grown.

The danger in continuing to search for a physical cause for a child's behavior is that the effort and feelings engendered by doing so diverts the parents from their primary task during this stage of development – helping to create strong bonds of love. Sometimes parents are carried far afield by their obsession with finding a physical cause for behavior they find undesirable. The children of these parents may actually end up disabled. Not because of any physical abnormality, but as a result of the deficiency of love and care they received by their parents, whose perceptions of them were distorted.

It is noteworthy that the outcome for children who do have serious physical disabilities correlates far better with their mastery of developmental hurdles than with the actual disability. The reason is simple. The way physically impaired adults view and manage their physical disabilities depends mainly on their maturity, emotional strengths, and personality skills. The individuals who end up most handicapped, whether or not they are physically normal, are those who failed to master these early developmental hurdles.

Nearly all children who are excessively active, irritable, and harder to soothe during early infancy have no physical abnormalities. These kids can do perfectly well as they get older. In fact, if their sensitivities are constructively channeled they can evolve into creative talents. These children's elevated drive and energy levels, so disturbing during infancy, can later become a capacity to work harder and more successfully.

Unfortunately, many of these harder-to-soothe infants do not fulfill their potentials. Their poor prognosis seldom has anything to do with the early irritability. It has a great deal to do with their parents' responses to them. The term "overactive" as a description of young children has assumed a negative connotation. Yet most successful people in all walks of life are basically overactive. They become immersed in the things they do and pursue their goals with enthusiasm, in spite of the hard work necessary or the obstacles in their path.

Even during the school years, many of the most active children are the most successful. A child can be extremely active, but if that activity is devoted to getting the job done, his performance in school will be fine. Beginning life with a higher irritability level is not a deterrent to good functioning later on, if these children have been helped by their parents to master the developmental hurdles leading to maturity.

The Fear of a Defect Causes a Defect – Is There Something Wrong with Nancy?

There wasn't anyone in Nancy's family who didn't agree with her mother's conviction that Nancy was an impossible baby. She seemed to cry most of the day, would spit up her food, and awoke frequently at night. Most disconcerting to Nancy's mother, who had always wanted a child, was that Nancy did not seem to like her. She ached to hold her little girl and have her cuddle and smile back. Nancy seemed determined to resist this. Her mother felt confused and began to view herself as a failure. She vacillated between blaming herself and blaming Nancy.

Although Nancy was only two-months-old, she was already a high-risk child. The main problem was the effect that her behavior had on her mother, rather than the behavior itself. Nancy was not receiving the daily love and acceptance she needed for the formation of good bonding. "But how can anyone love a child like that?" family members would ask when Nancy's mother complained to them about her child, and expressed some feelings of guilt.

Well, the relatives were wrong. It is possible to provide love to a child who stomps on our emotional blisters and seems to literally spit in our eyes, no matter how hard we try to please him. It may not be easy, but it can be done. There is a question I like to ask parents who tell me that it is hard to love their child. I ask, "I wonder why you feel that it is easier to be frustrated, stressed, angry, and unhappy than it is to be loving?" "Isn't loving a source of joy?," I inquire. Responding to their expression of bewilderment, I usually followed this question with its answer, "Loving our children is not hard, it is a joy." It only becomes difficult because our little ones are so good at stomping on our emotional blisters.

An understanding of how this happens provides parents with the opportunity to make an extremely important decision. They can surrender to the power of their emotional blisters and be steered by the feelings unleashed, or they can use this precious time with their little ones to begin to understand and master those nasty blisters. Is the effort worth making? Is there anything we can do in our own lives that we might rank as more important than meeting our infant's need for love? And will there ever be as much at stake? It may be hard to withstand the pull of our emotional blisters now, but that task is dwarfed by the parenting problems that we will likely have to face in the future if we do not.

A happy ending to a scary story

Most of us are willing to make an extra effort to accomplish tasks that we label as important. Some infants are irritable, cranky, and don't seem to respond comfortably to our love and care. Children not meeting our expectations are not a problem, but a lesson designed for our edification. And we might as well face this early on, since it will be a daily occurrence. This is the time for parents to make the same kind of extra effort that they do over and over again in other facets of their lives. They and their children will reap wonderful rewards from this effort, but will pay a dear price if they fail.

Nancy's mother was immediately relieved when she was told that the child's irritable behavior was due to sensitivities present from birth, and that Nancy was a fine baby who could do as well in life as any other child. With encouragement and some sound thinking, the mother was able to find a formula for providing love and care that was more compatible with her child's disposition. For example, Nancy cried intensely when she was snuggled closely, face-to-face with her mother. The mother discovered that when she bounced Nancy gently on her knees and allowed her to face another direction, Nancy enjoyed the interaction and settled down. Nancy's parents, working together, found numerous other ways to show her love and care. To their pleasant surprise, within a period of months Nancy's pattern of interaction began to fall closer to the norm. By the time she was one-year-old, Nancy was indistinguishable from other happy, loving kids.

I was able to tell these parents that their extra efforts had given Nancy the most precious gift that she will ever receive. They said that being able to fully love Nancy was probably the most precious gift they would ever receive.

The steps that Nancy's parents followed are the same ones implemented by Abe's parents. First, they learned the meaning of the problem, allowing them to make sense of Nancy's behavior. Second, they realized their real goal: finding a way of providing loving care to a very irritable child. Finally, armed with this knowledge, they formulated parenting strategies aimed at achieving that goal. They were able to use their creativity to find workable solutions to problems that would have guaranteed serious problems later on.

Step 1 – Understanding the meaning of problematic behavior, or discerning the developmental struggle that accounts for the behavior.

Step 2 – Understanding that the goal is nearly always synonymous with mastery of the developmental hurdle.

Step 3 – Formulating a parenting plan aimed at achieving the goal.

Points to Remember

- From birth, children's temperaments vary tremendously – some are placid and easy to manage and others irritable and tense.

- Differences in temperament are normal and not harbingers of later problems.

- Difficulties arise only if a child's higher level of irritability interferes significantly with his parents' capacity to remain loving and accepting.

Chapter 9

GIVING A HELPING HAND – THE ROLE OF THE OTHER PARENT

Question – My spouse just does not seem to have the motivation or ability to give our child the love and care he needs. I now know how important this is during this period of time and am concerned about the impact it might have on the formation of bonds. How should I think about this and what should I do?

Blame – The enemy of helping

Helping a loved one is not as simple as it might seem at first glance. The well-intended desire to help a loved one with a problem youngster too often leads to words that are interpreted as criticism and blame, and this becomes its undoing. In fact, many times the best, or only, help we can offer is to lovingly accept that we cannot help. **At all costs, it is essential to avoid blaming.** The opposite of helping is not the concession that there are times when we can do nothing to help. **The opposite of helping is blaming.**

When faced with difficult problems, we often fall into the trap of asking the wrong questions. Answers to the wrong questions lead us away from viable solutions. Topping the list of flawed questions we ask when we become aware that something is wrong is, "Who is to blame?" The appropriate question that should be asked is, "What does this problem mean?" Problems can't be solved until they are understood. Instead of trying to understand, we have a tendency to jump to blaming.

There is never a role for blame in parenting. It is always inappropriate and destructive because it complicates problems and never aids in their solutions. The blamed person is not better equipped to solve the problem. His already diminished capacity to function is further eroded by heightened guilt and anger. In addition, blaming is inappropriate because it implies that the mistakes made by parents with their children could and should have been avoided. This is always untrue. No parent would intentionally harm his or her child emotionally or physically if there were an alternative and the capacity to choose.

There are essentially two causes of poor parenting: ignorance and very painful emotional blisters. Blaming others for their ignorance makes no sense unless they are aware of their ignorance, have the ability to remedy it, and elect not to make that change. I have never found an actual example of this. When parents err, they are either unaware of their ignorance, or can't do anything about it because of the obstructive power of their emotional blisters. Parents with the necessary knowledge of good parenting, and sufficient freedom from emotional blisters to implement this knowledge, will always do so.

Question – What is the alternative to blame? I can't help blaming myself and others.

We are not to blame for our ignorance or for our emotional blisters. We did not choose to have them. We all do, however, have a faculty that allows us to become cognizant of both our ignorance and the constellation of emotions that bar us from wiser choices. If this were not true, there would be no possibility for growth. The capacity to understand that our beliefs may be in error, and then to choose accurate ones to replace them, combined with a willingness to make an effort to use this newly acquired knowledge in our daily lives, is the only path leading to growth.

If it were only ignorance that bared our access to the path of growth, problems would be quickly solved. The primary purpose of this book is to replace flawed information about parenting with accurate knowledge. This is the easy part. All that is required is a willingness to acknowledge mistaken beliefs and replace them with ones that make better sense. Parents who do not have painful emotional blisters are usually able, and even eager, to accept new information about parenting, allowing them to see the flaws in their previous thinking. Armed with this new knowledge, they willingly discard past beliefs and implement a parenting strategy that dovetails with their child's developmental needs. In my work with parents, this has been the easy part. It has been gratifying to see the rapid progress made by kids whose parents were able to quickly utilize new knowledge.

The other purpose of this book is to alert the reader to the negative impact that our painful emotional blisters have on the quality of our parenting and to find ways to diminish their untoward influence. This is much harder to do. Most of us are not even aware when this is happening. Dominated by the power of those blisters, our focus becomes directed at efforts to find relief. It is clear that the ability to relinquish poor parenting approaches and to implement better ones, is considerably more difficult when our emotional blisters become irritated. What can be done about these pesky feelings?

The main ally we have is our faculty for understanding. An awareness or ability to reflect upon these feelings allows us to recognize when they are coming into play. In theory, this is a simple matter. We should be aware that our parental blisters are becoming a problem any time our children's behavior makes us uncomfortable. Emotional discomfort is a reliable signal indicating that we have become a part of the problem. The greater our discomfort, the more likely our judgment will be significantly impaired.

I have repeatedly emphasized the impact of emotional blisters because in my experience they have been the main impediments to positive change.

COPING WITH EMOTIONAL BLISTERS – A BRIEF REVIEW

1. Be alert to their presence when parenting leads to confusion or discomfort.

2. When this happens, pause and ask the right question, "What does this mean?" rather than, "What do I do?" or "Who is to blame?"

3. If the answer to the question, "What does this mean?" is, "I am confused about my child's behavior," the solution is

straightforward. Try to link the behavior to the developmental hurdle that the child is negotiating. Read the appropriate chapter, if you have doubts.

4. If parental stress levels remain high, you need to direct your attention to your emotional blisters. High stress levels are associated with confusion. This is not the time to plunge ahead with more strongly enforced parenting schemes. Our best ally here is insight into the meaning of our child's behavior and its link to our distress. This type of reasoning is our best tool for coping with emotional blisters.

5. Making sense of our child's behavior and knowing what needs to be done is the best way to reduce stress. **When stress levels are high, it is time to stop, think, and ask, "What does this mean?"** Often, this cooling down period of clear thinking is sufficient to regain a firmer footing.

Points to Remember

- It is common for parents to blame one another, or sometimes their children, for their own discomfort.

- Blame, whether directed towards our children or our spouse, is never helpful and always makes matter worse.

- Families should be no-blame zones.

- Blame usually follows from confusion and stress.

- Clear, cool thinking is the best remedy to overcome blame and helps to define a more reasonable course of action.

CHAPTER 10

DEPRESSION – A COMMON EMOTIONAL BLISTER

Question – What about helping others without blame? Sometimes my spouse is depressed and not able to cope with the kids. I try not to blame, but often can't hold back because I feel so helpless. What should I do?

There are a number of different types of emotional blisters that interfere with good parenting. A common and often serious one that occurs during the first months of a baby's life is parental depression. There are numerous reasons for this. The arrival of a newborn places many psychological burdens on the parents. Their relationship with each other is forced to change. One or both of them may find that emotional needs previously met within the marriage are being frustrated. Old schedules and routines that lent predictability and satisfaction to their lives are disrupted and many need to be abandoned. The demands upon them increase and they are thrust into new roles with which they have had little or no experience. The infant's behavior also has a powerful impact on the parents. The child's seemingly insatiable needs, the intensity of his pain, and his complete helplessness and dependency, all serve to re-create and bring to the surface similar feelings within the parents. In addition to all of these external stresses, there are powerful biological changes that predispose mothers to depression.

The problem with tackling depression is that most of the commonsense tactics don't work. Encouraging our loved one to try harder, snap out of it, or see the bright side of things, may hurt more than help. Understanding our spouse's pain, instead of blaming or cajoling, makes better sense. There are many very effective treatments available for this problem that can dramatically shorten the period of suffering. Opportunities for treatment of even moderate postpartum blues should not be missed.

What can we do?

If we had the magical power to eliminate the pain from our spouse's life, we would. If we can accept what we can't do, we are freed to do what we can. There are important things we can do to help our spouse. The depressed parent needs love and understanding from us. The many pressures we experience, as well as the behavior of our spouse who may be completely unable to reciprocate our love, make this a formidable task. It demands that we bring a high level of motivation to this important endeavor.

If our loved one is competent and motivated to provide care, this should be encouraged no matter how meager that care might be. This is important for two reasons. The child obtains love and attention that would otherwise be absent, and the act of caring itself may foster the emergence of stronger feelings of love. We should never discount the ability of an infant to gently lull his parents into a mutually rewarding interplay of love. The least-desirable alternative for the infant is isolation.

Question – Is there anything more a loved one can do until relief is obtained either by treatment or, for milder episodes, until there is a gradual remission?

If the love and care provided by one parent is deficient, the other parent or another relative should pitch in. This job is too important to be overlooked, even for a short period of time. Generally, this is not what happens. Emotional unrest is like a communicable disease – it spreads chaos and distress from one to another. When one parent drops the ball, the other may feel overwhelmed and let it roll. As a result, the job of parenting at this crucial time may not get done.

It is hard for one parent to do two or more jobs during a time of turmoil. I want to emphasize that the stakes are very high and the investment is worth making. In the business world, we might be very willing to undertake an exhausting job if we knew that a few months of very hard work would pay off to the tune of a million dollars. The satisfactory completion of this job is worth many times that in terms of the far-reaching consequences for our child and our family. In later years, we may even look back and say to ourselves, "It was our finest hour."

Points to Remember

When your partner can't do the job

- Avoid blame.

- Provide large doses of the best medicine we have – love and understanding.

- Enlist the help of others, especially to combat depression.

- Don't overlook your child and his continuing, desperate need for love and attention.

CHAPTER 11

EARLY SEPARATIONS – VACATIONS AND OTHER TIMES AWAY FROM THE CHILD – THE FIRST SIX MONTHS

It takes time to build bonds, time full of loving and caring for our children. Time can also erode bonds, time apart from our children. These bonds are important, but they are also very fragile during the first year of life. When our children are older, their bonds with us are much stronger and can survive a great deal of pain, including more prolonged periods of separation. **During the first six months of life, our infants cannot endure separations of more than a few days before they are overwhelmed by our absence. Absences of this length, as well as repeated interference in the continuity of the parents' care, impede the mastery of this developmental phase and have a variety of unfavorable consequences.**

Question – I now understand the importance of bonding and how this is achieved. I know that more love and contact with our child is better than less love and contact. I am wondering about the effects of vacations and other separations upon bonding. Are there guidelines that can help to clarify this issue?

Whose clock – The child's or the parents'?

Separations are a part of reality. Much of the time its measurement and the interpretation of its meaning are based on how it is perceived in the eyes of the beholder, rather than by the precision of clocks. The estimate of passing time during separations varies dramatically, depending upon many factors, including age, vulnerability, state of helplessness, past experiences, and current situation. No one needs to be reminded that time seems to move slowly when we are in either physical or emotional pain. In marked contrast, we are often oblivious of the passage of time when in the midst of a joyous experience.

We know that the damage done by the disruption of bonds during the first year is of great magnitude. It is therefore important that we do everything possible to keep this to a minimum. To accomplish this, we need to know the length of separation that is likely to fray and sever these ties of love. This issue is especially important in our society. Families today often consider options that will take parents away from their children for variable periods of time.

The saying, "absence makes the heart grow fonder," may be applicable to separations from an older child. But a more accurate expression of the impact of separation on children during the first six months of life might be, "out of sight, out of mind." Each time this happens, each time the parent is away for the amount of time it takes for bonds to fray, it becomes more difficult to restore the bonds. In addition, the helpless infant will avail himself of a variety of less adaptive methods to allay his distress.

Bonding is based on the child becoming comfortable with a specific face and style of care. Disruptions in the continuity of this care, even when this merely consists of repeated movements from parent to babysitter, may dilute the strength of emerging bonds. These types of changes are often stressful for adults. The elevated discomfort the child must experience erodes his potential for trust and delays the formation of the basic building blocks required for the later development of self-esteem.

GUIDELINES FOR SEPARATIONS DURING INFANCY

Continuity of care is especially important during a child's first six months. Separations of more than one day should be avoided. These would tax the child's budding ability to hold on to the essential feelings of closeness and trust. As much as possible, parents should limit their absences to evenings or parts of days. Many children may have the ability to withstand more prolonged absences without damage. But since so much is at stake, it is wise to err on the side of safety. As the child's bonds grow stronger and his coping mechanisms increase, he will be able to tolerate, and even profit from, longer well-timed separations. This period of increased vulnerability passes quickly and parents will soon have ample opportunities to vacation apart from their baby.

If the infant's mother needs to be away from her child for more than a day, the child should be left in the care of another "mother." I am using the term "mother" to connote the other person, or persons, with whom the child knows and is comfortable. If the father has participated in the child's daily care, bonds will have been established between the two and his substitution for the mother during her absence would be a good choice if this can be arranged. If both parents must be away for more than a day, the selection should be made from the persons most familiar with the child and the child's routines. Whenever possible, it is preferable for the care to be given in the child's own home and the caretaker should be given as much information as possible about the baby's routines, habits, and other characteristics.

Parents often feel more uncomfortable about leaving an older child with a caretaker than an infant. They are mistaken about this. It is far easier to deny the pain we are causing others when that pain, and the effects of that pain, are not immediately evident. By the time our children are two-years-old they have developed a hearty set of lungs and the smarts to let their parents know how strongly they object to being left. Parents can leave, but not without the child being able to get his revenge. In contrast, the infant seems outwardly content as he passively submits to movement from one caretaker to another.

The difference in responses of children in these two age groups is not due to the lesser harm occurring to the infant. It is a reflection of the older child's greater ability to vocalize and protest his hurt and direct his anger at its source.

During infancy, these separations impair the initial formation of trust. It is noteworthy that the one- to two-year-old who has securely bonded during infancy will protest vociferously when left with a stranger. In marked contrast, a youngster of the same age whose bonding was sabotaged by early and repeated separations may seem on the surface to adapt very nicely to changes in caretakers. Parents may be pleased with this, not realizing that these children have not bonded securely, and as a consequence, lack a basic building block of good personality development. Their apparent ability to accept separation, a trait seen in many children who attended day care during their first year, may be a sign of poor bonding and not an indication of real independence. It is easier for children, and adults as well, to shift from one person to another if their ties of love are not strong. But this is based on vulnerability rather than being a sign of strength.

Real independence, self-control, and self-esteem rest on a solid foundation of bonding and trust. Younger children, who have bonded securely and are on the path towards the development of trust, are still very helpless and will object to separations. But their strong foundation of security will allow them to gradually develop the skills needed to achieve complete independence and finally full emancipation.

Points to Remember

- Decisions about separation need to consider the impact upon the child.

- During the first six months of life, separation of more than one day may not be advisable.

- If separations for longer periods are necessary, a caretaker should be chosen who already has ties to the child and is aware of the child's routines.

Chapter 12

AN EARLY RETURN TO WORK?

Question – If extended separations can diminish the strength of my child's bonds with me, how might my returning to work during this phase of his development affect him? Can substitute care provide the love and attention required to forge strong bonds?

The guideline about the primary caretaker working during this period is quite clear. If at all possible, avoid it. If we constructed a graph depicting the importance of parents' contact with their children from birth through adulthood, and gave year eight a ten rating, then the first year would deserve a rating in the hundreds.

The outcry from parents and others to this guideline is often loud and angry. After all, many mothers of newborns want to work and a considerable number need to work to support their family. It is easy to understand the variety of personal, financial, and political issues involved in this decision. The purpose of this book, however, is to clarify parenting from the perspective of the child. It is not to make a value judgment about the other priorities of parents.

This book was written solely for the purpose of providing information to parents about the developmental needs of their children. There are many other interests apart from parenting that motivate their choices. Parents must decide how they will mesh the multiplicity of these other agendas with their roles as parents. Information about this helps them to make more informed decisions.

It is important to elaborate a clear formulation of both the needs of their child, and the optimum solution, even if most parents cannot always reach this high standard. Failure to do this would leave many parents who do have the capacity to take positive steps without the necessary knowledge to do so. This information is also useful for parents who find it impossible to optimally meet their child's needs because of other important demands on their time. A better understanding of the most favorable strategies can help them to find compromises and alternatives that will come closer to the ideal.

Sometimes, parents have little interest in information that may call into question their cherished theories. They tend to search for information that supports their beliefs. An unwillingness to evaluate new information or opinions is nearly always a symptom of one type of emotional blister or another.

The One-Mother Rule

Question – I have been told that it may be constructive for very young children to get used to more than one person. What do you think?

The one-mother rule as the ideal arrangement for children during this phase of development is not arbitrary. It is derived from an understanding of early development. From the infant's perspective, having one mother with him during most of each day, giving the love and care needed to build strong bonds, is the ideal. I am using the term "mother" for the person who functions in the role of giving love and care on a continuous, daily basis.

We would certainly understand and be completely accepting of a mother who looked adoringly into her child's eyes and said, "Dear baby, more than anything in the world, my first choice would be to give you the daily love you need. But we must eat, and to do that I must be away from you for most of your waking hours." We would understand that this is a realistic decision and be completely accepting of it. But if her infant could process her language he would not be at all accepting or understanding.

Understanding the Child's Point of View

Children's perceptions of events are based on the developmental hurdles with which they are struggling and the level of cognitive functioning available to them. From this standpoint, his mother's decision to return to work is highly undesirable, regardless of its realistic necessity. It is the daily rhythm of anticipated care and loving responses that is the stuff from which bonds are forged. The movement from one caretaker to another disrupts the harmony of that rhythm. Infants are extremely sensitive to changes in their care and have very meager abilities to discharge the stress that is engendered by these changes. Even adults find changes in their lives, especially ones involving people they are close to, extremely stressful. And when all else fails and that stress level gets too high, an adult can always shout, "Stop this merry-go-round, I don't want to put up with it anymore!" The infant can do nothing. He helplessly submits to the hurt and its ominous long-term consequences. He cannot speak for himself and there is no one else to speak for him.

The ties of meaningful love that are the first stepping stones towards trust, self-esteem, and maturity cannot be forged from a succession of faces, even when those faces convey love. The child must have the opportunity to do what Henry Higgins sings about in the musical *My Fair Lady* – "I've grown accustomed to her face." It is one face and one touch that love requires rather than a series of faces. It is the increasing trust and the feeling of being accepted and loved by that one specific person that leads to a solid sense of security and self-esteem. It is hard enough for the child to learn that there is one reliable face that becomes associated with love and care. To accomplish this satisfactorily with an array of faces and changing routines will tax the capacity of many children. There will come a time in our children's lives when it is constructive for them to become more deeply involved with a variety of individuals. This is not the time.

Effective loving takes time and commitment. How meaningfully can that love be communicated when it is sandwiched fleetingly between other priorities that consume most of our energy and time? Even those few precious moments when we are finally with our kids are contaminated by the thoughts of the many other things that must be done. Parents who are busy with other activities most of the day will too often think of their babies as one additional chore that must be attended to before they can rest. We are all exquisitely aware when the person whose love we crave is looking through us, rather than at us, or telling us by their look that we are a bother and source of pain to them. This is the opposite of love and when repeated becomes indelibly imprinted into the infant's impressionable mind.

Substitute Care – Weighing the Alternatives

The Least-Bad Alternative

Question – I can understand the drawbacks of separations from our children during this early period. But sometimes a daily caretaking arrangement cannot be avoided. What do you think about a single caretaker arrangement?

This is obviously a better arrangement than one in which a larger number of babies are contained in one setting. If the best alternative – a loving, full time parent – is not possible, then this arrangement is the second best choice. The first choice is a full time parent. The love that imbeds within children a firm conviction of their intrinsic value can only be conveyed by a look or touch that communicates a sense of unconditional love, forever. It is that message that creates strong bonds. Later in life, our children will need to learn how to hold onto that message during the long hours that we are apart from them. There will be nothing to hold onto if the bonding was not forged securely during infancy. Only the parents can communicate, "You are mine, precious to me, and I'm yours forever and ever."

Even the best substitute caretakers cannot convey this message. The child is not theirs and they are ever aware that their contact with him can be terminated at any time. Many factors, such as the whims of the parents, the possibility of finding a more convenient or less expensive arrangement, or the decision to stop working for a while, create an atmosphere of impermanence to the arrangement. It is unusual, for even more mature adults, to allow themselves to become fully committed to someone they know may soon be completely absent from their lives.

What about Larger Child Care Settings?

There are significant drawbacks to the best kinds of substitute care. The dangers for infants in less-desirable settings, such as the larger day care facilities, are much more ominous.

The very helpless, vulnerable infant will have slim pickings if he is in a group of other infants. How likely will he be to obtain the special attention, stimulation, and love he must have to take that first secure step towards maturity?

Well-intentioned parents may attempt to minimize the dangers of substitute care by searching for a setting that meets their standards for good care, warmth, and stability. Their attentions are commendable and this type of planning and exploration should always precede the placement of children into caretaking facilities outside of the home. Good intentions, however, are not enough. Parents should be forewarned that despite their extensive research about the quality of the day care facility they select, there is no assurance that the best choice will have been made. There are so many unpredictable variables that come into play. It is extremely difficult to accurately evaluate the actual quality of individual care by even careful observations. In addition, changes in staff are not uncommon.

Question – You have mentioned your concern about repeated changes in the lives of very young children. Can you help me to better appreciate what this entails?

In order to appreciate the impact of repeated changes it will be helpful if we can imagine them from a young baby's perspective.

Three Strikes and You're Out

The Sims, a young professional couple, began to make careful plans for substitute care arrangements several months before the birth of their first child, John. The parents met with the prospective caretaker several times and were convinced that she was an extremely pleasant, kind, and dedicated person. They observed her interactions with two toddlers already in her care and noted her warmth and patience. Mrs. Sims returned to work when John was three months of age. She was completely comfortable with her decision. Naturally, John had to adjust to the abrupt loss of his mother and a new person who was suddenly in his life for most of his waking hours. But John could not communicate this to anyone. **STRIKE ONE!**

The first doubt about the quality of John's care occurred when Mrs. Sims came early to pick him and discovered that his bottle was being propped. Troubled by this, she spoke to John's caretaker and then tried to push the matter out of her mind. She was not able to avoid a recurrent feeling of uneasiness about not knowing what happened during the many hours each day that John was away from her. Her anxiety returned with throbbing impact after she met with another woman whose child had been in the home of the same caretaker. This woman told her that the caretaker was a warm and kind person, but seemed to prefer toddlers and had given very little attention to her infant.

After a panicky discussion with her husband, Mrs. Sims decided to find another caretaker for John. Now she had less time to carefully explore other alternatives. John was placed in a neighborhood day care setting recommended by a family member. Naturally, John had to adjust to the change in caretakers, routines, and setting, but he could not communicate this to anyone. ***STRIKE TWO!***

After just a few weeks, Mrs. Sims knew that this arrangement was not adequate. She found herself preoccupied during work with thoughts about her son and was not sleeping well at night. Neither was John. She was relieved when a friend at work, having had a similar experience, encouraged her to contact an older woman she had used who was willing to care for children in their own homes. The friend could vouch for her skill and love of infants. From Mrs. Sims's perspective, this would work out beautifully and was well worth the added expense. This woman reminded Mrs. Sims of her own grandmother and seemed to take an immediate liking to John. Naturally, John had to adjust to another change, but he not communicate this to anyone. ***STRIKE THREE!***

John was now five-and-one-half-months-old. The phone rang in the Sims' home at about 8:00 on a Sunday evening. The caretaker sounded distraught and explained that she would not be able to take care of John for at least one month. A close relative had become seriously ill and needed her help.

At 9:00 P.M., Mrs. Sims was not thinking of John. She was thinking of how she would find another caretaker for tomorrow. She was thinking of many things all at once but most of all about her job, which would suffer if she did not find someone quickly. Naturally John would now have to adjust to the next tidal wave of changes as well as his own stressed mother, so different from the mother he had known when he was only two-months-old. But he could not communicate this to anyone.

Mrs. Sims was able to find another day care provider and John did not seem the worse for the ordeal. "How wonderfully compliant he is," she thought. John seemed to accept all of this, but what else could he do? Several years passed before John's behavior began to reveal trends that stemmed from this series of separations. He became a hard-to-manage four-year-old and did poorly in kindergarten. During the early grades he had difficulty learning and continued to display an attitude of not trying and needing to have his way.

It is noteworthy that his attitude of not trying and needing to have his own way mirrored the example he had learned from his parents when he was accumulating his strikes. His parents, of course, had no way of knowing this and attributed his problems to a variety of causes. They tried to alter his diet by reducing the sugar content, then used time-outs to modify his behavior. Each seemed to work for awhile, but his problems continued. They finally consulted a child psychiatrist who told them that John had an attention deficit disorder and needed to take Ritalin and engage in a number of other therapeutic programs. John submitted to this as well. He could not tell anyone what had happened. He did not know himself since it happened when he was preverbal. It happened at a time in his life when only his parents were in a position to think clearly about what he needed from them. Although they loved him and were well-intentioned parents, they had no awareness of the impact their decisions were having upon his early development.

As the years passed his problems continued. Teachers and others were bewildered about this since the Sims seemed like such loving and reasonable parents.

Sound Decisions Are Based on Knowledge and Reason

Question – Sometimes parents are bitter and resentful when they are stuck at home with their infants. Isn't it better for these parents to be working?

Some of the concepts I have described may cause some parents to feel uneasy. They are not intended for that purpose. The prerequisite for learning is a willingness to discard old beliefs for new ones that we decide are more valid. Learning cannot occur if we are not willing to consider concepts that may make us uncomfortable. I am presenting this information because I believe it will help parents to make decisions that are more likely to dovetail with their children's developmental needs. One thing is clear: Sound decisions cannot be made if we are not willing to consider ideas that differ from ours.

I have mentioned this before but it bears repeating. There is no room for guilt or blame in parenting. We did not choose to adopt beliefs that are invalid, nor do we choose to experience the array of uncomfortable feelings that interfere with sound parenting. Flawed information causes the former and emotional blisters the latter. We are, however, blessed with minds that provide us with a special capacity to think about our beliefs, discern their validity, and deal with the emotional resistances that stand in the way of their replacement when we find them flawed. There is a tendency to overlook, deny, and sometimes ridicule concepts that cause us uneasiness. Let us be alert to the emotional blisters that prompt such attitudes, since they are the most pernicious obstacles to learning and growth.

There are many parents who must work. It is imperative for these parents to comprehend the significance of this first developmental hurdle. Neglecting to clarify the importance of early bonding may enable parents to avoid some feelings of uneasiness they might otherwise experience about returning to work. But it leaves them bereft of the knowledge essential for them to use the limited time they do have available in the most effective manner.

Other parents work during this very early period even when it is not absolutely essential for economic reasons. This decision is sometimes supported by the contention that these mothers would be resentful and unhappy if they remained home. Advocates of this position claim that these mothers are happier, and therefore more motivated, to provide higher quality care for their children if they find fulfillment in work.

Knowledge about bonding reveals the flaw in this reasoning. It is easy to overlook the many obstacles to good bonding that follow from the decision to return to work during this developmental phase. Many of these have been addressed. Certainly there are infants who are better off with good substitute caretakers. These children have mothers who are so extremely depressed or angry that they might be physically or emotionally abusive. In these instances the decision to work is reasonable, but from the child's perspective it is not the best arrangement. A happier, working mother, rather than a depressed, abusing one, may be the better of two undesirable alternatives. But it is not the ideal alternative.

The ideal alternative is a happy, full-time mother.

None of us enjoys finding out that our decisions are based on faulty reasoning. For this reason it is common for parents to convince themselves that making the better of two undesirable choices is the same as making the best choice. Some parents work because they must, but many work by choice. These parents need to fully understand all the ramifications of this decision. Would they want it otherwise? Would they prefer to remain unaware of important information that will bear upon the future well-being of their children?

The Hidden Message Transmitted In an Early Return to Work

Children always become much more like us than the way we want them to be. We transmit a very powerful message to our infants when we choose to work in order to avoid feeling miserable by staying home. In words, the message might sound something like this, "Being at home with you makes me miserable; I feel better if I can get away from you during most of the day. My own desire for pleasure comes first and you are in the way of that."

Love is the appreciation of the intrinsic value of another being. Wanting to be away from our children during the time that our presence in their lives is so important implies a devaluation of them that is the opposite of love. Bonding suffers and the negative image implied by this message becomes embedded in the their impressionable minds, becoming their own self-image.

Parents are usually bewildered when their kids of ten- or fifteen-years-old are selfish and unwilling to think about others. The parents fail to understand why their kids may be so demanding and intolerant of anything that stands in the way of their immediate pleasure. They wonder where this comes from and are at a loss to know how to deal with it. They don't realize that the picture they see of their kids saying, "My own immediate desire for pleasure comes first and you are in the way," may be exactly the same message that they transmitted to their children when they returned to work. They don't realize that the pain engendered in their infants by that message was far more intense than the pain they are now experiencing as they try to cope with the noncompliance of their child who is now age ten. And they are completely unaware that the early hurt inflicted by that message was not a one-time-and-it-is-over kind of hurt. It weakened bonds leaving a legacy that may follow and plague the child into adulthood. They can't possibly realize any of this. Their child had no way of telling them when he was an infant.

A JOB WORTH DOING WELL

Some jobs are more important than others. The job of creating the strong bonds that become the foundations of self-esteem and trust must rank very high on the list of important life tasks. Its impact upon a child's future functioning and happiness is enormous. It is a job that has much at stake but it is also one that is remarkably gratifying and fulfilling. Can there be any valid reason to want to miss the opportunity to watch our own child emerge into a person, knowing that the essential ingredient for this remarkable transformation is our love? In addition, unlike other jobs that can be put off for another day, in a twinkling that precious time has passed and we will have missed the only chance we will ever have to do it right the first time, when it counts most.

This special altruistic commitment of our time can only be given productively very early in our children's lives. The ramifications of that commitment, however, will continue to be felt by them as well as by us for the rest of our lives. The form of our commitment changes, as our child grows older and stronger. Soon enough parents will have ample opportunities to pursue other interests that may take them away from their children for longer periods of time. It is only very early in their lives that our children need a fairly continuous infusion of attention and love. As the first building blocks of development become stronger, children will be able to, and even profit from, learning to deal with the more extended periods of time that they are apart from us.

GUIDELINES FOR WORKING PARENTS

Question – I have no choice and must work. Now that I understand the importance of this first developmental hurdle I would like to know the most reasonable way to implement my return to work. Are there principles that will be helpful?

Some parents have no choice. They must work a major portion of each day. The following is a summary of the general guidelines that may help them choose the least-damaging alternatives:

1. It is extremely important for all parents, but especially for those who decide to work, to thoroughly understand the developmental hurdles their children must master during this period of their lives.

2. The choice of a caretaker is obviously extremely important. In addition to the type of personality that would be most desirable, parents should try to make sure that the first decision would be the only one. Repeated changes should be avoided. These are far more harmful than they may seem at the time. The least-bad alternative is for the caretaker to come into the family's home and have few duties apart from her involvement with the child.

3. The impact of the impending change is muted if the caretaker has had the chance to observe and learn some of the child's habits and the style of care used by the parents. This also gives the child a chance to get to know the caretaker

before his mother departs. It is always easier for children to weather disruptions when some components of their lives remain stable. Gradual changes are always easier than abrupt ones.

4. Large day care settings, in which their infant must share the staff members' attention with a number of other children, would be the least desirable. An exception might be made only if we are convinced that the level of daily love and attention given by one person will be higher in the day care arrangement than it would in other available alternatives. This is rarely the case.

5. Bonding is the most important gift parents can ever give to their children. Working parents should be prepared to organize their lives so that this gift becomes their priority during the brief amount of time they have for their kids. They should search for as many opportunities as possible to build strong bonds.

    In two-parent families in which both parents work, this should be a family project. Mother and father will need to cooperate with one another to this end. This task in their busy lives is difficult since the pressures of time are often extreme. When the burdens are not shared, stresses and resentments build with unfavorable consequences for the child as well as the parents. Starting from birth, fathers should be encouraged to establish their own strong ties with their child. An attitude of, "I'll get to know him when he is old enough to play ball," is especially problematic when both parents are working.

6. Parents need to monitor their child's progress during this high-risk period. It is easy for them to overlook signals that mean that all is not well. These signals are not usually clear during the first year of life. After nine hours of inadequate attention and love from his caretaker, our little girl cannot say, "Gee mom, why are you doing this to me? Don't you know that this babysitter lady is not meeting my needs?"

The best way to pick up signs that all is not well is to spend some time each day with the caretaker. If we watch and listen we will detect if the caretaker is fatigued, depressed, or not motivated. These problems will not come to our attention if we are not willing to see and acknowledge them. It is important that the caretaker's life with our child not be separated from ours. The caretaker is a valuable storehouse of information about our child's progress and problems.

Babies do not talk but they communicate in many other ways. Feeding problems sleep problems, increased irritability, apathy, and withdrawal need to be watched for and heeded. Some of these trends occur in all children, but they should alert us to the possibility that our child's care may be deficient.

Points to Remember

- During the first year of life, it is best for a parent to be the full-time caretaker.

- If this is not possible, parents need to maximize the amount of quality care they provide.

- Parents should choose a caretaker who has the capacity, motivation, and time to provide quality care.

- The early months fly by quickly and the impact of deficient love and stimulation during the first year can never be totally remedied.

Chapter 13

SUMMARY – BONDING – THE FOUNDATION OF A STABLE PERSONALITY

The bonding process is the first step that must be taken in order for children to move securely onto the path to maturity. It begins at birth and a fairly solid foundation should be established during the first year. It is upon this foundation that all later strengths are built. Once in place it supports the development of trust, self-esteem, and the many other traits and skills acquired by children as they negotiate subsequent developmental hurdles.

If this foundation is faulty, the child's path towards maturity will be blocked. Each subsequent stage will be more difficult and leave new scars. Later attempts to remedy the consequences of poor bonding may be partially successful, but can never entirely heal the wounds from this early, preverbal period of life. The long-term ramifications of poor bonding read like an encyclopedia of the most serious emotional disorders. Children who are school failures, adolescents who are antisocial, and adults who become seriously addicted to drugs represent some of the detrimental outcomes of inadequate bonding.

There has been continuous debate about the timing of the onset of human life. Theoretically, the child's life begins at conception. Nearer to the time of birth he has the capacity for an independent physical existence. It is not, however until a link of love has been forged to another that the bud of "humanness" first begins to blossom. The child is becoming a person and all this happens so quickly. It unfolds in front of us but we may often fail to appreciate its significance.

To Sally, Dan's mother, it seems as only yesterday when she remembers being in awe of this new life that was her child. It is morning and Dan is now eight months of age. As Sally holds him she marvels at the changes that have occurred in such a short period of time. She is proud of his physical growth and development, but there is something else that is even more exciting and wonderful. Dan knows her and loves her. Dan is capable of a rich variety of expressions and sounds that communicates his feelings to her. At birth, she loved him because he was hers. Now, he is another real person in her life and it is a source of joy that she is at its center.

PART THREE

LEANING TO BE A SEPARATE PERSON – BASIC TRUST

ONE YEAR TO THREE YEARS

PART THREE

SECTION ONE

LEARNING TO BE A SEPARATE PERSON – THE TASK AND ITS IMPORTANCE

Question – My child is one-year-old and I am confident that he is strongly bonded to us. Can you clarify the developmental mission that lies ahead for us as he enters his second year?

Dan has mastered the first developmental hurdle. He is securely attached to his parents. They are his whole world. With each day he has become more cognizant that it is not just any face, but a specific face, that he associates with his contentment. With this comes a new insight about the world. That certain face, the source of so much of his well-being, regularly disappears. He is compelled to deal with a problem that cannot be avoided because it is an integral part of human existence – **the problem of being alone.** There are a variety of typical responses he will display as he struggles with this new problem. The outcome of this struggle is influenced dramatically by his parents, who will shape another important part of the foundation of his personality.

Chapter 1

IN THE STILL OF THE NIGHT – THE TERROR OF BEING ALONE

There are moments during our sleep when in the midst of a pleasant dream we are enveloped by feelings of contentment and calm. It was at just such a moment that Sally's tranquility was shattered by a piercing noise. There could be no doubt about its source. Her sleep had been interrupted many times in the past by such a noise. Like a cold bucket of ice being dumped on her warm body, it tore her away from a place of calm contentment that for some time had eluded her during her waking hours.

The noise was grating to her ears and unrelenting. With one eye, Sally looked at her husband lying next to her. "He surely must hear it," she thought. Well if he did he was not letting on. His eyes remained shut. In the darkness she left her bed and in a swirl of unpleasant feelings advanced towards the noise.

When she saw him in the dim light of the room, her anger reached a height rarely attained during the daylight hours. Dan's screams abruptly stopped when he saw his mother cross the threshold of his room. At one year of age, he was adept at pulling himself up to a standing position. When Sally could see his face more clearly her gaze was drawn first to his smile. Relatives and friends thought that smiling face was cute and adorable. But at that moment, it was not a pleasant sight to Sally. To her it was the face of a malicious persecutor.

She throttled an impulse to pry his little fingers off the crib's handrail and pound him down upon his mattress where he belonged, and then flee. But to where? Anywhere, to get away from the room, the house, as far away as possible, to get a full night's sleep. As Dan watched his mother enter his room his perception was very different from hers. He bounded up and down with glee. Dan was bubbling over with happy relief because he could see the wonderful familiar face of his mother growing nearer.

Would Sally's thoughts have been different if she had been able to read his mind? If she could translate his feelings into adult concepts she might discover something like this, "Mom, I went to bed feeling okay because you seemed so close to me. I felt your presence with me and my whole world was light and happy. Then I awoke in the still of the night and everything had changed. I was enveloped in a sea of interminable darkness and nothingness from which there was no escape. You were not there. I tried to think of you, to bring you back to me, but without your presence I could not recapture the glow of your warmth that permeated every part of me before I fell asleep. You had become a distant flickering candle growing ever fainter. If it went out, there would be nothing and I would be nothing. I would be alone. There would be only darkness forever and ever. The smile that you see is a smile of joy because your appearance at the door made my whole world bright and happy again."

Chapter 2

LEARNING TO BE ALONE – THE TASK AND ITS IMPORTANCE

Dan's view of the world is dominated by the new developmental hurdle he is facing.

At each stage of development, children's perceptions are influenced by the emotional challenge they are facing. Dan's perceptions of his mother in the still of the night are understandable, though obviously incorrect. It is not true that calamity would befall Dan if his mother had not appeared and he had remained alone. It should be noted, however, that many adults much smarter than Dan have identical perceptions when they feel abandoned by a loved one. They have not yet mastered the developmental hurdle that Dan is facing for the first time.

Many of Dan's other thoughts about his mother's appearances and disappearances are also inaccurate. When he awakens to find himself alone he is certain that something hateful and mean is happening to him. That's what he feels and feelings count for nearly everything when you are only one year old. He vacillates between believing that the badness that caused this to happen is within himself and believing that it is within others. His anger is powerful and seems an alien force that will repulse and harm others. In all this and more he is wrong.

This array of distorted perceptions, the feelings generated by them as well as the resulting behavior, means that Dan is struggling with the second developmental hurdle. He is coming to grips with being alone. Dan cannot master this problem on his own. Its solution will be influenced by the many interactions that will unfold between Dan and his parents during this period of his development. Unfortunately, his mother has no understanding of this as she strides into his room. She has only one agenda – to shut him up as quickly as possible and return to sleep. Her obliviousness to the actual meaning of his behavior combined with her own emotional blisters color her perceptions.

This episode, and countless ones similar to it occurring on a daily basis, provide opportunities for Dan's mother to help correct the distorted perceptions that account for his elevated distress. This is not likely to happen if her responses are colored by her own distorted perceptions. Unless corrected, these responses and the feelings accompanying them will tend to support and reinforce her son's distorted perceptions rather than help to eliminate them.

Sally has the opportunity to influence his thinking constructively, but her lack of knowledge combined with her painful emotional blisters interfere. Sally's mind has been taken over by her own distorted perceptions and her thoughts reinforce his. As she enters his room, she momentarily does hate him and wishes that he were not there. Her perceptions, fueled by anger and desperation, sabotage her capacity for reasonable thinking and effective parenting. She has lost her ability to appreciate that Dan is just a loving little boy who, upon awakening and finding himself alone, is consumed by the nightmarish thought that the source of everything good in his life, his mother, is gone forever. She will soon regain a more realistic perception of her son, but this moment of opportunity to help him to master the second developmental hurdle will have passed.

As a consequence of her feelings and flawed perceptions, she will have missed one small chance to help her son to cope with the problem of being alone. She will have missed one small chance to help Dan understand that he can trust that he is loved, and that his mother will return even during those long, dreadful moments of darkness in the still of the night. Sally will have many more opportunities. But time passes quickly and if she misses too many of these, she will leave Dan with a problem that will haunt him for the rest of his life. The following chapters provide information that will help parents understand this developmental hurdle, be better equipped to help their children negotiate it successfully, and counter the impact of their own emotional blisters.

Points to Remember

- Towards the end of their first year, children become aware of that their parents are separate from them and are sometimes absent.
- This awareness forces them to face the fear of being alone.

Chapter 3

UNDERSTANDING WHAT NEEDS TO BE DONE

Question – You are suggesting that our responses to the many issues that arise with our children during this period should address the underlying developmental hurdle and not solely the behavior that has elicited our attention? I have never thought about this before. Can you clarify this further?

The motivation to quiet our children and return to sleep is natural, but there is another mission we have during this period that must not be overlooked. During the first developmental period our love helped our infants to know that they are persons and that their existence has intrinsic validity. **The second crucial lesson for our children to learn is to manage being alone.** Many experts speak of this as the development of trust. Children are learning to trust that they are loved and well, even during those periods when they are absent from the source of that love. They are learning to trust that they and their parents can survive being apart.

Dan is learning to trust that his world and the people in it are safe when he awakens in the still of the night and sees only darkness. As this knowledge begins to crystallize in his mind, he will find it easier to quell the bit of alarm he feels upon awakening alone in the middle of the night and he will be able to fall back asleep without needing reassurance from his mother's presence. The mastery of this developmental hurdle is the next essential building block in the construction of a stable, mature personality. Bonding allowed him to know that he is loved and valued. **Trust will provide him with the capacity to hold on to this truth when there is nobody close by to affirm it.**

This explains why a parental focus that is exclusively confined to the child's behavior may lead parents astray. A surface change may be temporarily pleasing, but unless it is accompanied by real developmental progress the outcome may be ominous. The importance of addressing the underlying developmental hurdle needs to be emphasized. There has been considerable debate and concern about the development of self-esteem in children. Many parents, and even experts, imply that praise and positive reinforcement can establish self-esteem. It is not my intention to derogate praise. When authentic, it is an important part of any loving relationship. It would be naïve however to imply that praise builds self-esteem. Real self-esteem rests on a foundation of knowing that we are valued and loved, independent of successes or failures. It does not require the continuous adoration and love of others for it to survive. It is easy to feel good when we are praised. The ability to maintain our emotional balance in the face of harsh criticism or repeated failures is the key element in good self-esteem. This requires mastery of this developmental hurdle.

Children who fail to master this development hurdle continue to need approval, love, and gratification from others to maintain their emotional balance. The years pass quickly and they reach adulthood, but like Dan at age one, they require the presence of a supportive person to feel valued and to stave off a sense of helplessness. Their need for reassurance that they are loved and valued is insatiable. Their hearts, like Dan's, light up with joy for the brief moment that they are sure that they can see love in the eyes of the person closest to them. But too soon it is gone or deemed insufficient, leaving them again feeling unloved and worthless. This chapter describes the process that leads to self-reliance and solid self-esteem.

Question – Can you help me to understand what it might be like for children who have not solved this early problem?

Laura, an adolescent with a problem that never went away

Laura was fifteen and afraid of many things. She was afraid of what others might think about her, afraid of being alone, and afraid of making a mistake. She was so afraid that she stayed by herself most of the time and preferred to remain at home. Laura had been afraid for as long as she could remember. She always felt better when she was at home with her mother. Her fear and helplessness became more pronounced about a year ago when her mother took a job. Laura recalled how terrible it was for her on the first day that her mother left for work. She had always been comforted by knowing that her mother was close by to help her. Speaking about her mother's return to work, she said, "I was afraid that my mother might not be thinking about me as much as she did before. I don't know how well I can get along if my mother is not thinking about me. It makes me feel frightened."

In reality, Laura was a bright youngster who was fully capable of functioning well on her own. This was completely contrary to her feelings. She believed that if she was really alone with no one to help her, she might lose control of herself and "do stupid things." With her mother close by, she knew that she was loved, but this knowledge did not help her when they were apart. At one point she commented upon being alone, saying, "It is worse than being dead." The passage of time had not significantly altered Laura's original perceptions of being alone. Her perceptions and reactions to being alone were understandable at one year of age, but were a crippling handicap when still present at fifteen.

Good parenting is based on understanding

Without understanding, well-intended efforts and even real love may go astray. Confusion often leads to stress and misguided parenting ploys. Helping our children during this period begins with an understanding of the central developmental problem they are facing. Armed with this knowledge, parents will be much better equipped to respond with confidence and competence. With reasonable help from their parents, these normal developmental problems are easily negotiated the first time they are faced. If they are not solved they persist and interfere with subsequent progress. Children reach adulthood still in terror of being alone and many continue to be saddled with the few maladaptive ways of coping that were available to them when they were so young and immature. We should not be surprised at the level of irrationality displayed by many adults threatened by rejection.

In the next chapter, Dan's parents will learn to spot the behavioral signs of his struggle with the second developmental hurdle.

Points to Remember

- Children need their parents' help to successfully manage learning to be alone.

- Parents must help their children to gradually accept periods of being alone and to have confidence that they are safe, are still loved, and that their parents will return.

PART THREE

SECTION TWO

UNDERSTANDING THE MEANING OF CHILDREN'S BEHAVIOR DURING THIS PERIOD

There is a series of steps that lead to good parenting decisions. The first is to understand the developmental hurdle your child is facing. The second is to make sense of the behavior that is being generated by that hurdle. The final step is to use your understanding to adopt parenting strategies aimed at helping your child to achieve a successful resolution. This is the same method we generally use in the other parts of our lives in order to function successfully. In this chapter, we will address the very typical responses of children struggling for the first time with the problem of being alone. These are commonly called the signs and symptoms of separation anxiety.

Chapter 4

SEPARATION ANXIETY – FACING BEING ALONE FOR THE FIRST TIME

Question – I have some knowledge about the second developmental hurdle. Can you help me to understand the changes occurring in my child's thinking and the types of behavior I am likely to see as he struggles with this developmental problem?

The First Loss

If parents know what to look for it would be easier for them to make sense of their children's behavior. In response to a real or perceived loss many adults manifest an array of typical symptoms. The most prominent of these include sadness, sleep disturbances, reduced appetite, heightened irritability, and often an excessive need for approval and gratification. Between six and twelve months old, most children begin to manifest similar patterns of behavior. It is important for parents not to be confused or upset about these changes. These patterns of behavior mean that their children are coming to grips, for the first time in their lives, with a part of human existence that no one can avoid. **This is the reality of our separateness from others and the fact that we can be completely alone. The behavior this struggle generates is called** *separation anxiety.*

Separation anxiety is an entirely normal phenomenon. It becomes evident as children advance cognitively to the point when they are increasingly aware that they are separate from the persons with whom they have bonded. Earlier, the infant did not have the mental faculty to know that the love and attention that he craved actually emanated from a source that had a separate existence, and as a consequence he did not experience separation anxiety. With the development of better mental skills, he acquires the capacity to discern the difference between the moments when his mother is there to gratify him and other moments during which she is absent, but he can picture her in his mind. At these times gratification does not occur. As this scenario unfolds over and over again, a frightening concept coalesces in his mind. He is becoming aware that those he loves are separate from him and therefore can be lost. The distress ushered in by this realization is considerable and easily understood. Many adults, nearly all of us to some extent, respond with similar hurt when faced with the prospect of being left alone. No wonder Dan cries when he awakens alone in the dark, at an age when he has extremely limited resources to help him cope with this very frightening ordeal. As the months unfold there will be a variety of ways that this problem can be played out and his parents will play a crucial role in determining the outcome.

Chapter 5

IDENTIFYING THE SIGNS OF SEPARATION ANXIETY

Nighttime Awakening

Nighttime awakening, including difficulty and unwillingness to go to sleep, will usually be the most common signal to parents that their child is experiencing separation anxiety. It is helpful for parents to be aware of the normal fluctuations of sleep patterns during this time frame so that other types of nighttime awakening will not be confused with separation anxiety.

During the first three to four weeks after birth, the pattern of sleep and wakefulness follow the innate rhythm of each child's hunger. The infant will awaken several times each night to feed. Between the third and fourth month, the number of nighttime awakenings for feedings gradually diminishes and are finally eliminated altogether. During this period both the length of sleep at night is extended, as well as the period of wakefulness during the day. Most parents eagerly watch this progress, anticipating the time when they will be able to reclaim the night for themselves. Usually, by four months of age the baby has gone a number of consecutive nights without awakening to be fed. Parents begin to breathe more easily and allow themselves to hope for a full night's sleep. When a month goes by without any nighttime awakenings, they are convinced that the ordeal of getting up at night is over.

Typically, at some point in the latter part of the first year this bliss comes to a jarring halt by a new bout of nighttime awakenings that is often even more intense and unpredictable than the first. There are significant differences between the two. The first was precipitated by hunger and generally relieved quickly by feeding. The new brand is ushered in by separation anxiety and requires a more complicated prescription for its relief.

STRANGER ANXIETY

The fairly rapid transition in early infancy from awareness of only sensations to an appreciation of one special person distinct from others, is fascinating and is nearly always overlooked by busy parents who take this progress for granted. Smiling in response to seeing another's face is the first evidence that the infant is able to single out people from other external stimuli. This needs to be distinguished from the indiscriminate smiles that begin soon after birth and are elicited by a variety of external and internal stimuli. By the second month, most children will show a smiling response. They will smile at any face that is brought into their line of sight. This landmark on the path towards becoming a person means that the infant has begun to associate parts of the face with feelings of comfort and contentment. It's a signal that bonds of love are being forged.

During the second half of the first year, the infant begins to bestow his smiles on others in a more discriminating fashion. Before this time, when Grandma visited from out of town she was delighted when our very diplomatic baby responded to her cooing with a wide grin. A few months later, he is in the throes of separation anxiety and disaster strikes. Grandma picks up our dear little baby expecting the same warm greeting. She has traveled one hundred miles anticipating his smile. She coaxes him with her usual, "goo goo," but after a peek at her expectant face, his expression becomes contorted with distress and he lets out a loud frantic wail. Using every trick she learned with her own kids she tries to soothe him, but the harder she tries the harder he cries. She finally hands him back to his mother. After one reassuring glance at his mother's familiar face the crying stops abruptly and the smile returns. Grandma, who has forgotten her own experiences long ago, is thinking, "What has that daughter in law of mine been saying about me?" The baby's mother, seeing her distress blurts out, "Oh he is doing that to everyone who is a stranger to him." She stops quickly as she realizes that these words coming from her might be as jarring as the baby's screams.

CHANGES IN APPETITE OR FEEDING TIMES

Changes in appetite or feeding times are the other less common signs of separation anxiety. One of the reasons that parenting is so perplexing is that it is hard to know if we are doing a good job. There is no paycheck at the end of the week and children rarely pat us on the back and say "well done" as we tuck them in at night. Since there is one aspect of the job that they can quantify, food intake, we tend to use it as a parental rating system. A system that uses love instead of food during this period would be much more accurate, but this would be difficult to implement even if parents had enough insight to try. Parents feel pride when their kids consume their food with gusto and steadily gain weight. It is therefore a disappointment when their pride and joy, the champion eater of the neighborhood, becomes squeamish, picky, and more irritable at meals.

CHANGES OF MOOD OR DISPOSITION

A change of mood or disposition may also be a sign of separation anxiety. We all experience stress when we are facing difficult challenges. The ones we encounter during our adult lives may seem formidable, but they pale in comparison to the task faced by our little babies as they tackle this developmental hurdle. They are facing being alone for the first time. This is stressful and as they struggle with separation anxiety our kids may become more demanding and harder to please. They may be less accepting of changes in routine. Their capacity to entertain themselves may be lost and replaced by clinging behavior and needs for reassurance. It may seem as if they have tied an invisible cord to us and will yank on it with a cry the moment we seem to be gone. Leaving them with substitute caretakers often becomes an ordeal.

Question – How will this information about separation anxiety be of help to us?

In the first chapter, I addressed the "rule of comfort." Confusion is the enemy of good parenting. Parents are generally confused and upset when their kids seem to be sliding backward towards more immature forms of behavior. Replacing confusion with understanding is the first essential step towards reasonable problem solving. Faced with new and often upsetting trends of behavior, parents need to begin by asking the right question. The wrong question is "What should I do?" The right question is "What does this mean?" What does it mean when our kids seem to have lost new skills and there is a shift to less adaptive and more babyish patterns of behavior? A backward movement in a child's development always means that there is a developmental hurdle that has become a problem for him. Armed with this understanding it is never hard to identify the new problem, or an old one brought back to the surface by some stressful situation that accounts for a child's regression.

Points to Remember

- Parents can better respond constructively and comfortably when they understand the meaning of their child's behavior.

- Learn the typical array of behavior children manifest as they struggle with their fears of being alone.

Chapter 6

THE ABSENCE OF SEPARATION ANXIETY

Question – I have noticed that some children don't seem to experience separation anxiety. What does this mean? Are they more independent?

Although it is a ubiquitous problem, some children seem to move through this stage of development without any signs of separation anxiety. Parents are often delighted by this turn of events, relieved that they are not forced to expend time and effort coping with the nighttime awakening and clinging behavior that characterizes the lives of other kids as they struggle with separation anxiety. There is a wide spectrum of normal manifestations of separation anxiety, but its absence can have unfavorable implications. It can be a reflection of very inadequate or even absent bonding rather than a sunny, confident disposition. Adjusting very smoothly to repeated separations and movements from one caretaker to another might indicate the absence of a deeper commitment to anyone. These children are not displaying the typical signs of the second developmental hurdle because they have not mastered the first. They show no fear of being left alone because they have never adequately bonded to anyone.

This has been called pseudo independence. These children go through life with the emotional worldview of an infant before bonding. Like an infant, they require a fairly continuous supply of gratification to maintain their emotional balance. When one source of gratification is not available they merely shift to another. Their commitment, if we can speak of one, is to continuous gratification rather than to the person who supplies it.

Their appearance of independence is illusory. They remain dependent upon external supplies of gratification and have not made the transition to people. That transition is an essential first step on the path to mature independence. Children who have not made that transition are barred from so much of what makes human life rich and fulfilling. Moving forward on the path that begins with bonding leads to the most-valued facets of human life – the capacity to love and appreciate love, kindness, true self-esteem, the pleasure of being useful and productive, remorse when we hurt others, and so much more. Kids diverted from this path tend to view others in their lives as readily exchangeable sources of gratification. If one source does not supply the desired goodies, it will be quickly discarded in favor of another.

Understanding this process helps to make sense of the inexplicable obsession of many addicts with the next fix, even when it is obvious that their lives are being destroyed by drug use. They are no more able to accept giving up their fix than is the very young infant who must have a feeding. The infant's future is hopeful since he will soon be taking his first steps on the path towards maturity. The addict has missed that opportunity.

It needs to be emphasized that there is a wide variability to children's responses to their encounters with new problems. The best way to estimate any child's developmental progress lies in a global assessment of all facets of his functioning, rather then basing it on the observation of just one component of the child's behavior. Some kids tackle this second developmental hurdle without the usual manifestations of intense anxiety. Their progress can be confirmed by their increasing self-reliance combined with rich, warm involvements with the important people in their lives.

Dan's parents are learning about the meaning of his cries in the middle of the night. They now understand that these cries are not merely manipulative efforts that can be overlooked. Their new insights make them better prepared to help their son master the problem of being alone.

POINTS TO REMEMBER

- Children's reactions to separation may vary wildly.

- The complete absence of a reaction to separation may indicate that the infant's attachment to the parents needs to be strengthened through and emphasis on love and attention.

PART THREE

SECTION THREE

GETTING THE JOB DONE

LEARNING TO BE ALONG – THE DEVELOPMENT OF BASIC TRUST

Question – Can you help me to understand how we can help our child to learn to cope with being alone?

Chapter 7

LEARNING THAT OUT OF SIGHT DOES NOT MEAN GONE FOREVER

How would Sally have responded to Dan if she had read the first sections of this chapter and could fully appreciate the meaning of his cry in the still of the night? Would her attitude and behavior have been altered if she understood that his crying was a manifestation of separation anxiety and if she realized the importance of this developmental hurdle?

If Dan had the ability to choose his mother's response and the power to dictate it to her there is no question about his preference. He would insist that she gratify his plea for her to be with him. Actually he would go one step further and demand that she remain with him permanently. He would have no understanding, or even interest in, achieving mastery of the developmental hurdle at the root of his distress.

Only Sally can assume the responsibility of getting this important job done successfully. Dan was crying in the middle of the night because the discovery of his mother's absence made him feel alone, helpless, and in danger of never seeing his mother again.

Chapter 8

BEGINNING ON THE PATH TOWARDS SECURE TRUST

For now, we are interested in helping Dan take the first step. It entails learning that his parents are available to help him when they are out of sight. This may seem very simple to us but it is a remarkable achievement for our very young children. Until this time, children are not able to abstract the existence of anything that is not actually visible. They have no way to know that objects out of sight continue to exist.

This did not matter very early in their lives. Then, their only interest was to obtain gratification. The symptoms of separation anxiety indicate that it has begun to matter very much. They have come to understand that there is a special face that is associated with love and care. How frightening it must be to awaken, picture the face, and realize that it is gone, and from the child's distorted perspective, gone forever. Our task is to help our child to feel less uncomfortable at those times by learning to trust that the special face will return.

The first step towards the development of this trust relies upon the trustworthiness of his parents. Their reasonable balance of love and frustration helps him learn that he is safe, loved, and accepted even during those periods when mommy and daddy are not with him. The imbedding of this trust within the child is called *object constancy*.

Children with object constancy know that their parents love them and they are not in danger when they are alone. As the months and years pass, this foundation of basic trust becomes strengthened and they learn to handle longer periods of being alone. This important building block is essential for the development solid self-esteem and confidence.

Points to Remember

- Learning to be alone is an extremely important developmental hurdle.
- As children take their first steps toward negotiating this hurdle, they need parents who are available and responsive.
- This is not a time for long separations, erratic schedules, or other distractions.

Chapter 9

FINDING THE BEST BALANCE BETWEEN FRUSTRATION AND GRATIFICATION

Question – I understand the concepts but I still need help with the details. How are we to determine the balance of frustration and gratification that will enable our child to tackle this developmental hurdle?

Our goal is to help our child to appreciate that he is loved and safe during those times when we are not in his immediate presence. In the first phase of his development, bonding, our parenting techniques were balanced dramatically in favor of attention and love over frustration. This was done in order to forge strong bonds. If that one-sided balance persisted into the second phase we might effectively protect him from experiencing separation anxiety, but real growth would be impossible. Problems must be faced in order to develop the skills needed for their mastery. Therefore in this second phase a shift in that balance needs to occur.

The guideline for the mastery of separation fears is to provide the balance of love and frustration that helps our children to reach object constancy. The key principle is to allow them to experience enough separation anxiety that they will have the opportunities to work on its mastery, but never so much that it will overwhelm them and impede forward progress.

Question – All of this is informative but you have not answered my question. How do we to gage the proper balance between love and frustration?

I have always found that when parents are equipped with an understanding of what is needed, and are relatively free from the adverse effects of emotional blisters, they do quite well. A best recipe for each child cannot be provided since each child is unique and his needs are continually shifting. Parents who base their strategies on understanding and love will nearly always find an appropriate balance. Knowledge about developmental problems helps to guarantee that understanding. Two examples of balances tipped too far may clarify what is needed.

A balance tipped too far towards indulgence

If Dan could have his choice, his preference would be to have his mother with him constantly, or at least as much as possible. The consequences of this wish being granted would be disastrous. His continuing need for persistent closeness would become his jailer, restricting his actions and sabotaging most facets of his development. The joys of exploring the world and experiencing a multitude of relationships would be impossible. Even his original motive for choosing eternal closeness, the sense of safety and the elimination of separation anxiety, would elude him. Regardless of the number of moments that Dan's parents try to reassure him by remaining near, he would never be able to dismiss the dreaded thought, "What if they are not there tomorrow?" Vows of unending love and endless reassurance never suffice to allay the fear of abandonment in persons whose separation anxiety has followed them into adulthood.

There is no way of avoiding or getting around the problem of being alone. It must be faced and mastered. The best time for children to do this is the first time they experience it. Postponing the inevitable creates ripples of disturbing currents in the developmental process and maladaptive compensating mechanisms that compound later attempts to achieve a satisfactory solution. Most parents know this intuitively, yet many indulge their child's desire to maintain the illusion of eternal togetherness. Their motive is usually thinly veiled. They try to mute the sounds of their child's fears to avoid having these awaken similar fears within themselves. They only succeed in prolonging the problem and the pain into adult life. The message communicated by the parent who tips the balance too far on the side of indulgence is, "Poor baby, I see how much you hurt when we are apart. I understand that suffering because it awakens similar feelings in me. Don't worry; I will keep you with me forever so that neither of us will have to feel that terror again."

A balance tipped too far towards deprivation

Bereft of an understanding of the meaning of Dan's cry in the middle of the night, Dan's mother might have her own inclination about the best way to deal with this manifestation of separation anxiety. After seeing his smile and concluding that he is "just trying to manipulate me," she might be tempted to act on her wish to get a good night's sleep by slamming the door and just letting him cry. Parents as a rule find their kids' behavior and sounds as they tackle separation anxiety extremely disconcerting. They complain of exhaustion and experience considerable stress. This is not caused by the actual difficulty of the job. Theoretically the task of caring for a one-year-old is simple and can be an enormous source of joy.

The task becomes difficult because the child's behavior stomps on the parents emotional blisters. There is a coded message contained in our child's cries that diverts us from the task of parenting and leads instead to a desperate need to eliminate the pain. One form that this escape takes is indulgence, or tipping the balance too far towards eliminating all anxiety. The other is to flee. We flee by closing the doors of rooms, or of our ears and minds. We do this to dull the pain caused by those cries. We also escape by blaming our one-year-old for our distress and believe that our anger is justified. Finally many parents flee, literally, by leaving their little children in the care of others for the major portions of each day. They often find temporary relief by escaping, but they may have tipped the balance too far in the direction of deprivation.

A balance of parenting that gets the job done

Question – What is the best balance for a successful outcome? I now realize that you cannot write a specific prescription, but are there any general principles that apply?

The optimum balance of love versus frustration to master the problem of being alone can be summarized by two guidelines.

The first guideline is the rule of a little at a time

We need to begin with small doses of separation and only gradually increase their size and frequency. This needs to be monitored to ensure that the amount does not precipitate so much anxiety that progress is blocked. This makes common sense. We would err badly if we attempted to teach our child to swim by heaving him into the deep water and praying that he stay afloat. After being pulled out there would be little likelihood that he would be eager to return for another try. On the other hand, we would be critical of parents who responded to their children's anxiety about going into the water by saying, "You never have to worry about water again. I'll protect you from that fear, we will just not think about it again." Later in this chapter I will illustrate the actual implementation of this guideline. The guideline itself is extremely important since it applies equally to most of the skills that are not easily mastered by children.

The second guideline is that this process unfolds in a setting that remains understanding and loving

This cannot be emphasized too strongly. Let's see why. Adhering to the first guideline will mean that Dan's mother will begin by allowing him to experience small doses of separation anxiety. As progress occurs she will gradually increase the dose. Dan will not be grateful of his parents' reasonable efforts to help him to master the problem of being alone. From his point of view it would be so easy for them to entirely eliminate the hurt by remaining with him. He will, therefore, interpret even these small doses of separation as a hateful abandonment of him. **This image of them as mean, abandoning people will be confirmed if his parents cannot undertake the endeavor in a setting that remains understanding and loving.**

An important part of the mastery of each developmental hurdle entails the correction of infantile, distorted perceptions. There will be little chance of correcting these if our children see and feel animosity or an actual desire by us to be away from them. Responses of anger or actual withdrawal will confirm our children's infantile belief that being left alone means that they are hated and are being abandoned. This brand of response also steers our children's thinking towards another ominous conclusion – that there must be something bad or deficient about them that accounts for our terrible mistreatment of them. **This is avoided when we combine small doses of separation with an attitude that remains loving.**

The scenario I have described in general terms unfolds over and over again in the daily routines of every one-year-old. Our children awaken from their naps and we do not immediately magically appear. We go to the bathroom, attend to cooking, talk on the phone, or involve ourselves in the myriad activities that take our attention away from them. If the two guidelines are followed, each of these events can be a constructive learning experience, gently nudging our children towards mastery of this developmental hurdle.

Naturally, in the beginning, children's tolerance for any separation is limited. Distorted perspectives fueled by powerful feelings are not easily dislodged. But each day our children are repeatedly made aware that their interpretation of separations is wrong. Our love and availability during and immediately following the separations will begin to dispel their belief that these short separations mean that someone is abandoning them and cannot be trusted. Bit by bit they will come to realize that in their family, with their parents, they can be confident that out of sight does not mean gone forever. Our children cannot be spared from the reality of being alone. It is a fact of life. But they can be helped to know that being alone does not mean that they are hated, abandoned, or in any real danger.

Separation Anxiety and Emotional Blisters

Warning! Beware of emotional blisters

Most parents find the first guideline – a little at a time – easy to understand and implement. The second – remaining loving – is more difficult. If parents are asked about this they often give the same response. They say that it is hard to remain loving, calm, and understanding when their kids are crying or afraid. I have always found it curious and interesting to think about this. They are saying that it is easier to be angry, frustrated, and unhappy than loving, calm, and content. Why would so many reasonable people believe that it is easier to be frustrated, angry, and unhappy than to be calm and loving? The answer once again clarifies the main obstacle to good parenting. Our children's behaviors, in this case their protests and cries of separation anxiety, stomp on very painful emotional blisters. The people we love most are usually the ones who are most adept at striking at our most sensitive parts.

There are many things in life that we would change if we could. Our child's suffering falls high on that list. It moves to an even higher position when their suffering stomps on our emotional blisters, creating similar pain in us. When this happens, we have two choices. I am hoping that after reading this book parents will choose the more constructive alternative and use their own distress as a signal to alert them to the task that needs to be addressed with love and reason. The shift in thinking that this entails proves to be an effective way of replacing stress with reason and calm. The alternative is to be prodded by pain to abandon the guidelines of effective parenting.

Contrast the impact of the messages communicated to our children when we are stressed with the ones they receive when we remain loving. The child's anxiety is generated by his mistaken belief that being left alone means that he is being discarded and in danger. The loving parent, by building trust, makes a lie of that equation and gradually frees the child from his fears. The calming look of love that he sees at the very moment that he is being left alone imbeds confidence that being left alone does not mean gone forever. It provides trust that he is loved during the period of time that his parent is not actually in his presence.

Parents who lose their capacity to remain loving as they interact with their children during this phase send an entirely different kind of message to their children. At the moment of separation the child sees an angry expression, instead of a loving one. Or equally destructive, a message that says, "I wish I did not have to put up with you, you are a burden to me that I would rather avoid." This fairly typical response by harried parents confirms the child's belief that he is actually in danger of being abandoned and that it is his fault. Regardless of age, we all have the ability to accurately interpret the meaning of the nonverbal messages transmitted when our loved one says good-bye and closes the door. We can easily discern the difference between, "I love you and will soon return," and, "I don't want to be with you."

Points to Remember

- During the first eight months, children need parents who can tune in to their needs.

- Parents must find the optimum balance between gratification and frustration.

- Using the rule of a little at a time in a loving setting will enable a child to learn feel less threatened when he is alone.

- Long separations or excessive indulgence may impede a child's progress towards independence and hamper self-esteem.

Chapter 10

STRATEGIES FOR NIGHTTIME AWAKENING

Question – I now have a good understanding of this developmental hurdle. I know the meaning of my child's cries in the middle of the night and that my long-range goal is to help him master separation anxiety. I am still not sure about the best ways to respond to some of the behavioral manifestations of separation anxiety. For example, are there some insights that might point me to practical parenting ploys for nighttime awakening?

Being prepared and understanding – The best tool to neutralize our emotional blisters

Once more Dan's mother has been awakened by his cry in the middle of the night. As before, Dan has pulled himself up and is grinning as his mother enters his room. This time, however, Sally is better prepared to tackle what lies ahead. She now knows that his cries, as well as the smile of relief that appears on his face as she enters his room, are signs of separation anxiety. This knowledge allows her to put aside her initial impulse, after being pulled out of a pleasant sleep, to find someway to "just shut him up" so that she can get back to bed. She understands her long-range goal and knows the guidelines that will lead to this successful conclusion. And she is confident that as Dan acquires trust and achieves object constancy, he will be no longer be overwhelmed by separation anxiety when he awakens in the middle of the night and finds himself alone.

Being prepared with this knowledge is helpful to Sally. It allows her to anticipate nighttime awakening and other manifestations of separation anxiety. Being forewarned reduces the confusion and frus-

tration she might have felt as she faced these patterns of behavior without this information.

She also knows that the gains made by Dan in his struggle to master separation anxiety are gradual, so she is patient and avoids falling into the trap of blaming herself or Dan for slow progress. She is optimistic about the outcome and confident that each time she responds constructively he is making a small step towards her ultimate goal, becoming a secure, self sufficient person whose self-esteem and well-being does not depend on others.

Being prepared is never complete assurance against the pernicious influence of emotional blisters, but it is the best available ally. We all have persistent vulnerabilities that were built into our personalities when we were young. The pains and struggles of our kids invariably bring these to the surface. Anticipating and accurately detecting our emotional blisters when they appear is the most effective tool we have to reduce their destructive impact. With practice we can reduce their control over our lives

But what do I actually do?

Question – I still want to know what I actually do. Instead you repeatedly address the problem in general terms. Are there parenting guidelines that you can tell us?

Of course there are. I have found that these guidelines are the easy part. The purpose of this book is to tackle the hard part – the sticky emotional context in which this all unfolds. It is a bit like the story of Brer Rabbit and the Tar Baby. Since he was made of tar, the Tar Baby obviously could not answer Brer Rabbit. Brer Rabbit did not understand this and became increasingly confused and then angry. As he tried harder to elicit desired responses and attempted to physically coerce a reply from the Tar Baby, he became trapped in the tar and found himself in danger. My primary goal is to help parents understand the developmental issues so that they can avoid the sticky emotional traps. I have generally found that parents who avoid the traps will be able to adhere to the guidelines, even if they have not been provided with a list of actual parenting ploys.

I have promised the guidelines and will provide them, but first a peek at the progress being made in the home of Dan and his parents.

Enlisting Father's help

Understanding the importance of this time in Dan's life, his mother had convinced her husband that it would be wonderful if he shared in the joys of helping their son to become a secure person. As part of the bargain, she agreed to forego a scheduled visit to her mother so that he could watch the playoffs. That clinched it. He agreed to take one turn each week.

When the cry awakened him, Bob looked instinctively at the clock – 2:30 A.M. If he weren't able to fall back asleep after the ordeal, it would mean four hours of looking at the ceiling and then off to work, tired before the day had begun. He muttered to himself and when his eyes accommodated to the dark he glanced hopefully at his wife. Her eyes were shut tight. Knocking over everything in his path, he got out of bed. He convinced himself that he was justified in putting on the bright light at the head of Sally's side of the bed because of the danger of bumping into something and breaking a leg. He waited and watched as she gradually pried open her eyelids. At just the right moment, he bent over so that his mouth was close to her ear and bellowed his question, "What do I do now?"

Sally recalled some of the frustration and helplessness she had felt before she began to appreciate the meaning of her son's cry and knew first hand why it had the strength to knock even mature individuals off balance. Bob had been transformed by the cry in the middle of the night from an understanding and loving father into the image Bob's own mother had painted of him when he was a monster two-year-old. Sally was able to avoid the clash of wills that is so typical of these stressful moments. She calmly arose from bed and explained with patience and warmth that they could tuck Dan in together that night and perhaps tomorrow after dinner she would be able to answer his questions about Dan. In the surreal atmosphere of the early morning hours, Bob saw a halo around her head. She seemed like a princess or goddess and he vowed to be eternally grateful that he chose to share his life with her.

The next evening Sally helped him to understand that there is no simple recipe for this task. Dan, who is now age one, is changing daily. Each day a variety of factors influence his level of adjustment – minor illnesses, emotional upheavals in his parents, other pressures such as weaning, and advances in his cognitive skills. Younger children experiencing higher levels of separation anxiety obviously need the balance of parenting to be tipped further towards gratification than does an older child who has better coping skills. We might respond to the nighttime cry of a stable two-and-half-year-old with a firm, "We will see you in the morning." To do the same repeatedly to a one-year-old in the throes of separation anxiety would be devastating to his development. The younger, preverbal child will need more concrete assurance that he is not alone than will an older one.

When Sally stopped speaking, Bob said, "You're sounding like Dr. Raskin. He always seems to emphasize understanding and comfort rather than how-to details. I do feel more comfortable about all this, but you still have not given me the kind of details that I like to have when I tackle a job." Sally thought a moment, smiled and said, "That will take a whole chapter and a nice dinner out."

PREPARATIONS FOR SLEEP

The parenting strategies for nighttime problems are not confined to the hours that our kids are sleeping. Many of the things we do during the day and before bedtime will influence the outcome. Our goal is to help our children hold on to the knowledge that we have not disappeared forever from their lives when they awaken in the darkness of the night. It therefore would make sense to spend time with them when they are ready to go to sleep. The gap from daytime activities when our children are with us continuously, to the nighttime when they are alone, is bridged more successfully by the wonderful moments we can spend with them before they get tucked in. Depending on the age, looking at pictures, reading stories, and a multitude of other loving interactions make it easier for our kids to nod off with a warm picture of us firmly planted in their minds. This time together also provides opportunities for the types of mental stimulation that encourages cognitive development.

The Nighttime Bottle

Since our intent is to help our children master separation fears, not avoid them, it makes sense to refrain from giving them a bottle to have with them as they fall asleep. A better feeding strategy is to give the nighttime bottle a half-hour before sleep. A bottle given to ease the child into sleep is functioning as a pacifier. Tranquilized by the bottle, he is able to blot out any awareness of the impending separation. As he falls asleep with a nipple dangling out of his mouth, he is oblivious of being alone. Everyone seems to gain by this arrangement. Parents are able to eliminate the tedium of having to spend time with a fussy baby and the baby is able to make the transition from daytime activities to sleep without stress. But both parents and baby will pay a price if this is used repeatedly. The reality of being alone cannot be put off indefinitely. Later in the night, he will awaken alone in the midst of darkness and we will have missed one small opportunity to nudge him in the direction of achieving a constructive resolution of this important problem. An understanding of the developmental hurdle allows us to think more realistically about our many daily contacts with our young children.

Settling Down

After tucking Dan in for the night, Sally tiptoes out of his room, keeping the fingers of both hands crossed. In the kitchen with Bob they glance at each other each knowing exactly what the other is thinking, "Will Dan allow us to finally spend some time together or will the ordeal begin?" A minute passes and all is well. Just as they begin to relax they hear the telltale sounds of stirring that they have learned is usually a harbinger of the lusty cries soon to follow. They are prepared for this and are ready to implement the guidelines for dealing with separation anxiety: **a little at a time combined with love.** They allow Dan to fuss and even cry for a minute or two. Sometimes he can achieve a sufficient level of comfort by himself so that he can fall asleep. They certainly want to encourage these efforts. Mastery requires facing difficult issues a little at a time, enough that gains are being made but never so much that the child is overwhelmed.

Dan is only age one and has not had much practice dealing with separation fears. His anxiety and discomfort quickly escalate to an intensity that he cannot dismantle without help. If his parents did not intervene, eventually the crying would turn to whimpering and then subside altogether. At this point Dan would be in a state of frightened exhaustion and we would have lost a round to separation anxiety.

Dan's parents are in tune with his level of development. After a very brief delay they return to his room to say a few soothing words and provide another comforting tucking in. They may have to repeat this a number of times until he is able to fall asleep. The weeks pass quickly and, with his parents' help, Dan's skills improve. His parents monitor this progress and respond accordingly, always aware that there will be ups and downs in his progress.

We all have the ability to sense the proper balance of frustration and gratification needed to make progress. A bit of patience and understanding is required in order to incorporate this into our parenting methods. Parents generally err for two reasons: their preoccupation with their own needs and desires, or the influence of emotional blisters. As a consequence, they might lean on the side of too much frustration by ignoring their child's distress, or in the other direction by indulging him. Erring on the side of indulgence at this point usually takes a number of obvious forms. These include repeatedly taking their child to bed with them or supplying a variety of pacifiers to quell his anxiety instead of helping him to master it.

THE CRY IN THE MIDDLE OF THE NIGHT – GUIDELINES

They had reached dessert and Bob was speaking to Sally, "You have still not told me what I need to know. What do I do in the middle of the night when it's Dan and me alone?" Sally responded, "If you hear him begin to fuss or whimper, cross your fingers and hope that he will be able to settle down on his own without needing reassurance. Crying that continues and becomes more intense means that his fears have become too much for him to handle and your presence is needed. Let him know that you have not disappeared forever by saying a few words and tucking him in. Sometimes this is enough and you can quickly return to bed.

"Unfortunately he will often not let you off so easily and the moment you leave his room the howling will start all over again. There are a number of ways I handle this, but you may devise methods that you prefer. As long as you incorporate the two guidelines it will work out well. For example, you might sit quietly in his room, allowing him to see you but offering no additional gratification. This would be in accord with the rule of a little at a time. Dan will be reassured that you have not disappeared but he will not get everything he wants. In fact, when he sees you, his crying may become even more intense. If his cry could be verbalized in adult terms he might be saying, 'How can you sit there and not give me love on my terms? I want more. I want to be held and fed and more! It makes me very angry.'"

At this point Bob interrupted his wife, exclaiming, "But apart from getting cold, what will I be accomplishing if I'm just sitting there?" Sally replied, "You are combining both guidelines by remaining loving as you give Dan a little less than he is demanding These experiences will help him learn that getting less than he wants is not synonymous with being unloved. Your calm and loving presence will communicate some very important messages. You will be saying, 'I love you very much and will remain here a while so that you can continue to see me. I realize that at this point your separation fears are still very intense. If I left your room it would make it harder for you to let go of the idea that separations are the same as rejections. **I am confident that my adherence to the rule of a little at a time combined with an attitude that remains loving will help you to feel increasing comfort with ever larger doses of separation.** As you develop more skills we will tip the balance of frustration versus gratification further in the direction of frustration than you would like. I will do my best however, to never let it swing so far in that direction that it impedes your progress and reinforces the distorted perceptions at the basis of your separation fears.'"

"How many times would I have to do this?" asks Dan's father, as he visualizes himself being used as a yo-yo by the little guy. "When I reach the third or fourth time I'm going to begin to feel used and manipulated."

Sally, with confidence, said, "We are the ones in charge of how this unfolds. If the rule of a little at a time is followed, there is absolutely no danger that this will go on indefinitely; time and his developmental gains, both cognitive and emotional, are on our side, the side of growth. The security our love is instilling will lessen Dan's need for concrete evidence of our presence. We are the ones who are responsible for helping him inch a little bit at a time towards our goal, the elimination of his fears of being separate and alone. Parents get into trouble only if they are not able to use a loving, balanced approach. This happens when parents indulge their child's desire for excessive and prolonged closeness or when they allow him to be subjected to too much distress too soon."

Points to Remember

- Sleeping difficulties are typical symptoms during this age period and indicate that children are struggling with a developmental problem: the fear of being alone.

- Children struggling with the concept of being alone need their parents' help in order to successfully overcome this fear.

- By understanding the issues, remaining calm and loving, and with some added common sense, parents will do fine.

CHAPTER 11

MANIPULATION?

The issue of manipulation needs to be addressed because it is so often used by parents to explain their children's disturbing patterns of behavior, such as nighttime crying, and can become a rationale for parenting responses that completely miss the mark

Question – How can we be sure that our child is not manipulating us?

Let us once and for all eliminate the erroneous, but not uncommon belief, that children can manipulate parents. Our children are utterly helpless and completely dependent upon us. Their distorted perceptions, actual helplessness, and lack of cognitive skills prod them into responses that their parents find disagreeable. By no stretch of the imagination can any reasonable person believe that at these moments we are dealing with cunning minds, using Machiavellian tactics to devise plans to drive us crazy or thwart our will. If we decide to excessively gratify our child's whims, we are completely responsible for this. We are never justified in claiming that our little kids have manipulated us. Appropriate parenting decisions are based on reason and love. Poor parenting decisions can be attributed to ignorance or emotional blisters, but never the manipulative behavior of our children.

Parents like to believe that they have been manipulated because it allows them to shift responsibility for their poor parenting from themselves to their children. As a consequence, the kids have to bear the brunt of both the poor parenting and the blame for the poor parenting. When we spoil or excessively gratify our children, for example, by repeatedly taking our little kids into bed with us, it is never because we have been manipulated. Dan did not cry in the middle of the night because he had concocted a plan to torment his parents until they gave him what he wanted. He was crying because of his separation anxiety.

It would be altogether fitting to put to rest forever the notion of children manipulating their parents.

CHAPTER 12

NIGHTTIME AWAKENING AND OTHER SIGNS OF SEPARATION IN OLDER CHILDREN

Question – You have given me the knowledge I need to respond to nighttime awakening in a younger, preverbal child. Is there additional information that I may find useful for older children, or when the balance of frustration versus gratification should move further in the direction of frustration?

Separation anxiety makes its appearance in the later months of the first year of life, and with the parents' help it will be essentially eliminated by age three. As children move closer to their second birthday, they acquire new skills that their parents can enlist in their efforts at helping them to master separation anxiety. Their general awareness of the world about them becomes expanded and they acquire the use of speech. Speech allows parents to directly communicate the constructive messages that before relied exclusively on the parents' demeanor and behavior. The emerging ability to think clearly about their feelings, thoughts, and behaviors is an important vehicle for progress. Parents need to encourage the use of this new skill to start their children on the path towards the development of a capacity for insight. The words may vary but the message is the same and is aimed at correcting distorted perceptions.

Before Dan became verbal, his parents could only communicate through attitude and behavior that they could be trusted to be there and that they did not disappear forever when they were out of sight. With his development of speech they can actually use words to express these sentiments. For example, after tucking him in, Sally can say, "Mommy will be in the kitchen, if you need me I will come." Or upon arriving at his doorstep in response to a cry, Sally might say, "Its okay, when you stop crying I'll tuck you in." Well-chosen words will always be a verbal elaboration of the two guidelines. The use of words has the added advantage of helping our children to gradually develop the knack of being able to do the same. We must remember however that words even for adults are often unable to counter the power of fear, and in the end it is **our child's accurate reading of our motives** that is most effective vehicle for the creation of trust and the elimination of distorted perceptions.

The progress children make often seems slow and erratic. Even very appropriate efforts by parents to reduce their child's anxiety are usually not immediately successful. For this reason parents should evaluate their parenting by their ability to adhere to the two guidelines, rather than by their child's response. Sometimes an episode of crying may not end until our child finally tires and settles down to sleep. If we can accept our limitations and remain loving and calm throughout, we will have remained on course. Our loving calmness is showing our children that we are confident that they have the capacity to learn that they are loved and safe even when their desire for closeness on their terms is being frustrated. This is not the kind of constructive message children hear if, prodded by emotional blisters, parents become angry or need to distance themselves for their own comfort.

We cannot always eliminate our child's anxiety and agitated behavior, but we can try to control our own. The nonverbal message communicated by our calm presence says, "I love you very much. You will learn to trust our love as you see repeatedly that it can be relied upon and is not diminished by your discomfort. Through a veil of fear and anger you will see the truth, that I have not disappeared or abandoned you. Gradually your distorted perceptions of being abandoned, unloved, and worthless will be replaced by confidence in us, our love, and in your own increasing capacity to handle the stress of being alone."

CHAPTER 13

DAYTIME STRATEGIES THAT HELP TO MASTER SEPARATION ANXIETY

Question – Now that I can see how important it is for children to master this developmental hurdle, I wonder if there are other strategies I might use during the time that they are up and about that may be of help.

Parents have a tremendous capacity to use their ingenuity and common sense to find unique solutions to problems, if they understand what is needed and avoid letting their own feelings interfere. Once I have introduced them to the concept of devising strategies to help their kids to feel more secure when they are alone, parents have usually been able to carry the ball on their own. I begin by explaining that younger children cannot abstract the existence of things and people once they are out of sight. For example, if a toy is removed from the hands of a six-month-old and placed behind a pillow, the child will not reach for it. If this is done several months later, the same child will usually immediately look behind the pillow to retrieve the toy. This cognitive advance is associated with gains made in the emotional side of his life as well. He is learning to retain an image of his parents during periods when they are not immediately available.

This knowledge can be used to devise forms of play and other activities that will help in the mastery of separation anxiety. Games that have been played for centuries with very young children, such as peek-a-boo and retrieving objects, are examples. These games, always enjoyed by preverbal children as well as their parents, should be encouraged since they help to master the fear of things going away and never coming back.

Peek-a-boo, played with younger children, usually consists of the parent covering their child's eyes or their own face and asking, "Where is Mommy?" After a brief pause the hands are suddenly removed and the mother says, "Here I am." The kids love this and the game ends only when the parent becomes too tired to continue.

What accounts for our child's special interest in this game? All day long, in a variety of different ways, he finds himself a passive participant in a frightening and confusing experience. He may be completely content, basking in the love and care of his mother, when suddenly she is gone. The frustration of his wish for permanent possession of the source of so much pleasure leaves him helpless and angry. No matter how hard he wishes for it, he does not have the magical power to bring her back at will and the absence seems an eternity. When he plays peek-a-boo, all this is turned around. As the game unfolds he has the wonderful ability to make her go away and reappear. He is also learning about seeing and not seeing, coming and going, and being gone and returning.

Children are not able to tell us directly what they are thinking. But we can learn so much by watching and thinking about the meaning of their behavior. For example, their choice of play at each stage of their development offers good clues about their emotional life as well as providing us with useful information about their cognitive development.

Another playful behavior, more usually a source of consternation rather than pleasure for parents, is also linked to mastery of separation fears. There is generally a gleam in his eye and smile on his face as he tosses things to the floor at the same time his mother is trying to get food into his mouth. His grin widens when Mommy returns the object so that it is within his grasp, allowing him to repeat the process. His mother is tempted to baby proof the table so that she can be relieved of making this extra effort. It's hard enough to get the spoonful of food to the target without the added burden of having to pick something up from the floor after each mouthful. This activity is neither trivial fun nor designed maliciously by the child to drive his mother crazy. It is enjoyable precisely because it gives him some sense of mastery of things going and coming back. This type of activity is useful and should be encouraged to the extent that parents have the time and patience to play along.

Pull toys are one of the first types of toys enjoyed by toddlers. In the daily routines of a toddler, his mother dashes past him like a car on the highway. Our little guy, who has only recently acquired two-legged mobility, may reach out to grab her but he is too slow and too small. She is gone. This is reversed when he plays with a pull toy. He becomes the one who leads and the toy dutifully follows. He can hear it even when he does not see it as he marches along with the toy rolling along behind. Some parents, after becoming aware of this concept, have humorously suggested placing a cowbell around their own neck during this period. The clanging sound of the bell in different parts of the house, they suggest, might lessen their child's need to keep them close enough to be seen.

Parents will discover an endless array of opportunities during the daily routine to initiate games and other parenting techniques that are tailored to the situation and their child's level of development. For example, verbal children and their parent can take turns closing their eyes and describing the color of the other's clothing. We can devise a variety of imaginative interactions with an older child that will more directly address the child's nighttime fears. The sequence might begin by reminding him of going to bed and then asking, "When you are in your bed and can't see Mommy, where do you think I am?" The child will answer, or be coached to answer, "In your bed, Mommy." We can then accompany our child to our room saying, "Yes, this is where I am, right in my own bed." This simple and enjoyable interplay helps him to conceptualize his mother's continued existence when she is not in his sight.

A variant of this activity begins by directing our child to lie down on his bed, explaining that we will lie down on our own bed and play a game. We would then call out, "Where am I now?" An addendum to this is to count to ten and then tell the little fellow to come to Mommy's bed so that he can see her again. This type of play can be concluded by saying, "Now you know where I am at night when you don't see me. It's scary to not see anyone when you get up at night, but you know where I am, right here in my bed."

Waiting is hard for all kids, but especially difficult for children who have not mastered separation anxiety. A moment seems an eternity if the mother's absence engenders fear that she will never return. There will be innumerable opportunities to help dispel this concern. By adhering to the rule of a little at a time, we can instill trust that at the end of the moment we will still be there. This exercise occurs repeatedly during our daily routines when we might say, "You play here for a little while; Mommy has to look at something on the stove and will be right back." This template can be used to provide other similar experiences. For example, incorporating this concept into a play form we might say, "Let's play a game. Mommy will go to the kitchen and count to ten and then return, when I come back it will be your turn."

As our child progresses, we can extend the length of separations during these interactions and enlist his participation in the endeavor. This exercise would begin with an explanation that we were going to help him to learn to wait by saying, "Here are some toys, let's see if you can play by yourself for three minutes or until the buzzer goes off, and then I'll return and play with you." Puppets and dolls can be used imaginatively with an older child still struggling with separation problems. In utilizing them, the parent acts the part of the child and the child is encouraged to take the role of the mother. Using the mother puppet, the child is coached to tell the baby that it is time for the baby to go to sleep. Taking the part of the baby puppet, the mother cries and says that she is afraid of being alone. Through the mother puppet, the child is encouraged to say, "Don't worry, don't be afraid. Even if you can't see Mommy she is in her bed and will be with you all day tomorrow."

The stories and rhymes that children love can also provide us with insights about their inner feelings and thoughts. Children enjoy hearing certain stories over and over again for the same reason they choose forms of play. The unfolding of the story themes provides mastery in make-believe of the events that they are finding so troubling in real life.

It is interesting that a widely known bit of English literature has separation as its central theme – the nursery rhyme *Mary Had a Little Lamb*. Let's see why this is so.

> *Mary had a little lamb,*
> *Its fleece was white as snow;*
> *And everywhere that Mary went,*
> *The lamb was sure to go.*

In her daily life, it is the child who attempts to follow her mother and feels in danger of losing her. In this first verse the helpless condition of the child is reversed. Everywhere that Mary went the lamb, which represents the mother, was sure to go.

> *It followed her to school one day.*
> *It was against the rule.*
> *And made the children laugh and play,*
> *To see a lamb at school.*

Children must at some point face the reality of their separateness from loved ones. A milestone in this developmental process is the first day at school.

> *And so the teacher turned him out,*
> *But still he lingered near,*
> *And waited patiently about,*
> *'Till Mary did appear.*

Acceptance of the separation and the capacity to wait until reunification is possible is a requirement for mastery of this developmental hurdle.

> *And then he ran to her, and laid*
> *His head upon her arm,*
> *As if he said, "I'm not afraid,*
> *You'll shield me from all harm."*

Mastery depends on children learning that they are safe when they are apart.

> *What makes the lamb love Mary so?*
> *The eager children cry.*
> *"Why Mary loves the lamb you know,"*
> *The teacher did reply.*

Ultimately, it is the strength of love that paves the way for the successful mastery of separation anxiety. Children first learn to trust their parents and then to trust their capacity to cope with being alone because their parents' love has been reliable. That is the teacher's lesson. Why can Mary attend school? How is she able to listen to the teacher and learn her lessons for those long hours that she is away from home? The answer is simple. She trusts that she is loved. This is an essential skill for successful adaptation at school, but this is often overlooked when parents and educators are attempting to understand the reasons that a child is not profiting from his early school experience.

I have addressed this topic in detail to show parents how understanding their child's developmental problems can help them to creatively devise helpful parenting strategies applicable to each of the problems their children will face.

Points to Remember

- There are many useful parenting strategies to help children progress.
- Helpful strategies must be based an accurate understanding of the meaning of children's behavior and a clear conception of parenting goals.

Chapter 14

A BRIEF REVIEW OF PARENTING

The thought sequence I have used to delineate helpful strategies to master separation anxiety can be applied by parents to clarify and respond helpfully to the variety of other issues that arise and commonly bewilder and frustrate them. The steps that comprise that sequence have been mentioned before and deserve to be repeated.

Step 1 – Understand the developmental hurdle with which the child is struggling. In this chapter it is learning to be alone.

Step 2 – Understand the meaning of the behavior. Nighttime crying during this period is nearly always a manifestation of separation anxiety.

Step 3 – Understand the goal. The goal is to help our child master this problem and gradually learn that he can trust and be confident that he is loved and secure even when he is alone.

Step 4 – Getting the job done entails our combining love with responses aimed at the mastery of the problem.

We will rarely miss the mark if this simple process is followed. The hardest part is to remember that thinking and understanding must precede acting.

CHAPTER 15

PACIFIERS AND SEPARATION ANXIETY – THUMB SUCKING AND SECURITY BLANKETS

It's not very hard to understand the meaning of the array of behaviors elaborated by kids as they struggle with each developmental hurdle. Kids lack the resources for adaptive responses when they face new developmental hurdles. Their behavior at these times nearly always falls into one of three categories: protest, rebellion, or pacification. Adults generally respond in one of the same three ways when, in spite of their chronological age, they are overwhelmed by problems that should have been mastered early in life.

During this developmental phase, children latch on to a particular group of pacifiers to quell their frustration and anxiety. Any assessment of the appropriateness of pacifier use depends upon whether it helps or hinders their mastery of the developmental hurdle with which they are struggling. A particular pacifier that may be entirely appropriate at one age might need to be discouraged a year later.

Pacifier use was already addressed in the previous chapter on bonding. During the earliest months of infancy, children have few ways to cope with the buildup of tensions. Being provided with the plastic variety of pacifier that is sucked helps many active infants to be soothed. This will not impede developmental progress unless its use is extended beyond the fifth or sixth month, when children can be encouraged to learn more effective methods of coping.

Question – I understand the signs and symptoms of separation anxiety and our goal. Before it is achieved, kids can be expected to experience high levels of stress when they are alone and look for ways to soothe themselves. Some kids suck their thumb, others use special blankets. Should these types of pacifiers be encouraged or discouraged? Are there helpful guidelines about pacifier use during this phase?

The reduction of stress, every one does it

Most people don't tolerate stress very well and will go to great lengths to reduce it. There is a spectrum of ways that we deal with stress, ranging from adaptive to extremely maladaptive. If kids are saddled permanently with maladaptive methods for stress management they will encounter many problems as they wend their way along the road of life. It makes sense, therefore, to help our children discard poor methods in favor of ones that support more adaptive patterns of behavior. For example, overeating, drug or tobacco use, or tantrums for the management of stress are far less adaptive than jogging, meditating, or even watching television when these are used to wind down. Good parenting is aimed at helping children master a sequence of developmental hurdles. An important part of this mastery entails the adoption of more adaptive methods of stress reduction and the elimination of those that are less adaptive.

Dan's parents are helping him to master separation anxiety, but this takes time. Perhaps in six months his skills will be sufficient for him to quell the mounting anxiety and go back to sleep on his own. But now, at only fourteen months of age, he has not yet reached that point. This night he has awakened and finds himself at the mercy of emotional pain that is rapidly threatening to overwhelm his meager emotional resources. What is he to do? Perhaps his mother will come and the dreaded feeling of being alone and helpless will quickly abate. But she is not here now and the wait seems interminable. What can he do to take away the hurt?

What would you do or what could you do if you were helpless, frightened, and alone, lying on your back in a crib with no capacity for speech and the physical limitation of a one-year-old? It is common for children as well as adults to fall back upon methods of tension relief that proved successful in the past, regardless of their functional appropriateness in the present. Dan is only age one, therefore his repertoire of coping methods is very limited. Of the few available, one leads the rest on his list of favorites. From the earliest moments in Dan's life, his relief of tension was associated with sucking. The stimulation of his lips and mouth and the ingestion of milk, together with the comfort of closeness with his parent, have been associated with feelings of well-being, security, and pleasure.

Dan's places his thumb in his mouth. Thumb sucking allows him to recreate those wonderful feelings and his crying subsides.

THUMB SUCKING AND THE CONCEPT OF A LONGITUDINAL ASSESSMENT OF OUR CHILD'S PROGRESS

Question – Are you implying that thumb sucking is useful? Should it be encouraged?

The answer to this question requires an understanding of another important concept. Behavior must be assessed longitudinally. Behavior that is normal at one point in a child's development may be a sign of a developmental delay at another point.

It is difficult to draw definitive conclusions about a child's level of adaptation based on a one-time observation of the behavior. Behavior must be viewed developmentally to access its actual implications. Even a well-adjusted ten-year-old will sometimes act like a much younger child. Only by following behavior over time can we safely conclude that a particular form of behavior is problematic. Even the most mature of us, under sufficient stress, will manifest maladaptive forms of behavior. It is entirely normal for children to move up and down on the adaptive-maladaptive scale on a daily or even hourly basis. **A trend of maladaptive behavior deserves our concern only when it remains unchanged or worsens over time.**

Newborn babies sometimes suck their thumbs and many children will continue to use their thumbs to relieve the buildup of stress during the following months. During this early time frame they lack the more sophisticated methods available to older kids. In fact, the primary method of getting gratification and reducing stress during the first year entails the sucking that accompanies feedings. Therefore thumb sucking is entirely normal at this time and is not a harbinger of future problems. It is also not surprising that children will continue to use this device to reduce the stress engendered by separations, beginning in the later part of the first year and continuing into the second.

Parents who understand this will be able to correctly interpret the implications of thumb sucking during this period as a sign of their child's struggle with separation fears. They will know that their parenting needs to be directed towards the mastery of separation fears and the development of trust and object constancy. As this is accomplished and anxiety subsides, thumb sucking can also be expected to diminish. Persistent, repetitive thumb sucking extending into the fourth or fifth year should alert us to the possibility that our child is not winning his struggle with this developmental hurdle. Trying to eliminate thumb sucking without attention to its actual cause would be like desperately trying to paint over a crack in our home's foundation so that it won't be noticed, or taking an aspirin for pain and neglecting to fix a broken bone.

Guidelines for making a developmental assessment of children's behavior

Understanding the concepts of child development allows parents to think about behavior on a continuum rather than in a static manner. There are relatively few accurate conclusions that can be drawn from a cross-sectional glimpse of a child's behavior. The implications of thumb sucking will change as a child's development unfolds. Behavior that is constructive at one point and deserves to be accepted as an age-appropriate method of stress reduction, may be far less desirable later.

The concept of developmental assessment leads to a series of typical questions parents might ask themselves when faced with behavior that they believe might require some type of intervention. Using thumb sucking as an example, these questions include, Is the behavior increasing or decreasing in frequency? Has its intensity changed? What types of situations seem to elicit thumb sucking? Has this changed? Does the thumb sucking occur in response to more trivial situations of the kind that most children of a similar age can usually manage quite well? Is the thumb sucking standing in the way of the development of new age-appropriate skills? Is it preventing the child from learning to face and handle increasing amounts of stress? Are there other signs of developmental lagging and immaturity? If the thumb sucking has increased in frequency, have there been sources of external stress in the child's life that might account for this change? (Examples include separations, illness, beginning preschool, toilet training, increased parental demands, or admonitions.) Has either parent been under stress, depressed, angry, or less responsive for other reasons?

Knowing what to do requires asking the right questions. Knowledge about developmental hurdles is a prerequisite for asking ourselves the right questions, ones that provide the answers needed for good parenting decisions. Parents need to remind themselves that their primary mission is to help their child master developmental hurdles. Finding a way to eliminate thumb sucking that does not include consideration of the underlying developmental hurdle that needs to be mastered bodes poorly for a favorable outcome.

Two examples will help to clarify the concept of longitudinal assessment of behavior.

Janice, a little girl who learned to relinquish her love for her thumb

Everyone noticed how much Janice loved her thumb. She was an active and happy nine-month-old adored by her parents. She sucked her thumb when she was hungry, when she was tired, and any time she just did not feel good. She even put her thumb in her mouth between spoonfuls of food when her mother fed her.

Her parents gave her an appropriate balance of love versus frustration and she gradually developed trust in her parents as well as in her own ability to handle increasing doses of being alone. Soon she began to acquire speech and became interested in toys and many of the other things that occupied her world. The thumb sucking persisted into her third year but by this time its character, frequency, and intensity changed. During the day it was mainly confined to those periods when she was tired or very cranky. She nearly always sucked her thumb after her mother had finished her tuck-in ritual before going to sleep.

These changes in the characteristics of the thumb sucking were so gradual, her parents did not notice them. Parents often overlook favorable trends. Accomplishments, as well as the part the parents played in bringing them to fruition, are often taken for granted. Relatives and some close friends had noticed the bit of continued thumb sucking and expressed concern that if nothing was done the habit might become ingrained. They gave the parents a variety of suggestions "guaranteed to work." These included scolding Janice each time her thumb went into her mouth, pulling her thumb out, covering her hand with a mitten, and using bribes to encourage her to give up the habit. Since she was only age three her parents wisely decided to reject these suggestions, say nothing to her about her thumb, and observe her progress. They did continue to spend time with her before she was tucked in. Since she was verbal and curious they encouraged her to participate in the story reading by pointing to pictures and repeating parts of favorite stories she had memorized. Naturally the thumb would be removed by these activities. By the time Janice was nearly five years old, the bedtime thumb sucking had disappeared altogether. It never returned. She continued to love bedtime stories and when she became older enjoyed reading before going to sleep.

Ryan, a little boy who was never able to give up his love of his thumb

Ryan was seven years old. His mother described him as a loving and sensitive little boy. He did not like school and favored playing with younger kids. His recurrent complaint when he returned from school or play was, "Everyone is so mean to me." Even when he was not crying, a tear could be discerned, ready to surface. He worried a great deal, especially about his mother. He said, "When I am away in school I think that something might have happened to her." After school he preferred to remain at home and tended to trail his mother around the house. This irritated his mother who resented the incessant demands he placed upon her. Ryan sucked his thumb before going to sleep and he could often be observed at home and in school with a faraway expression on his face and his thumb in his mouth.

A developmental assessment

Both Janice and Ryan began sucking their thumbs during their first year of life. The similarity of their thumb sucking ends there. Janice's use of this device gradually subsided as she became older. Ryan's thumb sucking continued and at age seven he displayed many other problems attributable to persistent separation anxiety. He still needed repeated reassurances of love from his mother before he could settle down and go to sleep. When his nighttime anxiety was more intense, he stayed awake until his mother had gone to sleep in her bed so that he would be sure where she was. Many times each day he told his mother that he was afraid she wouldn't like him and that she then might go away and never come back. After being criticized by his mother he once wrote a note to her. In it he said, "Dear Mommy, if you don't love me, tell me and I'll leave. I know I won't be sleeping, so if you love me, come kiss me. I'll say that I'm sorry for what I did." There can be little question about the implications of this pattern of behavior. The years have passed since Ryan first faced separation fears, but they were still getting the best of him. Not having achieved object constancy, he was saddled with the excess baggage of persistent fears of being alone. In addition, this handicap contaminated many other facets of his life. He was uncomfortable with others, vulnerable to criticism, had few friends, and found it difficult to concentrate in school.

SECURITY BLANKETS AND OTHER SOFT FUZZY THINGS

Question – I now realize that my child's special blanket is being used as a pacifier. But I don't understand why blankets are so often chosen for this purpose during this period of development. What can you tell me about this?

The pacifiers used by many adults as well as children all have something in common. They each afford the user a form of pleasure that is similar to those he obtained during the earliest feeding experiences with his parents. As a baby feeds, he touches the softness of his mother's skin and her hair while feeling the pleasure of sucking and having warm milk flow into him. The sucking, feeding, touching, and loving become linked in the memory traces of this experience. Later, when he awakens alone and afraid in the middle of the night, he can find transient relief by recapturing some of the same sense of well-being he felt while feeding during early infancy. This is accomplished by resorting to an activity that has some components in common with that early experience. The two-year-old awakening in the middle of the night alone and in darkness may not have his mother immediately available, but he can find and touch something else that is soft and comforting. He has found a substitute that gives temporary relief, but cannot help him to master the underlying problem.

Children become attached to an assortment of things that can be used in this way. The smooth edge of a blanket is a favorite because it is so handy. This phenomenon is depicted by the Linus character in the *Peanuts* comic strip. Linus carries his blanket with him at all times and becomes bewildered and overwhelmed when he is separated from it. It is fairly common for young children to use these devices until they have mastered early developmental hurdles and acquired better mechanisms for the relief of tension.

Question – I now understand the reason children adopt security blankets, but I am still not sure how we should respond. Can you provide some guidelines?

The principles I outlined about thumb sucking apply equally here. The use of security blankets and other soft fuzzy objects, like thumb sucking, need to be evaluated developmentally. Certainly by the time a child reaches school age he should not be using these devices during the day and be less dependent upon them at bedtime. There would be no need to be concerned about a child reaching age four who still had a favorite blanket that he used exclusively at bedtime, if his overall development was progressing satisfactorily. The use of the blanket should subside altogether over the next several years.

POINTS TO REMEMBER

- Children use pacifiers for the same reasons that adults do: to relieve stress.

- Young children have undeveloped coping mechanisms for the relief of escalating tensions, so they resort to pacifiers.

- The acquisition of good coping methods requires the satisfactory negotiation of developmental problems. Helping to reach this goal is the parents' primary mission.

- Parents who rely too much on pacification may impede the formation of more mature coping methods.

- As children develop better coping methods, they will have less need for the more immature forms of pacification and will gradually relinquish them.

- If a child suddenly resorts to increased thumb sucking or a more intense use of other immature forms of pacification, the parents must search for the problem that has elevated the child's emotional unrest.

Chapter 16

SEPARATIONS OF ALL KINDS

BABY-SITTERS AND OTHER TYPES OF SUBSTITUTE CARE

There is a wide diversity of opinion about the guidelines parents should use when making decisions about separations from their children during the one- to three-year age period. The basic principles that help to clarify this issue have already been addressed. These are, a little at a time in a setting of love and acceptance, and a large enough dose of separation that progress is made but never so much that it impedes a favorable outcome.

Question – But what is that proper balance?

Once again an understanding of development is the only way to clarify this often-confusing issue.

THE CHILD'S CLOCK IS NOT THE SAME AS OURS

Separations must be measured with an appreciation of the developmental task being faced as well as the skills that are available for successful mastery of that task. I have already addressed the harmful effects of even very short separations during the first phase of bonding. Parents should be aware that a separation that is very short from their point of view might actually be of sufficient length to erode the bonds that are forming with their child during that very early time in his life. During this next stage, equal consideration must be given to the impact of separations. Between about eight months of life and usually extending until three years, our children are learning to face and handle being alone. Information about this developmental hurdle is a prerequisite for reasonable parenting decisions about the timing and duration of separations during that period.

Early in this phase of development, separation fears are intense. Even the routine daily separations necessitated by bedtime, telephone calls, and sudden trips to other parts of the house may tax our children's ability to maintain their composure. Any brief separation may be interpreted as a rejection. Only by understanding and appreciating this vulnerability are we able to balance the ratio of frustration and gratification so that trust is instilled and object constancy achieved. During this period, extended vacations away from our child, or even repeated shorter absences, may tip the balance too far in the direction of frustration, hurt, and perceptions of abandonment.

Understanding our goals, and being guided by the basic principles of a little bit at a time, it will usually not be difficult to steer a reasonable path. Each child is unique. There are probably many children who can withstand longer separations without being scarred, but since so much is at stake and the time moves by swiftly, it makes sense to err on the side of caution.

Therefore, during the six-month to sixteen-month period, separations should be confined to evenings and parts of days.

If longer periods are necessary, careful preparation should be undertaken to minimize the danger. Parents who at this point are muttering to themselves about the time and effort required of them to carefully implement the principle of a little at a time should be reminded that this is a very precious and vulnerable item we are talking about. Many otherwise reasonable parents respond to their fragile children with far less consideration and care than they would give to a valued inanimate possession.

With common sense and understanding as guiding principles, the months pass and very soon significant gains are made. By the middle of the second year, children are mobile and understand much more of the world around them. The length of separations can be gradually extended. Until age two-and-one-half to three, it would be best to avoid both parents being away for more than three or four days. Parents can gauge their child's general responses to separations and use these observations to adjust their decisions. For a variety of reasons even children who seem secure and are advancing quickly may backtrack, becoming more clingy and needing reassurance. This data should be factored into the equation for decisions about the length of anticipated absences.

Question – What guidelines can we use to minimize damage if separations longer than you have recommended are necessary?

Especially in the early stages there are a number of strategies that can be implemented to reduce the pain of routine separations and, more importantly, of separations that are longer than recommended but absolutely necessary.

Whenever possible, the substitute caretaker should be someone the child already knows. Ideally this person would be another family member or a close friend with whom the child is already comfortable. Unfortunately there are times when this more ideal choice is not available and a stranger must fill the role. In accordance with the principle of a little at a time, the child should be given opportunities to be with the new caretaker on a number of occasions before the parents' longer absence. One way to accomplish this is for the new caretaker to be in the home and spend time with the child, first while the parents are present, and then during short separations. During periods when separation anxiety is high, it is especially useful to have several sessions that include both the caretaker and the parents before the new caretaker is left alone with the child.

Separations are less jarring if the care is provided in the child's home. Children are comforted, as we all are, by familiar surroundings and their own things since this helps them to maintain links to their parents when they are away. In addition, the caretaker should be encouraged to learn as much of the child's daily routine as possible. This includes reading the stories that the parents routinely read, serving the usual food, and playing in the same places with the same toys.

Older, verbal children whose parents are away for more than several days can be encouraged to talk about their parents, and look at photographs of them and other possessions. Verbal children may be able to make profitable use of daily phone contacts with their parents. Before the separation, parents can practice using this type of communication with their children so that they will be more comfortable with it during the actual separation. Many caretakers might discourage phone contact believing that this will remind the kids of their parents' absence and be upsetting. Indeed these contacts will often be a bit disturbing for exactly the stated reason. Nevertheless they are constructive since they support the mastery of this developmental hurdle by dispelling the distorted belief that out of sight means gone forever.

Separations may foster developmental backsliding

Children are on a continual emotional roller coaster. Therefore adjustments need to be made for their fluctuating levels of functioning. Separations, and even many of the seemingly trivial daily events of everyday life, jar the fragile stability of very young children. It's not easy to be a tiny little guy with limited emotional resources facing a series of tough developmental hurdles. The progress made by children as they increase in chronological age is never steady. Parents react with dismay when kids who were doing well suddenly revert to behavioral patterns not in evidence for many months. Parents need to expect and be prepared for this at any age, but especially when gains have been recently achieved.

Any time children revert to older patterns or less adaptive trends, parents need to step back, take a deep breath, and do some thinking. It is usually not difficult to detect the life event or other circumstance that is at the root of the backward slide. With just a bit of understanding and reasonable parenting, children can quickly get back on track.

The prognosis is less favorable when parents are confused, upset, and react without thinking. Even many loving and intelligent parents will misinterpret these setbacks as being manipulative and sadly decide that some form of punishment is in order. I am not now, and will never, suggest that we give children whatever they demand because they are upset. That would fit into the classification of indulgence. Instead we should try to be in sync with our children, always nudging them gradually towards higher levels of adaptation. This may sometimes mean that a step backward needs to be accepted before steady progress can once again proceed.

Points to Remember

- When considering a separation, take into account the child's developmental needs.

- This is the period in which children are learning to face being alone.

- Learning to be alone is a formidable task, requiring parents to appreciate the impact that separations will have during this time.

Chapter 17

A RETURN TO WORK?

Question – I have remained at home with my child for his entire first year. What are the implications of returning to work during this second developmental stage?

Back to work? Not quite yet! The long hours of daily separation that work entails should be avoided during this developmental stage.

Understanding – A Requirement for Making Good Parenting Decisions

During the first six months of life, children need a steady daily diet of love and attention to establish strong bonds. The daily disruptions in care, together with the limited time and energy available when both parents are working seriously impedes the mastery of the first developmental hurdle. During the next developmental stage, usually extending from eight months to about three years, there is another important task that children need to master. They need to learn to handle being alone. Parents are nearly never aware of the dramatic impact that this process will have upon their children's later life. Self-esteem, the capacity for independent functioning, and even many cognitive skills such as abstraction are contingent upon the mastery of separation anxiety.

The important guideline that applies to this period is the rule of a little at a time.

The principle of a little at a time rests on a very simple observation of human nature. Tasks that are beyond one's ability to manage may become overwhelming and impede progress. Being away from our very fragile, helpless child for eight to ten hours, together with all the other disruptions that this entails, cannot possibly fall into the framework of the principle of a little at a time. Many children will not have the capacity to maintain a secure sense of belonging and continue their progress towards trust and object constancy when they are apart from their parents for this amount of time on a daily basis.

Question – What are the drawbacks of substitute care during this period?

The substitute caretaking arrangement dramatically reduces the amount of time that parents can spend with their children and lessens the likelihood that the time they do squeeze in will provide the love and special attention that is needed for the successful mastery of separation anxiety.

Parents attempt to relieve their uneasiness by striving to find "quality care." Most soon learn that this is not easily accomplished. But even the highest caliber substitute care is fraught with serious risks for young children. Anyone who has spent time with very young children knows that another person cannot duplicate the special care and love we give our own children.

We need to be honest with ourselves. Substitute care for children of this age is not chosen as an outgrowth of our understanding of their basic needs. It is a response to the needs of parents and others. If our little kids could talk and appreciate the implication of this decision, they would veto it immediately. If their little voices could be heard, they would sound something like this, "You've imposed this on us because of your personal wants with little thought about us and how this makes us feel. We did not invent it and don't want it." Unfortunately, children under age three may be the only group these days that doesn't have the political clout to be heard.

Being away eight to ten hours each day is just too much, too soon, at a time when children's coping skills are meager and the intensity of their separation anxiety is very high. Parents need to be reminded over and over again that when children are overwhelmed, their hurt is not a one-time phenomenon. If kids are presented with too much, too soon, they resort to a variety of less maladaptive methods to maintain their emotional balance. Some of these include withdrawing, the excessive use of pacifiers, and an exaggerated reliance on immediate gratification. Too often these patterns, once established, persist and interfere with the mastery of subsequent developmental tasks and later adaptation in school.

Question – When can I seriously contemplate returning to work with some assurance that this decision will not have a deleterious effect?

Back to work ever? Yes! There will be a time in our children's lives when the risks of substitute care are sufficiently reduced that returning to work will be a reasonable option. Usually by age three, children have the skills to adapt to this change. I am not saying that there will be clear sailing after age three. Nor am I implying that from the child's perspective this is the best alternative. I am suggesting that by three years old, many children will have the emotional skills to cope with this change.

When Substitute Care Is a Must

Question – Some parents must return to work before the completion of the second developmental hurdle has been achieved. What are the guidelines?

It is always nice to elaborate a top-of-the-line plan for children. Defining the best possible alternative is useful, even though we know that in the real world this may often be impossible. This endeavor can help us to sort out the best of the alternatives that are available to us when the top-of-the-line plan is impossible. There are obviously many reasons why the parents of a young child must work, and as they embark upon this path it behooves them to do everything possible to minimize its pitfalls.

Question – How would you rank the quality of care provided at daycare centers for children in this age category?

Before addressing this important issue, a few words about childcare workers are in order. I have worked with them for many years and have been impressed by their dedication and love of children. Their high levels of skill and motivation are not appreciated by most parents. Their responsive involvement in the lives of many children often proves invaluable. Despite this, daycare arrangements would not be my first choice of substitute care for very young children.

Daycare settings in which each child becomes one of a group can rarely provide the quality of special attention and one-to-one love that these young children need in order to thrive. There are many obvious problems in such an arrangement. There is a continuing turnover of staff. More than one individual may be involved with each child on a daily basis. Some caretakers may lack the motivation and special ability needed to provide the human qualities essential for the development of trust and subsequent self-esteem. Even exceptionally good caretakers may be too overtaxed by the demands of a number of children to be able to give each an adequate dose of the one-to-one attention necessary for developmental progress.

In a job setting with many children and other pressures it is nearly impossible to recognize and attend to each child's special and constantly changing needs. Children need care that moves in rhythm with these changes. They don't fit into the routines required in a program that must respond to an array of external factors. Children require a look from a special person that says, "I see you, I recognize you, and you are special and valued." Leaving this to chance is worrisome.

Our one-year-old telling us about this might say, "You guys are messing up real bad. I'm not a commodity that can be placed on a shelf until I'm picked up after what seems like an eternity. I have a mind that is being continually influenced by everything that is happening to me. Feeding, cleaning, and keeping me safe are not enough. I need you to smile back when I smile, to give me a helping hand when I need it, and a special hug when my spirits are low. This is a darn important job you are supposed to be doing. You can't do it part-time or as an afterthought. I need to be your top priority. My future happiness and the kind of person I will be are on the line."

Daycare arrangements place children in groups before they can possibly profit from this experience. This type of setting will impede the development of trust that depends on the sure knowledge of being special and loved. There comes a time during development when it is constructive for children to acquire the skills needed to socialize. During the first three years, smaller doses may be useful, but eight to ten hours each day is too much, too soon. The job of building a solid foundation of trust and confidence is too important to be done part-time and left to others.

Parents usually feel disturbed when they are reminded that they know virtually nothing about what actually happens to their very helpless preverbal children during the many hours that they are apart. Older kids at least have the verbal capacity to complain. The parents of younger kids must allay their anxiety by repeating the mantra, "I'm sure it is a wonderful constructive experience for them, everyone seems so nice." The same parents who give so little thought about placing their children in the care of others are usually very hesitant to do the same for some of their precious inanimate possessions, their homes, or their cars. Possessions can be replaced. The damage to our helpless children is forever.

General principles for easing the transition back to work during this period

Question – What can parents do to minimize problems if they must work?

1. **Place their kids on top of the list of their priorities.** Parents need to remind themselves of the importance of their time with their children during the limited hours they are together. The two essentials of good parenting, being reasonable and loving, are often the ones that are inadvertently abandoned in our busy lives. Parents who are reasonable and remain loving do a far better job of muting the impact engendered by a return to work. This is not easily achieved when both parents work. Too often the transition from full-time parenting to work means that our kids are brushed aside during the few hours that remain after our return from being away during the major portion of the day. It is difficult to garner the energy and the motivation to really focus on our kids after a long work day, especially when there is still so much to do and so little time to do it.

2. **Parents need to have clear criteria they can use in selecting their caretaker.** The personality and demeanor of the caretaker is important and should be carefully evaluated by the parents. Parents must not allow the pressure of making this

decision to get in the way of their assessment. Good caretakers love and enjoy children and have the knack of being in tune with very young children. Parents are well advised to observe the caretaker interacting with children before making any decision.

The best substitute arrangement is for the child to be in the care of one person and for the care to occur in the child's home. The recognition of each child's special needs is less likely to occur in a large group. It is also best if the care of the child is the sole or main responsibility of the caretaker.

The next best arrangement is for the child to be the exclusive responsibility of the caretaker in the caretaker's home. Third on the list of preferences would be a caretaker who has one or two other children in her care. As the group number increases, so does the danger of our child being overlooked and his developmental needs not met.

3. **Parents should prepare their child for the transition from home to substitute care.** A child's entry into the new setting is best accomplished in accord with the rule of a little at a time. During the first week the transition is easier if one parent remains with the child for a number of hours each day. Gradually, the hours away can be extended. Naturally, this requires careful planning and considerable commitment.

4. **The caretaker will be a key person in our child's life. It is essential to establish and maintain good rapport with her and continually share information about problems and progress.** Any information we can give to the caretaker about our child's habits and routines is always helpful. If the caretaker knows about our child's life, she will be more adept at responding with understanding. Whenever possible, the child should have some of his own toys and other familiar objects. Contacts by the parents during the day are always helpful, but often logistically difficult.

5. **Topping the list of helpful hints is the one that is most difficult to mandate: Children do well when we are doing well.** They feel more secure and are better equipped to master developmental hurdles when we are stable and secure ourselves. When they sense our confidence and trust our love, their own security becomes more firmly imbedded.

Substitute Child Care after Age Three

Question – I understand why it is best for my child that I remain at home during his first three years, but what are your thoughts about out-of-home care after age three?

By three years old, children who have successfully negotiated the early developmental hurdles usually have the ability to adapt successfully to a full-day nursery school experience. Preschool for three-year-olds and older, while not essential, offers obvious reward for the parents who can use the time for rest or work. It can also be a pleasurable and useful experience for the kids. It affords children the opportunity to become familiar with a variety of social roles that may help their entry into regular school. Skills already established can be tested and strengthened.

Children between three and five years old whose parents elect to remain at home will not be deprived in any way of the ingredients they need to continue to progress. In the following chapters I will describe the tremendous amount of learning that occurs between ages three and five, as children encounter and are helped to master new developmental hurdles. During this period the parents continue to play a central role in their child's development, whether they remain at home or return to work. Children can manage a full day away after age three, but this experience should never be viewed as a replacement for parents, whose roles remain central. The basic building blocks for the development of well-functioning individuals are laid down in the context of their daily experiences with their parents. Other influences may assist or hinder, but are peripheral to the central role of the parents.

During the past several decades there has been considerable debate about the special advantages afforded children by an early preschool experience. The Head Start program is one example. Some children do make advances that would not have been possible without that experience. These kids get a head start from this experience since it offers advantages that may be absent in their homes. Children under age three, whose homes are devoid of even meager amounts of warmth and stimulation, may profit from a setting in which they are able to obtain some of these essential elements. For these kids it is not the best alternative, but rather the best available one. The best alternative is loving and attentive parents. Researchers have found that many of the gains that accrue for these high-risk children are soon lost. The long-range outcome could be enhanced if resources were available for the staff of these preschools to reach out to the parents and encourage their involvement, so that they might continue to support and reinforce what Head Start had begun.

Points to Remember

- If possible, avoid going back to work during this period.

- Otherwise, careful planning is required to minimize its possible deleterious effects.

Chapter 18

DIVORCE

The Child's Perception of Divorce

Question – I have heard many conflicting opinions about the effects of divorce upon young children. Can you clarify its impact upon children in this age group?

The special problems for a child whose parents are going through a divorce will vary depending on the child's age, developmental stage, and available coping tools. Needless to say the extra burden it presents is significant at any age. It is not easy to be a very little child in even a stable, loving home. Fears and problems loom large and children feel so helpless and small. From the perspective of a child in his second year, the world is unpredictable, frightening, and ever changing. Since kids at this age have so few coping skills of their own, they depend completely upon the stability of their parents to provide an anchor for them. The love, attention, and confidence of their parents create a protective niche that is a prerequisite for developmental progress.

The upheaval of divorce is too often like a tidal wave engulfing and ripping apart the sheltering sanctuary needed for growth. In a multiplicity of ways, the worst nightmarish, distorted perceptions of the very young child are made real in the wake of divorce. The foundation of a strong personality is rooted in secure bonding and the development of trust. It is this solid base that arms children with the skills needed to face and cope with a world that will inevitably dish out a daily dose of separations, frustrations, and disappointments. Having an inner sense of stability in an ever-changing world is not a blessing given to everyone. It develops only gradually and derives from the successful mastery of early developmental hurdles. With the help of reasonable and loving parents, children become adept at managing increasing doses of separations and disappointments. They learn to shrug off these hurts because of the sure knowledge that in their lives there is the fail-proof knowledge of belonging and being loved.

Divorce changes all of this. Divorce shatters the conviction that there is a place where they can trust that they belong and are loved. Loved ones become angry and leave. These are not imagined or temporary separations, they are forever. The secure setting that had given the child's world stability is suddenly gone and replaced by a frightening realization that "we will never belong together again." The illusion of love forever, an essential tenet of the sheltered niche of security so necessary for developmental progress, has been shattered.

Following divorce – One catastrophe begets another

The impact of a real, permanent separation on young children is often overshadowed by another consequence of divorce that may be even more damaging. This is the alteration of their parents' moods and responsiveness during this stressful time. Even in stable and loving homes, kids are thrown off balance by the emotional vacillations of their parents. If these emotional swings are balanced by longer periods of stability, they may fall within the rule of a little at a time and act as a catalyst for developmental gains. In the aftermath of divorce, the balance tips precariously towards emotional deprivation and pain. This is not transient. The emotional ramifications of a divorce may last for months, years, often forever. It is no accident that divorce ranks extremely high on the scale of life's stresses, for people of all ages.

Under these circumstances, the young child will inevitably find the cards stacked against him in his struggle to master developmental hurdles. Trust becomes a fugitive illusion as he helplessly endures his entire world becoming unpredictable. There are real and dramatic changes in his basic love relationships. His daily routines are changed. A parent with whom he lived and loved on a daily basis is gone from the home. When he is with his parents, he may find them changed and far less understanding and responsive than before.

The substantive component of successful parenting is the loving and harmonious interplay between parents and children. Painful emotional blisters are the archenemies of love and harmony. There are few types of emotional blisters as painful as those associated with divorce. Children thrive on harmony. The pain, confusion, and anger of parents following divorce may bring to an end the harmony that previously existed and doom to failure the prospects of it being reconstructed again in the future.

GUIDELINES TO MUTE THE DAMAGE OF DIVORCE

Question – If divorce is inevitable, what steps might we take to make this easier for our children?

The importance of stable and secure parents – The essential guideline

The most important guideline is the one that parents find most difficult to follow. Children need stable, secure parents who are motivated to respond lovingly and reasonably to their children's changing needs. The emotional turmoil created by divorce leaves many parents overwhelmed and preoccupied with their own pain. Parents involved in a divorce never choose to experience this emotional upheaval. Emotional blisters are very powerful. The only defense we have against them is insight and understanding. Parents cannot wish away their pain and easily regain their stability. They can, however, attempt to use their capacity for understanding to think more reasonably about what they are going through and together find a more favorable path to see them through this difficult time. Too often efforts of this kind are too little and too late.

Feelings cannot be legislated. This is why courts don't have the power to remedy the issues that bear most directly upon the welfare of children. **Leading the list is the parents' capacity to remain as a stable, loving presence in the lives of their children.**

If the court discovered a previously unknown power, granting it the ability to legislate feelings based on the best interests of children, the first ruling would be the most important guideline. It would sound like this:

"It is hereby proclaimed that divorcing parents will henceforth be a source of stability, harmony, and love for their children. They will no longer fall prey to all of the trivial traps that ensnarl them. These create stress and anger that erode the harmony and love children need to thrive."

Parental cooperation – The second key ingredient

A fable with an important message

Before the parents could consider the court's first proclamation, it continued with the second: **"It follows from the first ruling that divorcing parents will conduct themselves in a cooperative, civil, and empathetic manner with their respective spouses or ex-spouses. They will do this regardless of the past animosity and conflict that prevailed during their marriages. They will do what the United States Congress has never been able to do, compromise happily so that the best interests of the people will be achieved."**

Do divorcing parents have the capacity to implement these two guidelines?

The group of parents standing before the court had listened carefully. The first ruling was greeted with nods of approval but with silent skepticism about its implementation. The court had barely finished the second when a tense undercurrent of increasing discord could be detected in the group. Soon audible voices could be heard. "Impossible!" "Appeal to a higher court." "It's a rigged partisan court, disregard its verdict."

A news commentator brought a microphone closer to one of the more vocal protesters to catch her words. The following were those that did not need to be censored.

"No way will I be nice to that jerk. Jail me if you like. Throw away the key. I'd rather rot in hell than be nice to that sucker. I'll get him yet. If he is listening tell him to be prepared. He won't get off so easily."

A man nearby was saying, "You people have not heard anything. They say justice must be blind; you people must have been deaf. Don't you know that if we could have been civil and made nice to each other we would still be happily married instead of having this shoot-out in court? Are they suggesting that I must communicate politely with my wife? It would be easier to flap my arms and fly."

Suddenly the crowd was hushed. The very distinguished chief justice stepped forward and began to speak. His voice was serene but firm. Everyone listened.

"We have just ruled, but you all know that we do not have the power to command you to provide your children with the special love and attention they need. It is our judgment, however, that you do have the capacity to implement the rulings just made by the court. We believe that within each of you is a flame of goodness. We further believe that it burns with sufficient brightness for you to put aside your anger and petty differences in this most significant facet of your lives – the joint creation of a beautiful human being. Doing this for your children and ultimately for yourselves will not be easy. The course you must chart will be lengthy and will have many obstacles that lie in wait for you. It is, however, manageable and will become easier with time. The rewards you will reap from the successful conclusion of this journey, as well as the journey itself, will be the most significant of your lives. Later, as you see what your efforts have wrought, we are confident that you will think, 'That was my finest hour.'

"You would not do less if you were partners in a very creative and profitable business venture. The personal feelings that you and your partner have about each other would be set aside and you would work cooperatively if a million-dollar business were at stake. Does the future happiness of your children count for less? We talk glibly about diverse groups and nations learning to live together in peace and harmony. These are often groups with competing interests. What hope is there for achieving harmony and cooperation between strangers if you cannot achieve it for the sake of a person you both love?"

The crowd listened and thought carefully about what they had heard. They realized that they had heard the truth.

A dream becomes a reality – The phone call

Jim had heard the proclamation and immediately knew its merit. Jane was not there at the time and he was not sure that she had heard about it. Based upon the history of the past three months, he was sure that his call would not be well received.

JIM: Is that you Jane? This is Jim.

JANE: Oh. *(Thinking: Why has he called this time? His accusations make me sick. What does he want from me now? I know that there will surely be an argument, there always is.)*

JIM: Jane, I'd like to meet with you so we can talk about Susie. Perhaps we can work out an agreeable arrangement ourselves and avoid the long, drawn out and very expensive court battle, which seems to be making us more contentious than ever. We both love Susie very much and I'd like very much to try to work things out with you.

JANE: *(Thinking: What he is up to this time?)* Jim, the last time I hung up this receiver I made it clear that I will not meet with you again without my attorney and a bodyguard by my side.

JIM: I fully understand and if that's your desire that's fine.

JANE: *(Thinking: He sounds different, I can't remember the last time I spoke to him without being shouted at. I do recall now a very dim memory of him once having been an okay guy.)* Jim, I'm not sure I'm using good judgment, but I'll meet with you.

A dream becomes a reality – The meeting

JIM: I've been thinking about Susie and what she really needs from us at this point in her life. She is two-and-one-half years old. Kids are so helpless and fragile at that age. I love her very much and she loves both of us, but it would be best if her living arrangements are as stable as possible. Of course I would like her to be with me but it is clear that she has been more involved with you on a routine daily basis. Her home base should be with you.

JANE: I'm so relieved. I was afraid that you were going to fight me about that. I know it's the right decision. She is a basically happy child, but this has been a very hard time for her, actually for all of us. She doesn't do well when there are lots of changes all at once. Since our separation, she has been a bit more edgy. You know, getting up more at night, making more demands, and at times having fits of irritability and being harder to please. I had been concerned that you were also going to blame that on me.

(Jane was feeling a bit less tense than when she arrived and thinking to herself, *I was picturing another terribly unpleasant scene, but it did not work out that way at all. Now that I can think more clearly about the whole thing I do remember the real fondness that Jim had for Susie and her bubbly enthusiasm when they played together. I had been pushing that kind of picture out of my head in order to harden myself for the ordeal that I thought was ahead.*)

JANE: Jim, I do know that you love Susie and that it would be important that she continue her involvement with you. I hope we can figure out a way to do that pleasantly.

JIM: Of course, that is exactly what I want and I will do everything in my power to achieve it. She needs a calm and harmonious setting and only our cooperation can make this a reality. I will always try to be open to your suggestions about anything I can do to achieve it. I hope that we can work cooperatively, both knowing that we share the same goals. This is what Susie needs most from us and it's up to us; it can't be mandated by the court. I am aware that my contacts with her can't be as spontaneous as they were when we were all living together. But if we can build a good working relationship we may be able to make adjustments that are in harmony with her developmental progress.

JANE: I am so happy that we met. I would not have imagined that we would have been able to work together and make decisions about Susie in this cordial manner. Let's meet again in a week to continue these talks. It will give us an opportunity to share the observations and concerns we each may have about Susie. Be well, Jim.

JIM: You too, Jane. I'll see you in a week.

DECISIONS – DECISIONS – DECISIONS

Armed with some reasoning skills and free from the crippling effects of very painful emotional blisters, parents can generally do a fair job at making appropriate decisions concerning their children. However, that is rarely what happens. The impact of divorce sweeps away their more mature faculties and leaves parents mired in crippling, painful feelings. Important decisions must be made, and some of them rapidly, at a time when the decision-making capabilities are at low ebb.

The questions themselves seem to defy acceptable solutions and necessitate facing issues that tend to elevate stress. Why did this happen? Who is at fault? What will happen next? Who gets what? Where does each parent live? Where do the children live? Who should have primary care of the children? How does the other parent continue to be involved in the life of the children? What are the responsibilities of each parent? What will others think about the divorce? And all this is complicated by the opinions of friends, relatives, lawyers, and even casual acquaintances.

Very stressed parents inevitably misread their children's needs, usually in favor of their own. If there is ever a time that the principle of thinking before acting applied, this is it. This is the time to take a deep breath and tap into whatever capacity is left for reasonable thinking. Applying this to the children usually goes a long way towards helping to make sense of what had seemed chaotic and overwhelming.

Who makes the decisions?

Parents commonly turn quickly to lawyers and the courts to make the important decisions. This is not the most desirable alternative. It is preferable for parents to assume this important responsibility themselves.

Especially during the first five years, but throughout childhood, kids need their parents to make important decisions. Relinquishing this role to others makes our children's world less predictable and safe. When our little kids are frightened and look into our eyes, they need to see an expression and response that communicates with conviction, messages instilling trust and security. Translated into words, it reads, "Don't worry, we are in charge. We will make sure everything will be all right; you will know that with as much certainty as you will know that the sun will rise tomorrow."

Parents cannot guarantee the stability and harmony children need if they don't feel fully in charge of all parts of their children's lives. That guarantee is too often shot to pieces by the process of divorce. Courts, laws, lawyers, and judges shoulder the task of making crucial decisions about children, a task that they are ill suited to perform. It is not my intent to be critical of our courts. They provide us with a legal system unsurpassed in the history of societies. The legal system, however, was not invented to make decisions about children and it is ill suited for that purpose.

A significant element of uncertainty and insecurity is introduced into the lives of all family members when the responsibility for decision making is transferred to court. If we could ask a young child what would be happening to him tomorrow or next week, and he could reply fully, his answer would be something like this: "I don't know, but I don't think or worry about it because I know that my parents are in charge and I can trust them to make sure everything will be okay."

When responsibility for decisions is shifted to others, parents no longer control or often even know what will happen. Children are always aware that their parents don't know and this uncertainty breeds stress and anxiety. In addition, the atmosphere of uncertainty that has descended upon the family does not evaporate when the lengthy legal process seems to end. Having used the court once in a futile attempt to right perceived wrongs and to find simple solutions for complicated human problems, parents are often tempted to use it again and again.

The stress generated from this uncertainty is intensified by the adversarial nature of the court process. This tends to exaggerate conflicts. It precipitates confrontations and erects barriers to more amicable styles of interactions. Let's face it, the courtroom is a battleground. Reasonable attorneys may try to negotiate, but they get paid to win by whatever means necessary. This may be the best method for achieving due process, but it is not conducive to creating the harmonious, stable, and loving setting that kids need for the mastery of developmental hurdles.

Decisions about children need to be flexible, changing as the children's development unfolds. The appropriate response in the morning may not be the same in the evening. Courts make their decisions with finality. When the final period is placed at the end of a document, the case is closed. The judge returns to his chambers, the lawyers to their offices, and the parents are left with a piece of paper to solve a complex and ever-changing human situation. Few if any of the important people issues have been solved, let alone addressed. Decisions made by the court may aggravate preexisting problems or be used by one parent to bludgeon the other. And this goes on and on. In our society today, when things go sour we look for someone to blame and search for a way to coerce him to make it right. The arena of choice for this madness has become the court.

The least-bad alternative for decision making

Once parents have definitely decided to divorce, the best alternative – a stable, loving, and lasting marriage – is no longer possible. At this point the best that can be achieved is to find and select the least-bad alternative. How is this done?

Problems that seem complex and overwhelming can be significantly simplified by a bit of knowledge and clear thinking. The thesis of this book is that an understanding of early childhood development is a prerequisite for reasonable parenting. The guidelines for good parenting in the aftermath of divorce follow from insight about the part parents need to play in order to help, not hinder, their children's continued mastery of developmental hurdles.

Parents are the only ones who can convey the sense of being protected, loved, and secure. **They, therefore, should endeavor to be the sole determinants of all decisions concerning living arrangements, visitations, and the endless other details involved in the daily lives of their children.** As much as possible, these decisions should be made the way we all would want our parents to make the decisions that affect our lives. **They need to be made by loving, reasonable parents in an atmosphere of harmony and mutual respect.** They also need to be made flexibly, so that necessary accommodations can occur in accord with the child's ever-changing developmental stages.

In theory, this is so simple. Armed with a bit of understanding about their kids' developmental hurdles and a willingness to adhere to the two guidelines for divorce, parents can usually avoid the many traps that wreak havoc with their kids' lives. The first of these principles is that the divorcing parents will be a continuing source of stability, harmony, and love for their children. The second is that they will conduct themselves at all times in a civil, cooperative, and empathetic fashion with each other. The rewards that will follow for themselves, as well as the children, are immeasurable.

And why not? Is there any conceivable reason for parents to create so much unnecessary grief for themselves and destruction in their kids' lives when this can be avoided?

If the parents can't cooperate

Alas! This is not the world of our dreams. Most parents would concede that the two guidelines concerning divorce have merit. Too few would be able to incorporate them in their lives.

Question – What are the alternatives if the parents are unable to work together in making important decisions about their kids?

The next-least-bad alternative is for the parents to choose, as a mediator, a person both parents believe has the expertise and impartiality to make these decisions based on one criterion—the best interests of the children. Both parents must trust this person and know that he, or she, has sound knowledge about child development. The parents should be prepared and willing to accept decisions that engender discomfort in one or both of them. Since the mediator, unlike the court, cannot mandate that the parents obey, they maintain ultimate responsibility and continue to be in charge of their children. The mediator functions as a consultant rather than as an enforcer.

There are other advantages to this arrangement. The court works in a ponderous manner and cannot make minor, or even major adjustments, if and when these are needed. By using an expert in child development, the parents have the flexibility of attempting to work out differences on their own, with the option of returning to court only if they find themselves unable to solve a particular problem. Decisions made in this manner are more likely to evolve from wisdom and knowledge, rather than from a battle and the law. The emotional climate surrounding this type of endeavor is nearly always less acrimonious than that of the court. The basic requirement for its success is the willingness of both parents to accept decisions that may make one or both uncomfortable.

Sometimes the court cannot be avoided

Question – Are there principles that will help us if our disagreements are so strong that we need the court to make the important decisions?

If parents insist upon using the court to make decisions about their children, a number of considerations may reduce the danger of damage. When the hometown loses at the end of the season, the murmur heard from the crowd is, "Wait until next year." The decrees of the court seldom satisfy both of the participants and it is not uncommon for the battle to be replayed again and again. There are few things as stressful as courts, lawyers, and the adversarial system. Many children are undoubtedly damaged by the continuing atmosphere of unpredictability engendered by the recurrent threat of returning to court. In most cases, the questionable advantages to the child from the possible modification of the original decree are usually outweighed by the toll this takes upon the entire family. Therefore, both parents should endeavor to avoid returning to court.

Decisions are easy – People are difficult – Which parent gets the child?

Question – You have still not told us what we want most to know. How do we decide upon the time allotted to each parent? Are there useful principles?

I have nearly always found that these decisions can be made quite easily. The obstacle is the common, mistaken belief that the proof of love for their children is measured by the amount of time that each parent has the kids. The parents forget how easily they decided to send their little ones to daycare, or the many days that they passed nearly oblivious of the child's presence in their home. These are often the same parents who complained bitterly about having to spend so much time with their kids and having no time to pursue their own pleasures. Suddenly, in the process of divorce, they are willing, even eager, to fight for what each considers a fair allotment of time.

Children know when they are loved and valued, we all do. It is the reality and trustworthiness of that love that children need. This does happen in a time frame. It is ultimately determined by the authentic quality of the love, not the sum of the minutes each parent has with the child. Parents who love their children will always find the time to convey that love. Parents never lose their chance for a wonderful life with their kids because of time considerations. They lose it because their own bitterness, anger, and divisiveness do so much damage to the developmental process. After this kind of prolonged early experience, why should parents expect that their kids will be able to have the ability or the inclination to have warm, meaningful contacts with them later in life?

Question – You still have not explained why you believe that these decisions are actually easy to make. Will you do that now?

During the first four to five years, it makes sense for children to have their home base with the parent who has been their primary caretaker. It makes no sense for very young kids to be shuffled back and forth, spending several days every week with each parent. It is seldom difficult to discern which parent has functioned as the primary caretaker during the early years.

Naturally, the nonresident parent should be encouraged and permitted to spend as much time as possible with the child. Using common sense as a guide, some overnight visits are fine. A bit of flexibility and understanding usually suffices to allow this arrangement to proceed smoothly for all. Problems arise only when very painful emotional blisters preclude reasonable cooperation between the parents. At times, this leads to the resident parent barring the other parent access to their child. Remedy by the court is the only path to a solution, but the outcome is generally very ugly.

With the mastery of early developmental hurdles, usually by age four or five, more extended overnight visits with the nonresident parent can be managed without disrupting the child's need for stability. By age seven or eight, children can handle, and may profit from, a joint living arrangement. The developmental tasks for children of that age, the acquisition of socialization skills in a complicated world, require identification with both parents. Parents who are able to cooperate and have some understanding of their child's developmental needs will have few problems making these adjustments.

Parents need to be reminded that it is the ability of both parents to help their children master developmental hurdles, rather than the amount of time that each spends with them that will determine the outcome.

Fairness – An elusive concept

Parenting requires a new definition of fairness. For our children, *fair* needs to mean whatever enhances the mastery of developmental hurdles. In the midst of divorce children desperately need to know that they are loved and protected by both parents. Any decision or action taken by the parents that conveys this is fair. Anything that runs counter is foul. And in this game it does not take too many fouls to put our vulnerable children in danger of being called out.

Parents nearly always mistakenly equate fairness with the amount of time each gets to own the child's body. Unfortunately, the conflict and stress produced by this flawed concept of fairness leaves children without the stability and love they need, and that is just not fair. Children know if they are loved and protected and this has no correlation with a measurement of the number of hours they will spend with one parent or the other.

It is essential for parents to redefine fairness if they ever hope to help their children to do the same. An inherent characteristic of the very immature is to equate fairness with getting what is considered to be "my fair share." This nearly always translates into, "more than I am getting now." Children do this all the time. They attempt to soothe their pain by getting more. A translation of the pouting cry parents hear from their kids, so grating to their ears is, "It's just not fair." The fair share they covet comes in a number of forms – more attention, more approval, and more of the gratification that they anticipate will take away their emotional pain.

Young children, at the mercy of their feelings, are dominated by these beliefs. That is the way children think and what accounts for their immature behavior. If the adults in their lives fall prey to similar beliefs, they will be of little help to the children. If the refrain kids hear repeatedly from their embattled parents is, "It's not fair, I'm not getting enough time with my child, or enough kindness, respect, or money from the other parent," the parents should not be surprised to hear an echo of this in their children's cries. Later, when the repeated refrain during adolescence is, "It's not fair, you are too strict, I have too much homework, I'm not getting enough of what I want, I'm miserable and you are to blame," they will know why.

When parents struggle to get more of what each considers their fair share of a child who cannot be sliced down the middle, they are modeling the infantile definition of fairness. Any doubts about this will be immediately erased by taking a video of them during this struggle and noting how much they look like little angry, pouting kids yelling, "It's just not fair!"

The court definition of *fair* also often strays far from the target. It is based on the laws and rules that must be followed. Neither of these perceptions of fairness has much to do with the actual developmental needs of young children: to have two parents cooperating harmoniously and fulfilling their children's needs for security, stability, and love. To accomplish this, each parent must give up his or her infantile desire for more.

A battle for the possession of Dotty

Who are the adults and who are the kids?

Ted was enraged. He loved Dotty very much and really enjoyed being with her. He recalled the many times in the past that they had played together. He had been so happy. This was all changing now and there was no question in his mind about the cause. Carol was making it her crusade to come between them. He had seen how angry Carol was each time she saw him with Dotty.

Ted tried to influence Dotty so that she would favor him, and Carol did the same. Each felt a lump in the throat and was a bit teary eyed with the thought of the possibility of losing Dottie's favor. The nightmare that would awaken both with a start always had the same central theme of being pushed out of Dottie's life.

Ted sensed that he was losing the battle for Dotty. He was now sure that when Carol was alone with Dotty that she was saying terrible things about him. He saw how much Dotty needed Carol and was afraid that she would use this power to turn Dotty against him. Some days he found it difficult to put the anger he felt towards Carol out of his mind.

This day, when he greeted them, he noticed a sly smile on Carol's face. As he approached, he was sure the smile was turning into a smirk. Carol looked at Dotty and said, "I'm sorry Ted, but Dotty does not want to spend any time with you today." There was a taunting note to her words. As they began to walk away from him he was buffeted by tidal waves of increasing anger. In his head the words, "It's not fair, it's not fair," echoed over and over. His emotions exploded and he found himself running after them and then pummeling Carol to the ground.

Mrs. Allen, their kindergarten teacher, was immediately aware of the commotion and quickly separated Ted from Carol. She was very surprised at the whole episode because it had been her impression that these two five-year-olds were usually very well behaved and kind. She surmised what had transpired and murmured to herself, "How silly and possessive these little children can be. Oh well, they are basically good kids, I'm sure that when they get older and wiser, they will learn to cooperate and not get so upset at the prospect of sharing a friend's attention with someone else."

They will get older but will they become wiser? A script of divorcing parents in the midst of conflict may be hard to distinguish from the dialogue of kids in kindergarten.

Dividing Children's Loyalties

The mastery of developmental hurdles requires a continuing, loving relationship with both parents. Divorce is an impediment to this. The problems of divorce are compounded if children are made to feel that they must choose which parent they favor.

I have often found that this happens when one parent has become disturbed about money arrangements or other perceived slights. Attempting to enlist the child as an ally in these altercations is always harmful and further erodes the potential for amicable, constructive dialogues with the other parent. The atmosphere of increasing acrimony that this encourages makes it a continuing ordeal for them as well as their children.

Children are completely dependent upon their parents. They feel insecure, unprotected, and confused when their parents tug at them from different directions. Communicated either subtly or overtly, the message transmitted to their kids at these times is, "Your other parent is an enemy of mine. If you remain a friend of my enemy you are in danger of becoming my enemy." Or, "If you like him, my feelings will be hurt and you will be the cause." This type of interpersonal dilemma is usually extremely disconcerting for adults; children are overwhelmed by it. They have been made to feel that the security and stability of their world will hinge upon their choice and either choice carries the threat of destroying that security.

Each parent should encourage and support their child's involvement with the other parent. There is nearly never a valid justification for one parent to communicate negatively about the other. Children should never be drawn into disagreements about child-rearing techniques, visitations, lifestyles, or money problems. The only exception to this would be behavior that is overtly abusive to the child. Even in this instance our concerns need to be directed to those whom we should enlist for guidance, rather than to the children.

Question – But what can I do if I am convinced that the child-rearing techniques that he and his new wife are using are way off base? I have attempted to talk directly to him about this but he is not receptive and he absolutely refuses to obtain counseling.

This is one of those times that we must accept that doing nothing is often the best available alternative. Becoming angry, having confrontations, venting to the children, or consulting lawyers only serve to further diminish the security of the setting. Whatever a parent might imagine would be accomplished by these and other attempts to nudge the other parent or their child to their point of view pales in comparison with the harm done. I am not suggesting that parents should not voice their opinions about the behavior of the other parent. I am saying that this should not be done in ways that are intended to influence children to be less loving or comfortable with that parent. For example, an appropriate response to the disappointment that your child might feel when the other parent neglects to come or call for a prearranged meeting might be, "Dad was supposed to come and didn't. That was a disappointment to you and it was wrong for him to say that he would come and not arrive." This combines telling the truth without attempting to influence that child's allegiance or love of the other. Contrast that with the following response clearly intended to change the child's feeling about the other parent: "Your dad infuriates me. I want to cry when I see how badly he treats you. It's terrible that we are forced to put up with his tricks. I wish you did not have to be subjected to this. He does this too often. We would be better off if he was entirely out of our lives."

Telling the Truth

Question – You mentioned telling the truth. Aren't there times when our children should be shielded? They are so young and vulnerable.

In my many years of involvement with children of all ages, I have never found any benefits that accrued from attempts to hide the truth from children. Deceptions, half-truths, and lies are never constructive for anyone. The mistrust and confusion engendered by this misguided attempt to protect is nearly always damaging. No matter how unpleasant the facts seem to be, they are far less disturbing to children than the bewilderment and distorted ideas created by deceptions or withholding needed information.

Therefore, as soon as parents have made a definite decision to separate or divorce, their children should be told so that they will be able to make sense of a very changed world. When parents listen and understand their child's language they will have little difficulty in wording their comments constructively. A simple statement to a younger child might be, "Mommy and Daddy are not getting along so we have decided to live apart." Naturally, the concept is very unsettling to very young children whose worst nightmare is often about loved ones inexplicably going away and leaving them alone. Not telling them does not make it less frightening. It only serves only to intensify their confusion and mistrust.

The parents' task is to help their youngster to know that their continuing love and protection can be trusted, even if their vows to each other proved to be untrustworthy. The task is not made simpler by trying to hide the truth. Older children are usually involved with various people outside of the immediate family, such as friends or teachers. It may be appropriate to inform these persons about the separation or divorce since this type of information is quickly disseminated. Older children may do better when they have actively participated in decisions about who should be told and how.

Telling the truth does not mean pouring out all of our thoughts to a very young child. Communication with children needs to be based on an understanding of their developmental stage and level of cognition. Obviously, an actual request for information from our kids always deserves an honest, appropriately worded reply.

Continuing Dialogue – A Prescription for Better Communication

We are often off base when we assume that comments we make to our children are heard and assimilated. The tendency to shut out anything associated with discomfort is quite pronounced in children. Therefore good communication with our children requires that we create an atmosphere that facilitates a continuing dialogue with them. This fosters the exchange of information in accordance with the principle of a little at a time. Placing an emphasis on listening and not preaching is essential for success. We should not lose sight that the goal of this dialogue is to build trust and security, rather than trying to knock some idea into their heads. Listening to them and understanding their fears and concerns are nearly always more helpful than dishing up a well-worded statement.

Kids are nearly never able to talk directly about their feelings. But given the opportunity, each child will find his own way of expressing the things that are important to him. By understanding our children's special language, and having the motivation to listen, we can tap into these feelings and thoughts. The endeavor itself has a healing quality. We all are comforted in the presence of another who listens with understanding and love.

This type of secure setting also encourages the mastery of developmental hurdles. This is our primary goal. Knowledge and information are important but they are not enough. Kids can be helped to learn the facts. What they do with them will be based on the level of maturity they attain. The real goal of parental communication goes far beyond the simple transfer of information. Our goal at each point in our children's lives is to understand and help them to successfully negotiate developmental tasks. To this end the emotional message communicated is more important than the information.

Distorting the Child's Role

Few have the capacity to consistently elaborate mature love to another. This would entail valuing our loved ones as they really are instead of seeing them as pawns in our own little games of life. Parents suffering from emotional blisters are nearly always intent upon finding relief for their own discomfort and may view their children as a means to this end. Using another for our own gratification is the opposite of love.

The forms this takes are varied and many of these are familiar to all of us. Lonely parents are tempted to use their children as companions and a source of friendship or love. During and following divorce, anger may reach high levels and children may be used as a vehicle for exacting revenge upon the other parent or become a direct recipient of the anger. In the frequent struggle over visitation rights, children are often overlooked and become little more than tools used by the parents for their own needs.

Avoiding the "who makes our child upset" syndrome

Parents often decide that their child's disturbing behavior, especially if it escalates at the time of visitation, is the result of poor parenting by the other parent. In spite of a long history of reasonable parenting by both, each parent has become sure that the other is botching the job of childcare and can no longer be trusted. They are nearly always in error about this. The dramatic changes that are imposed upon kids following a divorce are often too much for them to manage and elicit a variety of problems, often behavioral. Each parent, prodded by his or her own hurt and anger, tend to indict and blame the other. The validity of these flawed beliefs seems to be supported when they hear comments from their child such as, "I don't want to go," "I don't like it there," or "I want to stay with you." The rare instances that young children are actually being maltreated should not be overlooked. But in the main, these episodes of misbehavior that parents like to associate with visits to the "bad" parent are usually caused by the stresses of the divorce combined with the division of the child's loyalties.

Points to Remember

- Divorce is a child's worst nightmare.

- The impact of divorce is intensified by the parents' distress and disharmony between themselves.

- Children need consistent love, security, and appropriate parenting – all of which are usually in short supply during divorce.

- During divorce, both parents need to participate in the child's life, providing love and a presence of calmness and confidence.

- Regardless of their differences, parents must remain cordial and cooperative.

Chapter 19

SUMMARY – BUILDING TRUST – LEARNING TO BE ALONE

"Good night, Danny, Mommy loves you." "Good night, Mommy, I love you too, and I'll see you in the morning" Sally is once again in Dan's room tucking him in after a bad dream. A number of months have passed and a remarkable change has occurred in Dan's mind. He is nearly three-years-old now and is very verbal. He has also developed an inner security that was absent at the end of his first year. Dan is still a very little boy who is completely dependent upon his parents, but he is much more confident about being alone for longer periods of time. He now knows and trusts that he will do perfectly well during the time he is alone. He also trusts his parents and their love. He is able to rest his head on his pillow happily picturing his wonderful smiling mother, as he will see her in the morning.

He has successfully negotiated the developmental hurdle called separation. There will be problems ahead but these do not trouble his thoughts. Mommy has escaped from his grasp. She is gone. He has been forced to acknowledge that the imaginary silken thread he earlier had hoped would bind her to him forever, is broken. This bit of reality is no longer experienced as an ominous nightmare. He can relax and drift off into pleasant sleep since he now has something much stronger than a silken bond – he has new confidence in himself and trust in his parents.

JULIET: 'Tis almost morning; I would have thee gone;
         And yet no further than a wanton's bird,
         Who lets it hop a little from her hand,
         Like a poor prisoner in his twisted gyves,
         And with a silk thread plucks it back again,
         So lovingly jealous of his liberty.

ROMEO: I would I were thy bird.

JULIET: Sweet, so would I:
         Yet I should kill thee with much cherishing.
         Good-night, good-night! parting is such sweet sorrow
         That I shall say good-night till it be tomorrow.

                – *Romeo and Juliet,* Act II, Scene I,
                  by William Shakespeare

PART FOUR

**LEARNING TO BE A PERSON CAPABLE
OF REASONABLE BEHAVIOR – THE THIRD
DEVELOPMENTAL HURDLE**

ONE-AND-ONE-HALF YEARS TO FOUR YEARS

PART FOUR

SECTION ONE

LEARNING TO BE A PERSON CAPABLE OF REASONABLE BEHAVIOR – THE TASK AND ITS IMPORTANCE

Chapter 1

THE TERRIBLE TWOS

Question — My child is now two-and-one-half years old. He is a wonderful little boy who we love and who loves us very much. He is becoming increasingly secure and learning to manage when he is apart from us. Each day he learns more about his world and is very active and quite verbal. Can you clarify the developmental mission that lies ahead for us during the next few years?

Dan's parents, Bob and Sally, have helped him to master the first two developmental hurdles: becoming a person and learning to be alone. Now they are now facing a new problem. Dan is an energetic lad who seems to have no understanding of the word "no." Life with him consists of a series of tugs-of-war. At age two, Dan is a creature of impulse. He has not yet acquired the skills needed to get along in a world that does not immediately satisfy his whims. During the next developmental period his parents will need to help him accomplish that task. Their attitudes, and the parenting techniques they use, will influence the outcome.

Hell on wheels

Dan is an enormous source of satisfaction to his parents, Bob and Sally, but living with him is often an extremely disquieting experience. Friends and relatives find him "enchanting and adorable." They especially delight in his wonderful smile and the happy glint that they so often see in his eyes.

His parents are quite familiar with the happy glint, but they no longer find it so charming. On the contrary, when it appears they experience a sense of foreboding. In their minds it is associated with an endless series of images of chaos and destruction. Efforts to reign in their little dynamo seem futile, and a few hours with him leave them exhausted and often overwhelmed. They have seen the glint in his eyes, while his little hands reached prized objects, toppling and smashing them to the floor. They have seen the glint after hearing a shriek from the neighbor's youngster, meaning that Dan had struck again. A vivid picture of the teeth marks left in the little boy's arm still remains fresh in their minds. Nightmares about when the glint will reappear awaken them from sleep with a shudder.

It would be completely untrue to say that there is not another side to Dan. His parents always quickly point out that Dan has more than his share of redeeming qualities. During many of his waking hours he is a source of joy in their lives. And even the parents of the little boy he bit could not deny that he does look adorable and enchanting when he is sleeping.

As he headed in her direction, after one of his search-and-destroy missions, Sally thought fleetingly of the future and of the damage he would be doing if his size doubled and nothing else changed. His mother was his whole world but there was nothing, absolutely nothing, she could do to get him to mind. His charge picked up speed and she knew what she was up against. She remembered that in a recent episode her words of admonishment, finger wagging, and even the most upset expression she could project, did not deter him from bopping her on the nose with the same block she had prevented him from using to smash the television set.

This time, her loudest "No!" elicited only a smiling glance over his shoulder. His destination now became clear – he was reaching for her favorite ceramic platter. She knew that she would have to act quickly if she had any chance of rescuing it. Her loud frantic "NO!," combined with the sight of his mother swinging her arms wildly to catch his attention as she hurdled the furniture to reach him in time, produced only a flicker of hesitation. She watched the platter, as if in slow motion, hit the floor and shatter into tiny bits. "What am I to do?" she thought. "Why won't he listen to me? Does he hate me? How have I failed?"

In the evening after he was tucked in, Dan's parents often had nostalgic thoughts of the peaceful, serene time before his birth. Now they felt as if their home was no longer theirs. It had become Dan's battlefield and he tried to rule it like a fierce warrior. They tried to barricade him, contain him, and pen him in, but he never had any problem breaking through their lines. His war cry was piercing to their ears and they made attempts to mute it. But they inevitably tired before he did. Only when he begrudgingly drifted off to sleep did peace return to their home.

They would stand at the foot of his bed anxiously wondering what the next day will bring. They also wondered about Dan. Was there something wrong with him? They had heard about children who were hyperactive. Dan certainly fit that description. Did he need medication? Or was there something else physically wrong with him? Dan's father, Bob, remembered reading about children who could not behave properly because of food allergies.

Being willing to think before acting

A repetitive theme in this book highlights an interesting observation of human behavior. Many of us who are willing to think in some depth about other important parts of our lives, fail to do so when we are involved with the ones we love the most. I have begun each chapter with an attempt to clarify the *meaning* of our children's behavior instead of focusing immediately on "what to do." I am convinced that this seemingly small step is actually a giant one that parents usually overlook. Nearly all parents love their children. A bit of clear thinking about the meaning of their children's behavior can significantly enhance the quality of their parenting and provide some needed protection from painful emotional blisters.

Obviously, there are many times each day when time and circumstances do not permit more than a moment of thought before some immediate action is necessary. But in our daily lives with our loved ones, the important issues come to the surface over and over again, providing ample opportunities for some reflection and even discussion. I hope that after reading this book, more parents will take a few moments to understand what may be unfolding in their children's lives, especially when they find themselves confused, frustrated, or facing problem behavior that is not improving. Understanding the developmental meaning of their children's behavior during this period provides an opportunity to pursue goals more important than just "getting the child to mind." Successful actions require that understanding comes before deciding what to do.

PART FOUR

SECTION TWO

UNDERSTANDING THE MEANING OF CHILDREN'S BEHAVIOR DURING THIS DEVELOPMENTAL PHASE – LEARNING TO GET ALONG WHEN YOU DON'T GET YOUR WAY

Chapter 2

MAKING SENSE OF THIS PERIOD OF DEVELOPMENT

Question – My two-and-one-half-year-old is a terror. He understands everything but my words seem to have no impact upon him. Is this normal?

AVOIDING STEREOTYPING

Ever since humans developed the capacity to think, they have tended to stereotype people whose behavior made them uncomfortable. There probably has been no group that has been as excessively mislabeled as young children. *Bad, evil, spoiled, hyperactive,* and *willful* are just a few of the inaccurate labels given to kids like Dan, who leave their parents exhausted at the end of the day. Several months rarely pass without a newspaper account of a young child who has been severely mistreated because his parents concluded that demons or the devil had possessed him. And that is only the tip of the iceberg.

Dan is a normal little boy. Between one-and-one-half and three-and-one-half years of age, many kids are like charging locomotives without brakes. Dan does not have the apparatus to come to a halt when his parents say "stop." He could not accomplish this task even if he tried very hard; and kids of this age don't try very hard. They are creatures of impulse. Of course he loves his mother and thrives on her approval. But his powerful drive for immediate gratification will win nearly every time in a contest against any other motivation. At this age children are selfish, get very angry, and can be very cruel when they don't get what they want. They are not being bad. This is just the way they are, and no matter how disagreeable their behavior is to their parents, they cannot make it go away.

Keeping up with Dan sometimes makes the hours seem to stretch into days. "Will it ever end?" "Are we doing the right things?" his parents mumble to each other and to themselves. They try to dismiss the nagging thought that they are raising a kid who will be first on the most-wanted list in twenty years. What do they need to know to feel more confident that they are on the right track? How can they make sense of their child's behavior?

Question – Can you tell me about the issues that must be addressed that account for the typical behavior of children of this age? I know that effective parenting begins by understanding the meaning of our child's behavior.

Points to Remember

- The first step of good parenting is understanding the normal spectrum of behavior at each stage of child development.

- It's easier for parents to know what to do when they understand the meaning of the child's behavior.

- Often, behavior that is entirely normal may be mistaken for a problem that needs to be remedied.

Chapter 3

THE TWO THEMES OF THE THIRD DEVELOPMENTAL HURDLE – IMPULSE GRATIFICATION AND PERCEPTION DISTORTION

There are two themes of development that unfold together during this period that account for the array of behavior displayed by children between one-and-one-half and three years old. These themes in combination account for the behavior that parents generally label as needing discipline. Reasonable guidelines for dealing with this behavior should be based on an understanding of these themes.

Impulse Gratification – The First Theme

Once parents can put aside their tendency to jump to conclusions based on their own high level of discontent, they seldom have any problem making an accurate diagnosis of this theme. **Younger children, and for that matter immature individuals of any age, lack the tools needed to cope with not getting what they want.** Young children are creatures of impulse. During their waking hours they are continually beset by wants, which demand gratification. When these are not quickly supplied, they experience considerable duress, physical as well as emotional, and usually respond by making their protests known in the form of noise.

As hunger tensions become elevated, infants are rapidly overwhelmed by their feelings and let others know it. This characteristic of all infants and young children probably had survival value when our ancestors lived in caves, and later roamed the forests. Those infants who did not alert the adult world to their pressing needs were in greater danger of being overlooked and neglected.

As children become older, their adaptation requires that this characteristic be gradually modified. New skills are acquired for this purpose. The ultimate effectiveness of these new skills, combined with the array of attitudes, motivations, and behavioral patterns linked to this advance, will depend on the quality of parenting. The many messages, some overt and many implied, that are communicated to children as they interact with their parents in the arena of daily life, usually called discipline, has a far-reaching affect on their children's personality outcome. As parents attempt to discipline their kids, they are doing much more than "getting them to mind." They are programming an array of traits and skills associated with the problem of learning to live in a world that does not always fulfill all expectations. They are molding a human being. If this process unfolds favorably, kids become more and more adept at dealing effectively and comfortably with a world that can be guaranteed to frustrate them repeatedly on a daily basis.

Perception Distortion – The Second Theme

Question – My child is very verbal and seems to understand everything I say. I know that he has learned to be in better control of his impulses, yet more times than not he refuses to comply with even my most reasonable requests. I don't understand why he sometimes responds as if I were a monster who was threatening his life.

A characteristic of immature or infantile thinking is that perceptions are strongly influenced by feelings. This tendency, beginning early in our lives, remains a part of all of us and always leads to flawed assumptions about the world and maladaptive behavior as a consequence of those assumptions. This tendency is pronounced in very young children, adding another dimension to the task of learning to get along when they don't get their way.

Using adult language, let's see how this actually unfolds over and over again in the lives of young children. The typical pattern begins when parents decide to frustrate rather than gratify their children. This nearly always generates emotional pain in the children leading to the first of a series of distorted beliefs.

1. The child thinks, "If something has made me feel bad it means that I have been wronged." The flaw here is giving a personal meaning to any event that causes displeasure. Based on this error of perception, anything his parents do that displeases him is viewed as a grievous wrong that has been perpetuated on him. Children of this age have no ability to accurately evaluate the reasonableness of their parents' action. Even an innocuous statement that "it's time to eat" may be interpreted as "mean" if a child's preference is to continue playing.

2. The web of distortions doesn't end here. It becomes more entangling and pervasive. The distorted reasoning proceeds in the following manner: "If someone did something that made me feel bad it means that he did something wrong and deserves my blame." A new dimension has been added to the flawed assumptions. Blame has raised its ugly head. The tendency to blame others for emotional hurts is especially tricky since it precludes any movement towards personal insight and growth. Growth always entails internal change and cannot happen if one's focus remains solely on the perceived external source of the pain. Children will never develop the capacity for mature functioning if they continue to attribute the cause of their displeasure to others.

3. The final step in this maladaptive but all-too-common pattern targets for retribution the one who has been labeled as the cause of the pain. "If she is to blame for this horrific misdeed then I am justified in doing whatever is necessary to make her realize and acknowledge her mistake, and demand that she make it right." Carrying this thinking further, the reasoning might go like this, "I need to find a way to hurt her so that she will be fully aware of what she has done to me and never do it again. Being able to cause her pain also helps a little to compensate for what she has done to me."

Effective parenting and nearly all constructive discipline require an understanding of the impact of these distorted perceptions upon children's thinking and behavior, as well as methods to gradually replace these flawed perceptions with ones that are more accurate.

PART FOUR

SECTION THREE

UNDERSTANDING THE GOALS OF THE THIRD DEVELOPMENTAL HURDLE – LEARNING TO GET ALONG WHEN YOU DON'T GET YOUR WAY

The goals of the first two developmental hurdles – becoming a person and learning to be alone – were straightforward. They followed simply from an understanding of the developmental problem being faced. The goal of this developmental hurdle – learning to get along when you don't get your way—requires greater clarification. There are, after all, many reasons that children learn to get along when they don't get their way. Some of these are adaptive but others create many problems. For this reason a separate chapter has been allotted to address parental goals for this developmental hurdle.

Question – I think that I now have some understanding of this period of my child's life. I am familiar with the developmental hurdles that account for so much of his behavior. Can you clarify my goals?

Chapter 4

MATURITY VERSUS OBEDIENCE

Until now, the goal of this phase has been stated rather simply: children need to learn to get along when they are not getting their way. But this is not the whole story since it ignores the wide variety of motivations that may underlie their willingness to "get along when they don't get their way." There are many reasons why both children and adults "get along when they don't get their way." Many of these are not very constructive. Less-adaptive motivations rest upon the persistence of a variety of infantile perceptions and invariably detract from the quality of life. For example, many individuals try hard to get along because their fear of disapproval has persisted into adulthood. Pleasing others has become linked with being loved and valued; this is the hallmark of low self-esteem. Others are motivated to be compliant because they are still intimidated by disapproval and anger.

The optimum resolution of this developmental hurdle combines learning to get along when they don't get their way with the elimination of the distorted perceptions that surround this issue early in life.

Chapter 5

CLARIFICATION OF IMPORTANT CONCEPTS

Parents need to understand their goals, both long term and immediate, in order to parent effectively. The clarification of a number of important concepts will pave the way and is an essential step towards the delineation of effective parenting methods to achieve those goals.

Discipline

The process that unfolds in each family aimed at helping children to get along when they don't get their way is usually labeled discipline.

Some common myths about discipline

Question – I have always believed that discipline meant getting your kids to know right from wrong and making them conform to the right. Are you suggesting that there is much more to good discipline?

Yes, effective discipline is aimed at molding character, not merely coercing compliance.

Few parents give much thought to their long-term goals when helping their children learn to get along when they don't get their way. They don't even really conceptualize that that is what they are doing when they are involved with their children in what is commonly called discipline. If parents are asked about what they are trying to accomplish, they will usually respond that they are getting their child to mind, or to be obedient, or to be a good kid. Other parents address the unwanted attribute that they are trying to discourage. They comment that they are trying to get their child to stop being such a baby or to stop whining, or that they want to make sure that he does not grow up to be as sloppy as his father.

Even when parents reflect upon the style of discipline chosen, they seldom do so with an understanding of the actual developmental issues that need to be addressed. While many of these parents turn out decent kids, others are not so successful. An understanding of the developmental hurdles that account for their child's behavior and their long-term goals allow parents to tailor their responses more constructively.

Without this knowledge parents tend to focus exclusively on immediate compliance and overlook the long-term goals. I am not suggesting that children need not learn to comply. I am pointing out that too often the methods used to achieve compliance impede the mastery of developmental hurdles, and progress towards maturity is stalled. Efforts aimed solely at behavior control may produce transient surface successes, which may be poor predictors of later adaptive functioning. There is a very good reason for this.

The surface manifestation of compliant behavior tells us very little about our child's thinking. Ultimately it will be the tenor of their thinking, motivations, and actual skills that will determine the level of maturity they reach.

If the goal of discipline was solely to effect superficial manifestations of "good behavior," or to meet the parents' standards, every young child could easily be made "good." Parents would need only to impose their will strongly enough on their very dependent and helpless kids to obtain the desired results. Many parents favor this approach. It seems so simple and it avoids so much uncertainty and so many hassles. That it never really works does not diminish its ubiquitous use. A determined adversary could probably get me to say anything if he increased the intensity of the torture sufficiently. Would any of this change my character for the better?

The Difference Between Surface Behavior and Character Formation

Parents must remember that their long-term goals need to be aimed at character formation, not merely surface phenomenon.

For example, some children are "good" but can barely control their rage. Later, when the parents no longer have the leverage to successively manipulate compliance, their child's behavior rapidly deteriorates. I have heard many parents explain that they were able to keep everything under control until about age fourteen, when things went sour. Other children are "good" but have no sense of autonomy. Like robots, they move to the tune of whoever is pulling the strings. In adolescence, to the chagrin of parents, peers invariably begin to substitute for parents in the role of puppet master.

We should realize that we are after bigger game than superficial compliance. If we can keep our real goals in mind and remain aware of the developmental hurdles that need to be mastered to reach those goals, our disciplinary methods will be closer to the target.

The Difference Between Discipline and Punishment

The difference between discipline and punishment should now be clear. Discipline includes all those parenting strategies and attitudes that help children to master developmental hurdles. Punishment, in contrast, is the use of power, either physical or emotional, to coerce compliance. Any parenting technique that does not enhance the mastery of developmental hurdles can't be included in the category of effective discipline.

There is considerable ambiguity about the meaning of discipline. The main reason for this is that most people, including many educators, define discipline by the particular method chosen for its implementation, and the spectrum of methods is vast. How we do something is usually not synonymous with what we intend to accomplish. An understanding of our goals for the third developmental hurdle leads to a more accurate definition of discipline. Discipline is the process of influencing the development of our children's thinking. Its ultimate aim leads to a set of values or character traits that are associated with a high level of mature functioning in adulthood. These include responsibility, self-control, self-esteem, honesty, commitment, and many more. Anything parents do to further this process falls into the category of discipline. The mastery of this developmental hurdle has two requirements: an increasing capacity to handle frustration and the gradual reduction of the influence of infantile, distorted perceptions.

It is important to remember that the goal here is a state of mind, not merely behavioral compliance. Obviously there will be many times that behavioral compliance is mandatory and reason may dictate an array of responses aimed at this goal exclusively. The particular parenting response chosen may be necessary, but if it does not lead to mastery of the developmental hurdle it should not be considered effective discipline. **Real discipline molds character. It is not aimed solely at compliance or obedience, which may often be a poor measure of the development of a mature, effective personality.**

Question – You are suggesting that many children may be trained to comply, but this does not necessarily represent effective discipline. Can you explain by illustration what is meant by "doing the right thing for the wrong reason"?

Bob – A little boy who did the right thing for the wrong reason

Bob had become a good little boy because he was afraid. He was afraid of his parents' anger and afraid of the things they did to him when they were angry. He was a good little boy but inside was very angry. He hated it when he did not get what he wanted. But he was a good little boy and became better and better at preventing the hate from showing. He was a good little boy until his fourteenth year. That was the year that he realized that he did not have to be afraid of his parents anymore. That was the year he realized that his parents were more afraid of his anger and hate than he was of theirs. They tried, but there was nothing they could do to make him afraid again. That was the year he was free to do what he wanted instead of what his fear of his parents forced him to do. That was the year that he stopped going to school and began using drugs.

Question – Will you illustrate the difference between discipline and punishment?

A father who did not know that his discipline was actually punishment

Mr. Jones was quite proud of his parenting techniques and poked fun at friends and relatives who spoke about their ordeals with discipline. He believed that his son's "good" behavior was important and a reflection of him. He could not understand why he received reports from the school that his eleven-year-old son, Tim, who was so well behaved at home had become a problem in the schoolyard. When I asked him if he ever noticed any unruly behavior at home he replied, "Rarely, most of the time he is the picture of politeness." He added, "From time to time he might mouth off at me but a few swats always cuts that short. He needs to show respect to his parents. My right hand on his backside will see to it that he does. After an episode of that kind he generally retreats, crying and angry, to his room but when he returns he is well behaved and the air seems to have been cleared. I am sure that he has realized how much we value good manners and is ready to try harder."

There can be no disagreement with Mr. Jones's desire for his son to be polite and well mannered. Too many children grow up devoid of these important traits. We need to be cautioned that our well-intentioned efforts to accomplish this goal may have unintended consequences unless they also lead to the mastery of the third developmental hurdle. Politeness and good manners are very important attributes. Very little that is useful or even long lasting will have been achieved if these attributes do not rest on sound motivations and values. Parents are nearly always oblivious of this longer-term important facet of effective discipline. Many are fortunate and their kids move forward developmentally. Some are not so lucky and the outcome is unfavorable. Later, when serious behavioral problems arise parents are surprised and completely unaware of when and how they went astray. An interest in the process unfolding in their children's minds during this period of development might have alerted them to a problem that was not being addressed and guided them to a more effective path.

When Tim, Mr. Jones's son, spoke to me, he made no secret of what he thought about his father's efforts to make him polite. His answer also shed light on the meaning of his schoolyard misbehavior. He said, "I get mad at Dad. He makes me feel pushed around. When he yells at me or spanks me, I feel I want to hurt him back. I run to my room and at first I feel so angry and sad that I can't think. Then I imagine being older and very strong. I think about chaining him to a wall and leaving him there without food or water. I'd also stick needles in him and make him beg for mercy. After a while I feel better. I forget what happened and go out and play."

Tim's father may like to think that his parenting strategy is effectively influencing his son to be polite. In the immediate aftermath of its use, this seems to be confirmed. The "mouthing off" has stopped and Tim is once again relating to his father in what appears to be an agreeable manner. But Tim's father is not aware of the anger, humiliation, and helplessness Tim has experienced. Nor is he aware of the affect this is having on his son's personality development.

I want to emphasize once again that I am in favor of compliance and teaching children to show respect for their elders. In fact, I would probably have agreed with nearly all of Tim's father's values. I am pointing out another dimension of this process that should not be ignored – the underlying motivations that we are instilling into our children by our parenting methods. Tim is learning to get along when he does not get his way, but distorted interpretations of the process are being encouraged, not eliminated. Tim's belief that compliance is based on a power struggle aimed at humiliating and hurting his adversary is becoming a part of his character.

In the first chapter I emphasized that this book will not provide simple recipes for good parenting. In my experience, parents achieve favorable outcomes using a wide variety of techniques, often ones that I do not prefer. **Regardless of parenting style, children do well if they are helped to master the series of developmental hurdles leading to maturity.**

If developmental hurdles are not successfully negotiated, problems become apparent. This may occur quickly or after a delay. And when problems do arise the mischief done is compounded if parents repeat their past mistakes. If it was their car that was not working properly, or if they discovered a leak in the roof, they would get some information and do some thinking before embarking upon a course of action. But not with their child! Prodded by their emotional blisters and under the pressure of feeling that they need to do something, parents often opt in favor of doing what they did before, but more often and more intensely. In this they make the same error as our national leaders do with their pet projects. If the projects are not working, their option of choice is to fund them with more money.

The moral of this story is clear. In all endeavors, wisdom dictates that reason and understanding need to precede action. We get into water over our heads if we fall in love with our pet theories and are not willing to be flexible and shift to another philosophy when new data is obtained. If we were sure that one method was right, it would be easy. Mr. Jones would only be required to persevere using his theory about the effectiveness of the judicious use of his right hand as a guide. The flaw in this reasoning should be obvious. Many children punished consistently and severely for their "bad behavior" display a wide variety of serious problems later in life

A remedy devoid of an appreciation of the problem

A prescription for failure

Mrs. Smith considered herself a very enlightened parent. She was proud that she had never used physical punishment to discipline her daughter. Janet, who had just turned seven, had always been an excessively demanding child. When Janet was in preschool, one of her teachers had suggested that Mrs. Smith use time-outs as a form of discipline, and this seemed to satisfy everyone. Mrs. Smith found her child's angry defiance frustrating, so she was glad to have a device that rapidly removed its source from her presence. Janet would calm down very quickly during her time-outs, so her mother believed that this period by herself helped her to see that her behavior was inappropriate and to learn to control it more effectively. The preschool teacher had told her that the time-outs gave

Janet the opportunity to think more realistically about what she had done.

Assumptions we make about the impact we are having upon our kids are often inaccurate. Janet was not learning anything useful from her periods of isolation. Tears came into Janet's eyes when I asked her what she thought about when she was alone. She said, "When I'm there I think that if I got hurt no one would care. It would be scary and the hurt would go on forever. I am afraid that I was bad to her and she will never want to see me again. I think of this at night and I can't go to sleep. I think of Mom going away or of something bad happening to her. Then if something happened to me no one would help. I'm always afraid that I'll never see her again." These disturbing thoughts permeated much of her life and became more pronounced during her time-outs.

Janet's mother would do better if she were less wedded to her favorite parenting strategy. This would free her to make accurate observations and adjust her parenting to the actual needs of her child.

Self-Esteem

Everyone acknowledges the importance of self-esteem but there is little consensus about how it is achieved. Knowledge about the third developmental hurdle sheds needed light on that path. The goal of this third developmental hurdle is to learn to get along when you don't get your way. **And the ability to get along when you don't get your way is an accurate definition of self-esteem.** On daily basis, children face a seemingly endless series of experiences that are frustrating because of the discrepancy between what they want and what they get. Their craving for continuous gratification, approval, love, and success is repeatedly frustrated. Early in life they have rock-bottom self-esteem. Or stated another way, they have virtually no ability to get along when they don't get their way. Each disappointment causes intense emotional pain and is interpreted as a personal slight.

Helped by their parents to handle frustration and dispel the distorted perceptions that envelop their hurt, kids gradually appreciate one of the most important lessons they will ever learn. This is a basic truth about human existence that hardly anyone assimilates completely. **It is the realization that disappointments, frustrations, failures, and rejec-**

tions cannot diminish the intrinsic value of a human being. A failure or a rejection does not mean that we have less value. **Learning this is what it takes to get along when you don't get your way.** Too many children never achieve that goal. Many, perhaps most, move from childhood to adulthood continuing to believe a giant myth that gets passed down from one generation to the next. A cruel joke is played on so many by being programmed to believe that their value rises and falls contingent upon their moment-to-moment readout on the approval-disapproval scale. For so many this myth seems real and that is the definition of low self-esteem.

Question – How do I want my kids to view failure? I have been told that children need a lot of approval to build up their self-esteem. Is that accurate?

Failures or rejections are problems only if we continue to view them as we did when we were very young. **Failures are actually experiences that provide an opportunity for learning and growth.** They cause mischief only if used to measure our value. If our parents have helped us to fully master the third developmental hurdle, we are immune from this malady. We know our value transcends the successes and failures that are part of everyday life. The people who are most successful are those who are not deterred by failure. They learn and become stronger through the process of trial and error that is a prerequisite for ultimate success. Books written about the lives of individuals who have made major contributions to society show that most have been able to do this. They experienced severe setbacks that did not deter them from the continued pursuit of their goals. Failures did not engender despair and helplessness. Children who are most successful are also adept at doing this. They can persevere in the face of failure and external disapproval. Since nearly everything we do leads to failures, especially when we are learning a new skill, this attribute is essential for eventual success.

Many parents believe that they are building self-esteem by praising success. **It is perfectly reasonable to praise success but praising success does not build self-esteem.** It is very easy to feel good about ourselves when we are successful and receiving approval. The crux of self-esteem is the capacity to continue to feel good about ourselves when we fail. This is the goal. The guidelines and principles to achieve it will be addressed later in this chapter. These are identical to the guidelines that help children to dispel the flawed perceptions that they link to not getting their way.

Goals – The Third Developmental Hurdle

Simply stated, the goal is learning to get along when you don't get your way. But the optimum achievement of this goal requires an addendum. This achievement must include the correction of distorted perceptions that are normally linked to frustration and failure early in life. Our ultimate goal is the assimilation of values and strength of character rather than a superficial veneer of compliance. The next chapter describes the path towards this goal.

Points to Remember

- Children need their parents' help to acquire skills that will allow them to channel feelings more adaptively

- Children also need to gradually learn to interpret frustration more realistically.

- Parents must remember that their goal is to influence the development of more mature ways of thinking about frustrations, not merely to obtain compliance.

- Parents need to understand the distinction between discipline aimed at mastery and punishment with its sole goal of obedience.

PART FOUR

SECTION FOUR

GETTING THE JOB DONE – THE MASTERY OF THE THIRD DEVELOPMENTAL HURDLE – LEARNING TO GET ALONG WHEN YOU DON'T GET YOUR WAY

Question – I am fairly certain that I have made an accurate assessment of the meaning of my child's behavior. He is struggling with the problem of learning to get along when he does not get his way. I am also aware of my goals at this juncture of his development. These are to help him to develop the skills needed to master this developmental hurdle and, as much as possible, eliminate the infantile, distorted perception that complicates the task Are there general guidelines that I may find useful?

Chapter 6

ASSESSING AND ACCEPTING AGE-APPROPRIATE BEHAVIOR

The parents' first task is to make sense of their child's behavior. This is accomplished by recognizing the developmental problem that accounts for the behavior. At age two, children are demanding, aggressive, and overwhelmed by even trivial frustrations. Reasonable parenting begins with the capacity to interpret this behavior accurately. An accurate assessment of age-typical behavior allows us to avoid the misperceptions leading to frustration, mislabeling, and poor parenting.

The relatives who said that Dan was an adorable little boy with a wonderful smile and a glint in his eye were right. He is wonderful, just the way we should all want our two-year-olds to be. And all of the wonderful things about him did not emerge out of thin air. They gradually became a part of his personality because he has been fortunate enough to have two loving parents who helped him master the preceding developmental hurdles. He is outgoing, is capable of love, and is eagerly learning more about the world every day. Armed with knowledge about the next developmental hurdle, his parents will be able to build upon the strong foundation already in place. This growth-producing process will be hampered if they jump to inaccurate conclusions about his behavior or its motivation. Making sense of the typical responses of young children will help parents to avoid making this error.

Question – What is this typical behavior all about? So much of it seems bewildering and random. Can you help me to make better sense of it?

Children's Responses to Frustration

There are three typical ways that young children respond to frustration: anger, refusing to comply, and resorting to a fix. Their intense anger is nothing more than an infantile way of emphatically telling their parents to "give them what they want" to take away their hurt. Each child is in effect saying by his anger, "I will make sure you know of the gravity of your misdeed and demand that you make it right." The second typical response to frustration, refusal to comply, is intended to give the perpetrators of their frustration "a taste of their own medicine." The thought in the child's mind might be, "Why should I do what you want when you are so cruel and refuse to do what I want?" If all else fails, the fallback option is to turn to a "fix" for relief. These include pacifiers, bottles, food, and as the years go by, countless other devices that serve the purpose.

Children suffer and behave unreasonably when they don't get what they want because their perceptions of frustrations are dramatically distorted and they lack the skills and tools needed to cope with frustrations. With the passage of time most children acquire this skill and the main obstacles that remain are the distorted perceptions that they attach to this experience. For this reason a crucial goal of parenting during this stage of development is to help children correct these distortions. The difficulty for children when they don't get their way is never the issue itself. The exaggerated anger and hurt is caused by the personal meaning they attribute to the disappointment. A trivial disappointment acting as a catalyst for creative thought in one person is often an emotionally hurtful experience for another. The difference lies solely in the meanings attached to the experience. People who are the most content and productive are those who are able to fare well in the face of frustration and failure. They have learned to view frustration and failure realistically. Later in this section the method to accomplish this goal will be fully addressed.

Points to Remember

- Children's behavior is easy to understand when parents are aware of its meaning.

- The typical disconcerting behavioral antics of two-year-olds are usually precipitated by situations in which the kids are not getting what they want or are being asked to do something they want to avoid.

- Children's antics fall into three categories: protest, refusal to comply, and resorting to some sort of pacification.

- Anger in all its forms represents nothing more than the child's very immature method of demanding gratification.

Chapter 7

BEHAVIOR THAT IS NOT AGE-APPROPRIATE

What Does It Mean and What Should Be Done?

Question – But what does it mean if we notice behavior more typical of a younger age?

Earlier developmental hurdles that were not successfully negotiated sometimes account for the behavior manifested by children in this age category. If parents can detect this they will be able to respond more helpfully. When earlier developmental hurdles are not successfully negotiated, the problem remains as well as the array of typical behaviors associated with that problem.

During the first months of life, it was simple to determine the developmental task being faced. There was only one, bonding. At one year of age the diagnosis of the developmental hurdle causing our child's difficulties remained fairly straightforward. Once we have been made aware of the signs of separation anxiety, these are hard to miss. An accurate assessment of the developmental hurdle being negotiated becomes a bit more complicated during the second to fourth year of life. If earlier developmental hurdles have not been mastered, they will influence behavior at later stages. Some children of three years and older are still afraid of being alone. Some of the behavior of these kids with persistent separation anxiety may be manifestly similar to children who have moved on to the next hurdle. Parents will err if they neglect to make this distinction.

This dilemma is easily remedied. Children who have not yet mastered separation problems will always display some of the patterns of behavior characteristic of that stage. These include nighttime awakening, problems in separating, clinging, and other trends usually found in younger kids. Spotting these persistent patterns does not mean that efforts should not be aimed at the mastery of subsequent hurdles. It does demand that the approaches used are not ones that are likely to aggravate problems from a previous stage.

For clarity, I am addressing these stages of development one at a time. As children's lives evolve, there is naturally a varying amount of overlap. At times of stress, or when our kids are facing a new challenge, we should expect them to sometimes slide back to previous problems that we had hoped had been solved. We need the flexibility to shift our parenting accordingly. The basic thesis of this book is that good parenting requires some intelligent thinking, the type we apply to most of the other issues in our lives that we consider important.

Points to Remember

- Sometimes children reach two years of age having not yet mastered earlier developmental problems. For example, they may still have excessive concerns about being alone.
- Armed with a bit of information about children's behavior at each stage of development, parents are better equipped to detect these persisting problems and gear their parenting strategies accordingly.

Chapter 8

THE BASIC CONCEPTS UNDERLYING ALL EFFECTIVE DISCIPLINE

There has been a great deal written about effective discipline. Much of this is valuable information. But anyone who has studied the wide variety of methods that have been advocated, and the even larger number of approaches used successfully by parents, will come to one conclusion. There must be something in common being done by parents who turn out well-adjusted kids that is independent of the particular style of discipline chosen. In the pages that follow, I will describe a number of specific guidelines, but I believe that it is important for parents to grasp **the common denominator present in all successful approaches.**

The general formula for constructive discipline, and for that matter good parenting, at every stage is very simple in theory but, as we have already noted, may be difficult to implement. **Success requires only that parents be reasonable and loving.**

There are two goals that children need to accomplish to successfully negotiate this third developmental hurdle. First, they need to acquire the skills and tools necessary to be able to get along when they don't get their way. These are the array of devices that allow them to cope adaptively with frustration and stress. Second, they must begin to substitute a more realistic appraisal of frustrating experiences for the distorted infantile perceptions that had previously prevailed. The basic guidelines of love and reason are the essential principles for achieving both.

Learning to Tolerate Frustration

The principle of "a little at a time"

The first part of the equation, acquiring the tools to cope with frustration, is accomplished as parents, using reason as a guide, allow their kids to face doses of frustration in accordance with the principle of a little at a time.

This means that they allow their child to face enough frustration so that he is making gains but never so much that he is overwhelmed. The reasonable parent can gauge this fairly accurately and make needed adjustments. Parents rarely have any trouble understanding and using this useful parenting strategy. They have far more difficulty understanding and implementing the second part of the equation, correcting their child's distorted perceptions.

Understanding the meaning of distorted perceptions

Question – Why do children have such distorted perceptions and how do these perceptions get in the way?

The screeches of frustration we hear from infants are mainly a result of elevated tension. It is unlikely that very young babies have the capacity to reflect upon the implication of their pain. This changes rapidly as the infant's mind evolves. Very quickly, an increasingly complex pattern of thought becomes entwined with the central facet in the lives of our little ones – the cycles of pleasure and pain mainly associated with feeding and other forms of physical care. As the child's horizons extend to the shadowy figures that play such an important part in his emotional and physical life, these individuals take center stage in his emerging thoughts about pain and pleasure. There is nothing ambiguous about the themes of these early distorted thoughts. We can read them fairly accurately from a child's body language and as speech develops, they are quickly translated into words.

When children don't get their way, their level of tension rapidly increases and they can't help believing that it means that they are unloved and are being treated cruelly. This compounds their hurt

and rage and prods them into responses that are aimed at getting what they want so the hurt will go away. These distorted interpretations of frustration compound the problem of learning to accept frustration.

Everyone is familiar with these themes. They are a part of our daily lives. We all continue to carry within us residuals from our past. It never helps, but husbands do it to their wives, wives do it to their husbands, and parents do it to their kids. When humans don't get their way they take it personally, and feel slighted and hurt. Prodded by painful feelings, their thoughts are once again dominated by distorted perceptions and they fall back upon more childish methods of coping. They get angry, blame others, and engage in a variety of ridiculous maneuvers aimed at "getting the perceived perpetrators of the hurt to make it better so the hurt will go away." Failing this, they become intent upon hurting back to show that this type of outrage cannot be permitted to go unpunished. Carried to an extreme it accounts for much of the violence that occurs in our society, with a high percentage taking place between family members.

The pain that children feel when they don't get what they want is obviously not based on an accurate assessment of the precipitating event. An accurate assessment of being told that it is time to go to sleep, or that it is Brother's turn to sit in the front seat, would never result in such an outpouring of anger. This type of exaggerated response can nearly always be attributed to distorted perceptions. Young children are not capable of holding on to a realistic understanding of the ordinary frustrations of daily life. Instead these are interpreted through a haze of emotions that imbue them with personal meaning.

This means that their thinking becomes jumbled when they don't get their way. These actions of others are viewed as horrible acts of meanness, causing them to feel unloved and devalued. If we know how to listen and communicate with kids, they will often tell us about what they feel and think during these painful moments. In their own words they convey that not getting their way is like being discarded, ignored, insulted, annihilated, attacked, abandoned, and being left helpless.

The correction of distorted perceptions

Question – I now understand why it is so hard for my child to accept frustration. He views it as a personal slight. How can we undo the distorted perceptions that are an integral part of this infantile thinking? How can we help our children to know that their value and sense of being loved is intrinsically theirs and that it does not depend upon getting what they want in the form of gratification, attention, and approval?

We do this by breaking the link between feeling loved and valued and getting one's way. Children believe that not getting their way means that they are unloved and devalued.

For our children, the equation

Not getting my way = Being unloved and devalued

is the inaccurate equation that must be corrected.

It is obviously not true that our kids are less valued and loved when they don't get their way. Our task is to help them understand this important truth. The formula to achieve this goal is simple in theory. It requires only that parents adhere to the basic guideline of combining reasonable frustration with continuing love. This entails continuing to love their children and acknowledge their value when they are not giving them what they want and when their kids are not giving the parents what the they want.

This is the key component in effective discipline, and it is the reason a variety of disciplinary techniques can be successful.

Parenting techniques that are successful combine reasonable frustration with love. Learning that frustration does not mean being unloved or devalued is the key to the mastery of this developmental hurdle. It is also the basic building block of self-esteem.

Individuals with good self-esteem feel content, loved, and valued when they are not getting their way.

Combining love and wisdom – Helping to understand the concept

Question – I think that I understand the principle but I am still uncertain about how it actually works in real situations. Can you clarify this with an illustration?

Parents generally respond with some incredulity to this simple guideline of combining love and reason. They usually require many examples and repeated explanations and responses to their objections before they are able to see its validity. Their main objection is generally directed to the requirement to remain loving when their kids are being downright nasty. They are uncomfortable and even unbelieving that their most cherished weapon in their battle to tame their kids is misguided and should be discarded.

Permeating our culture is the notion that the way to motivate children to do the right thing is to intimidate them with the threat of loss of love or devaluation. "How else," they ask, "would you be able to prod kids to behave? Use the belt?"

Although all children, to varying degrees, will go through stages when it is perfectly normal for them to be motivated by their desire to win love and approval, it should be clear that this is not our long-term goal. **The child who grows up and is still doing the "right thing" to win approval is displaying low self-esteem.** Needing to please others for approval and love is the hallmark of low self-esteem.

The sequence of developmental steps leading to complete mastery of this hurdle and the development of good self-esteem will be addressed. The basic formula for achieving this goal remains the same throughout these steps. It is the combination of reasonable frustration with continuing love. An example will help to clarify how this actually unfolds in the minds of our children. Keep in mind that this process is aimed at correcting distorted perceptions, not solely at making our kids do what we want.

An example

Dan now has a younger sister, Irene. Their mother, Sally, is giving them lollipops as a treat. She has two lollypops, one red and one green. The last two times she gave lollypop treats to both kids she gave the red lollypop to Dan and the green one to Irene. Since both children coveted the red lollypop, she believed she was being perfectly reasonable when she elected this time to give the red one to Irene. Dan's shrieks of outrageous protestation had ear-piercing intensity.

At this point there should be nothing confusing about the meaning of Dan's disruptive and very disturbing behavior. Sally is trying to be reasonable and fair. She also knows that Dan needs to acquire the tools needed to deal with not getting his way and this would not happen if she indulged his whims. But from Dan's distorted point of view, a terrible act of cruelty is being perpetuated upon him. Not getting his way makes him feel overlooked, unloved, and devalued. After all, he reasons, "Before this interloper called Sister came along, I would be the only recipient of the prized red lollypops." His rage is the way he lets his mother know the enormity of her misdeed. It is also his way to prod her into making it right.

For Dan at this point in his life the equation, not getting his way = being treated unfairly and being unloved and devalued, still dominates his thinking.

Dan's belief in the validity of this inaccurate equation is firm and unshakable. How might Sally think about this? How might she respond? What can she do to help him to relinquish his flawed belief? How can she help her son to see the invalidity of this equation?

Sally understands the meaning of Dan's behavior and her goals. She knows that even if she tried she would not be able to supply him with the red lollypops he might desire for the rest of his life. Her job is to help him to accept green lollypops and eventually, as we all know, no lollypops at all. She wants him to know the truth that getting what he wants is not an accurate measure of his value or her love for him. Sally understands all this so she is confident about what needs to be done.

She gives the red lollypop to Irene and offers the green one to her shrieking son. She is prepared for what will follow. He hurls the green lollypop to the floor and continues the angry tirade directed at his mother. Sally knows that there is nothing she can say or do that will quell his anger. Perhaps as he grows older and becomes a bit more cognizant of the flaw in the infantile equation now dominating his mind, her words might be heard, but not now.

She says nothing and remains content, loving, and as grateful for his presence in her life as she is during the many more blissful moments they spend together. Dan continues to scream. If his actions became more destructive she would know how to respond. For example, she would certainly prevent him from attacking his younger sister or destroying an article of furniture. She is prepared to take any action that is reasonable. She is adhering to the guideline for mastery of this developmental hurdle. She is combining reasonable frustration with love.

Question – How does this work? What is the key to the effectiveness of this approach?

Understanding this requires a shift in the way parents ordinarily think. They must attempt to envision the thinking that is unfolding in their child's mind. Upon receipt of the green lollypop Dan believes that his mother has turned against him and loves him less than his sister. He is sure that he has been discarded and cast aside. These thoughts dominate his mind and influence his perceptions. In spite of the strength of his emotions, he retains some capacity to continue to assess the events that unfold. Through a veil of tears and anger he becomes dimly aware that there is a dramatic discrepancy between his belief that he is hated and the look of love and comfort his mother actually conveys. **The infantile link between not getting his way and being unloved and devalued is being broken by his mother's ability to combine reasonable frustration with love.** As this type of corrective experience is repeated he will gradually be able to substitute an accurate picture for the ones previously dictated by powerful feelings and distorted perceptions. Her continuing love is showing him that his belief that not getting his way means that he is unloved is wrong.

There are other important messages his mother's continuing love communicates to him that are constructive. Dan feels justified in his intense anger, but its presence makes him very uncomfortable. He is still very dependent upon his mother's continuing love. The anger that he can't yet control is like an alien force within him that has been exposed and that he is afraid will repulse those he loves and needs most. His mother's ability to combine not giving him what he wants with an attitude of continuing love in the face of his rage reassures him that his angry responses won't alienate her from him. He is discovering that his fear that his anger will make him less loved and devalued is another distorted, inaccurate perception. Her continuing love helps him to feel secure that his uncontrollable rage does not devalue him in her eyes.

The power of love to heal helps to remove yet another obstacle that stands in the way of progress during this developmental stage. The feelings of hurt and anger experienced by Dan when he does not get his way are very powerful, and he has no confidence that he will ever be able to control them. His mother's loving response shows him how comfortable she is in the face of his torrent of anger. Her comfort helps him to acquire confidence in his gradual ability to do the same. His mother is modeling a mature response to frustration that he will grow to appreciate and emulate. Many individuals reach adulthood still afraid of the power of their feelings.

Emotional Blisters – The Enemy of Reason and Love

Question – The guidelines for the mastery of this developmental hurdle seem so simple to do and I am convinced that it is the best approach. What are the pitfalls that may stand in my way?

By combining love with appropriate frustration, Dan's mother is helping her son to know that he is as loved when he is not getting his way as he is when his whims are being gratified. Unfortunately, this is not what happens in the homes of most children. The scene in these homes begins the same way. Like Dan, these kids also scream and yell when they don't get what they want. They are convinced that not getting their way means they are unloved and devalued. This is usually not true, but young children, influenced by powerful feelings and distorted perceptions, have no way of knowing this. And then what usually happens? Do most parents continue to combine love with reasonable frustration?

What do many parents do when their children don't get their way and scream and yell? Parents scream and yell. Their kids scream and yell because they are not getting their way and the parents do exactly the same thing for the same reason. When their kids scream and yell parents are not getting what they want. They want a better-behaved child who will refrain from tantrums that are stressful and time consuming. When parents get upset, yell, and punish their children **they have inadvertently reinforced their child's distorted perceptions.** When the kids don't get the red lollypop they believe it means that they are hated and unloved. **This belief is confirmed when parents respond with anger. Instead of combining reasonable frustration with love, these parents have combined not giving their kids what they want with anger and rejection.** The distorted belief that not getting their way means that they are unloved and devalued has become a bit more firmly embedded in their minds.

There is something else that is happening when parents respond to their child's anger with anger of their own. Keep in mind that children learn much more from watching our behavior than from what we say or teach. Our very young children get angry when they don't get their way because they take it personally. They can't do otherwise. Sadly parents are doing exactly the same when they get angry and retaliate in response to their kids not giving them what they want. **How can parents expect their children to learn to accept not getting their way when on a daily basis they have become examples of the very thing they would like to see eliminated from their children's behavior?**

There is a continuing debate about the influences that bear upon our young ones. Attention is often directed towards the effects of television, and later, of peers. These, combined with all of the rest of the external factors, pales in comparison to the role played by the parents. **Children become what we are when we are with them.** And the picture of ourselves with them may often be very ugly. They are taking a running movie of us that will eventually be played out for us on the big screen of adolescence.

Points to Remember

- All children, and to a greater extent younger ones, distort the meaning of many of the interactions with their parents, especially those that engender frustration or hurt.

- They read into these episodes an emotional meaning and conclude that they are unloved, less valued, or overlooked.

- This engenders pain and anger and leads to an array of disruptive forms of behavior.

- Children's propensity for this kind of misperception needs to be modified, which requires their parents' help.

- Parents who are aware of this important task are better prepared to help the child break his immature association that gratification means being loved and frustration means being unloved.

- Parents must, gently and in accord with the principle of a little at a time, provide a reasoned balance of frustration versus gratification in a setting that remains loving.

Chapter 9

PARENTAL ATTITUDES, FEELINGS, AND VALUES

A Key Element in the Successful Negotiation of This Development Hurdle

Perhaps the most important, but usually overlooked, facet of parenting is the patterns of messages parents communicate that either help to eliminate or to reinforce infantile perceptions. Our minds have the facility to tune in to the implicit meanings of the attitudes, behaviors, and communications of others. We know what they really mean regardless of what they may be saying. Children will detect our values and motivations and incorporate them into their own emerging personalities. When parents are combining reasonable responses with love, their children will understand that the frustration of their whims does not mean that they are unloved or less valued. They will appreciate this since it is actually what this type of response means and conveys when it is authentic.

People often behave in ways that make no sense. No one in his right mind would choose to be anxious or angry, yet many people do. No one in his right mind would choose to be violent or abuse chemical substances. And no one would mistreat the ones whom they profess are most dear to them. Many individuals are aware of the unreasonableness of their feelings and behavior but are unable to change. Others blind themselves to their own unreasonableness and only see the unreasonableness of others.

The cause of this sad state of affairs is very clear. All children grow up in years, but as adults they continue to perceive many elements of the world as they did when they were very young. None of us sees the world accurately. The infantile emotions and thoughts we carry with us from our early childhood distort the events that unfold around us, as well as our perceptions of the actions of others. These distorted perceptions are the usual ways that infants and young kids think. Their capacity for thought uncontaminated by powerful emotions is very limited. Gratification is equated with being loved and valued and frustration is equated with rejection and denigration. The extent that distorted perceptions continue to dominate the thinking of adults correlates with the mastery of early developmental hurdles.

Our thinking was shaped by our parents' attitudes and values. These were communicated to us during the myriad of daily interactions that occurred repeatedly. Similarly, our attitudes and values are passed down to our children and mold their perceptions of themselves and others. This explains so much of what we encounter in life that seems inexplicable. So the next time a friend, a loved one, a world leader, or one of the members of Congress appears like a very irrational little kid in the schoolyard, you will know why.

Distorted perceptions are passed down from one generation to another. Raising children is the second time around for parents. Their kid's behavior stomps on many old blisters that were never completely healed during their first time around, their own childhood. The discomfort engendered by their children's behavior precipitates parenting responses that communicate messages tending to confirm their children's distorted perceptions. Years later, parents complain about their children's behavior, completely unaware that this is a mirror of their own behavior during these formative years.

If parents become frustrated and angry when they are not getting what they want from their child, there are two children instead of one. When this happens between husband and wife, there are two children instead of one. The influence of distorted perceptions is not confined solely to parent-child interactions. Real conflicts and frustrations are an inevitable part of many facets of our lives. They often inflame our emotional blisters and lead to distorted perceptions and unproductive responses. There is only one tool available to help us at these difficult times. This entails tapping into a wonderful human faculty – reason and the capacity to choose based on reason. Since the strength of emotional blisters is considerable, we can't be assured that reason will always mute the pernicious effects of painful blisters, but it is the best resource we have. Thinking persons can develop the ability to make sense of their child's behavior as well as their own feelings, and use these insights to correct their own distorted perceptions.

Muddling on without stepping back to consider the meaning of our discomfort carries with it the risk that our thinking and actions will remain childlike. It is rarely difficult to detect this in others, but so easy to overlook in ourselves. This common charade of adults acting like little kids would be laughable if its ramifications were not so catastrophic, both in the lives of individuals and on a larger stage, the world scene. The only real solution to this basic problem is creating larger numbers of adults whose parents have helped to free them from the pernicious effects of infantile, distorted perception. The only time this can be done effectively is during our children's first time around with us, the earliest years of their lives.

Question – Earlier you pointed out that the long-range goal of parenting is to help our children acquire the character traits and skills that are needed for successful and happy lives. You suggested that these important attributes could not be taught the way we might teach history. Does the problem of distorted perceptions have something to do with this?

Yes it does. The persistence of distorted perceptions acts as an obstacle to the later assimilation of the values associated with good character. In all facets of our lives, the achievement of excellence requires a foundation of skills being first set in place. Children who have this foundation will appreciate and emulate examples of virtuous behavior they encounter in their lives. Others reach adulthood remaining unable to accept not getting what they want. They continue to be plagued by distorted perceptions that fuel their anger and preclude their assimilation of the values that comprise good character.

The case of the perception that would not change

Betty was a very unreasonable two-year-old. She did not merely like getting her way, she demanded it. Today she wanted to play with her mother's new dishes. She became enraged when she was barred access to them. At times like this, she could barely see the outline of her mother through the blur of her tears and power of her anger. Her distorted perceptions made her mother seem like a grotesque monster bent on torturing her.

Two years passed and Betty was enrolled in nursery school. She was an intelligent, attractive youngster but something had not changed during the intervening years. Betty pleaded with her mother to remain at home. When her mother refused, she could barely see her mother's outline through the blur of tears and power of her anger. Her mother seemed like a grotesque monster who hated her and wanted to get rid of her.

Another three years passed. Betty despised school and would rather spend her time playing. But even her play often became a source of pain for her when other kids did not allow her to be the center of attention. Today, she had turned in an assignment and her teacher was pointing out some errors. Betty wanted to put her hands over her ears so she would not have to listen. She wanted to strike her teacher or run from the classroom. Her perceptions had not changed with the passage of time and through the blur of tears and the power of her anger her teacher seemed like a grotesque monster who hated her and wanted to torment her.

Eight more years passed. Betty felt discontent much of the time and attributed this to her parents, whom she bitterly resented. She was convinced that her mother's mission in life was to make her miserable by imposing restrictions, by nagging, and by butting into her business. "Why can't they all leave me alone?" she often thought. "I'm happy when I'm with the other kids and we are partying. School is a drag and parents a pain. If only they would get off my back, things would be fine." Today her mother stopped her as she was about to leave the house to be with the other kids and gave her another lecture about the importance of school and told her that she should not go out until she had finished her homework. Betty did not hear a word. Through a blur of sadness and anger her mother appeared like a grotesque monster who hated her and was ruining her life.

Five years passed. Betty was twenty years old and had escaped from her parents by marrying Jim. Now she was home alone with her baby. She spent the day sitting in the kitchen, eating and feeling miserable. Her mind was filled with resentment towards her husband whom she pictured enjoying himself at work all day while she was stuck in the house with the baby. They had fun together before they were married, but now there was no time for fun. She hated Jim and she hated Tony, their one-year-old son, who made continuous demands upon her. She wanted to read a magazine and at that moment Tony began to cry. She had the urge to yell at him and shake him very hard. Through a blur of anger he seemed like a grotesque monster conniving to make her life miserable and he needed to be punished.

The years had passed but something had stayed the same. Betty's emotional perceptions had remained, as they were when she was two years old. And now she was responding to her own child in way that would pass her distorted perceptions on to him.

Points to Remember

- Children tune in to our underlying feelings, values, and attitudes during our interactions with them.

- These impressions become embedded into their emerging personalities and they therefore become much more the way we are than the way we tell them to be.

- Thus, when parents are frustrated with their children, they should use their discomfort as an signal to take a deep breath and give some thought to what is happening.

Chapter 10

A DEVELOPMENTAL REVIEW OF THE PROGRESSION LEADING TO MATURE SELF-CONTROL

The varying shades of an adult's personality and the variety of motivations that are at the basis of his behavior are significantly influenced by each step in the developmental process. This is nearly always overlooked and parents miss many opportunities to intervene constructively during the crucial early stages. They become cognizant of problems only late in the sequence when the possibilities for remedy are far more difficult.

In this section, I have addressed the category of parenting that falls more directly into the domain of discipline. If, however, I were asked by parents of a newborn child to address the contributions they could make to their child that would most significantly foster the development of adaptive behavior in later life, they would be surprised by my answer. It would begin with an emphasis on the foundation of effective discipline during the earliest developmental stages.

I would begin with the first stage, bonding, by saying, **"Provide your child with the highest quality of love and attention during the first year of life. Strong bonds are the foundation of effective discipline."** Bonding is the gateway that leads your child on his first steps towards becoming a person in the world of people. It is within this world of people that your child's mind gradually acquires the wonderful qualities we call human. These qualities can only be forged in the context of the web of love that begins during this very early time in his life. If that web is deficient, children may grow smarter and more adept at getting what they want. But they will be far less likely to assimilate qualities such as integrity, goodness, kindness, responsibility, honesty, and the many other personality attributes we might hope for them. These qualities require the nurturing of love in order to blossom."

The next important step in this sequence leading to mature self-control is taken during the second developmental stage and leads to the mastery of separation anxiety. Mature self-control cannot be successfully constructed upon a personality foundation that lacks the building block of trust. **It is impossible to function confidently and independently when plagued by the persistent terror of being alone and helpless.**

During the period that is covered in this section, children begin to become amenable to parenting aimed more directly at teaching self-control. Before this time these direct attempts to influence behavior have minimal effect at best, and if carried to an extreme can be counter productive. Younger children lack the skills to comply and persistent parental coercion may interfere with the mastery of the earlier developmental tasks.

The passage of time and the acquisition of new skills makes a difference. During the latter half of their second year, with the development of language, children become increasingly aware of their parents' wishes. They begin to discover that their need to obtain what they want to maximize pleasure and reduce tension often places them at odds with their parents. In the early confrontations that ensue, the strength of their powerful impulses nearly always trumps any nascent desire to conform.

Children telling us what they are thinking during this period might say, "Please don't be disappointed that I still cannot translate my increasing understanding of your wishes into compliant behavior. I do want to please you and part of me does try. But putting a brake on my impulses seems as hard as lifting a mountain. I need your continued protection and love and I hope that you won't be disappointed if I am not able to fulfill your expectations."

With the help of their parents, children between the ages two and three gradually acquire an increasing ability to tolerate frustration. At first this may be revealed merely by a slight pause in the discharge of their impulses, but gradually they become more adept at translating their desire to please into some instances of compliant behavior. Bonding, with its ties of love, acts as a powerful incentive for kids to move significantly along the path to mature functioning. Their desire for love and approval has begun to win out over the more primitive wish for immediate pleasure, at least occasionally. They are a long way from their final destination and gains at this point are tenuous, with much backsliding. They are learning to get along when they don't get their way, but this is still completely contingent upon the receipt of a coveted gift in return, approval and love.

Since these first steps towards self-control hinge upon approval, love, and gratification, anything the parents may do that erodes the quality of the love may precipitate a spate of misbehavior. For this reason, parents should anticipate that separations from their child, even a short vacation, might foster regression to more immature patterns of behavior. Other factors, including parental depression or involvement in other activities at the expense of time that had been previously spent with their child may have a similar outcome. During this phase the child's self-control is like a gift being given to the parents in exchange for approval and love. A perceived alteration in the quality or quantity of this gift leads to emotional hurt and behavior that takes a turn for the worse.

Children during this phase might say, "I am starting to get the knack of checking my own impulses in favor of some of your expectations. This is still very hard and I fail more times than I succeed. I hope that you will be guided by the principle of a little at a time and not expect too much of me. I still am pretty much convinced that not getting my way means that I am unloved and mistreated. I will need your help in order to gradually learn that I am loved even during those many times each day that my whims are frustrated. **I will not be able to break the infantile link between not getting my way equals being hated, devalued, and unloved unless you are able to continue to combine appropriate frustration with love.**"

Between ages three and five children usually have progressed sufficiently to take the next step towards mature self-control. **They are acquiring the capacity to get along when they are not getting their way, independent of the approval and other parental rewards they had previously needed to accomplish this task.** They may still feel personally slighted when they don't get their way but their distress at these times does not reach the level it did before.

These forward steps are a prerequisite for successful entry into school. Adaptation in school is not possible unless children can maintain some semblance of self-control for a fairly extended period of time. And this needs to be done without any of the rewards which previously acted as incentives.

Children at this time might say, "Life is easier now that I have more control over my feelings. I have a long way to go but most of the time I can get along when I am not getting my way."

The Role of Approval and Disapproval in the Acquisition of Mature Self-Control

Question – In your description of the progression towards mature self-control you mentioned that there is a role for approval and disapproval. Can you clarify this?

After learning about the third developmental hurdle Dan's mother had a question. She explained this to me saying that she fully understood her long-range goals. This was for Dan to be able to behave appropriately without the incentives of love and approval. But at three she could not imagine getting through a day without frequently voicing approval or disapproval.

She is absolutely right. Over an extended period of time the guideline of combining reasonable frustration with love will gradually erode the infantile link between not getting his way equals being unloved and devalued. As this unfolds we anticipate that his need for approval and other rewards to sustain appropriate behavior will lessen. But this is a gradual process. As this process moves along and even after its completion there will be countless times each day that it will be entirely appropriate to respond with approval or disapproval. This should be based on an honest assessment of our child's behavior rather than using it to manipulate desirable behavior.

I am certainly not suggesting that we banish approval and disapproval from our vocabulary. **My emphasis is that whether we disapprove or approve our love is unabated.** We are helping our children to understand that our honest evaluation of their performance has no bearing on being loved and valued. These are not gifts he must earn. They are his, now and forever. They can never be lost or reclaimed. No person or event can ever change that status.

It is perfectly reasonable to correct flaws in our child's functioning and to approve of successes. This all needs to unfold in the context of our continuing love which is unconditional. Our children need to know that their value does not rise and fall depending upon a moment to moment measurement of their performance. In other words approval is not linked to love or value. We are not using love or approval to manipulate behavior. We remain as loving when we disapprove as when we approve. This may seem like a subtle distinction but its importance can not be overstated.

Especially early in our child's development he will be gradually motivated to comply because of his desire for approval. Out task is to help him to understand that the reason to do the right thing is for its own sake. Parents are nearly always dubious that their kids will ever be able to appreciate the intrinsic rewards of mature functioning and are loath to letting go of their belief that they can effectively manage their children's behavior by giving and withdrawing love.

The motivation for the common trap that needs to be avoided is the appeal of using love to prod desirable behavior. If this ploy is used extensively, it will tend to strengthen our child's infantile perception that the path to love and feeling valued is based on fulfilling the expectations of others. Our children then remain dependent upon approval and crushed by criticism, a status synonymous with low self-esteem. This is avoided by adhering to the guideline of combining love with reasonable frustration. There is nothing ambiguous about the difference between criticism combined with love and criticisms meant to communicate the threat of the loss of love. We all understand this difference and have experienced it repeatedly. It never serves a constructive purpose in the lives of adults and should not play a role in parenting.

During childhood, especially early childhood, children will naturally be motivated by their desire for approval. This needs to be acknowledged but not aided and abetted by parents who may be tempted to use it as leverage to motivate compliant behavior.

Consistency – Not Always a Formula for Successful Parenting

Parents and educators often extol the virtues of consistency in dealing with children. This is somehow viewed as a magic formula for success and parents are told over and over to be consistent. We are attracted to the concept of consistency for the same reason we are enamored with punishment. Both are prescriptions for influencing our children's behavior requiring little thought.

It should be obvious that if what we are doing consistently is not helping our kids we are being consistently wrong. Children's needs are constantly changing. This occurs gradually as they move from one developmental phase to another; and more abruptly each day, depending upon the stresses and other problems encountered. For example, the appropriate response to a two-year-old who is having a temper tantrum because he did not get what he wanted may be to remain available but let him cry. The same youngster at 5:00 P.M. might do better if we directed him into another activity. Finally, the same child having a temper tantrum at 9:00 P.M. might require a hug and a lullaby. Many parents are in tune with their kids and make these adjustments very naturally. These are not parents who are trying to be consistent.

Points to Remember

- Early in life all children need approval, and this motivates them to please their parents.

- Although the need for approval persists throughout childhood, and to some extent into adulthood, children will encounter significant problems if their desire for approval is not gradually replaced by more mature and adaptive forms of motivation.

- Children who remain excessively dependent upon approval may when reaching adolescence switch the source of that approval to questionable peers.

Chapter 11

THE LITTLE DETAILS ABOUT DISCIPLINE THAT PARENTS ALWAYS WANT TO KNOW – ANSWERING THE "WHAT DO I DO NOW?" QUESTIONS

Question – I now appreciate the meaning of my child's behavior and understand the developmental hurdle that accounts for that behavior. In addition, my long-term goals are clear. I have a general idea how I will accomplish those goals, but I am still uncertain about how to tackle many of the problems that seem to arise every day. Can you fill in the details?

KEEPING CONFRONTATIONS TO A MINIMUM

Desirable versus necessary – A concept to help minimize confrontations

Based upon our appreciation of the limited skills of very young kids to comply with our requests, it is wise to place most of the things we want them to do into the category of "desirable" rather than "necessary." This is in accord with the principle of a little at a time. We are working towards better controls, but doing so at a rate that is commensurate with our children's actual level of development. Adhering to this principle will go a long way towards reducing the confrontations that make a battlefield out of the home and lead to an unfavorable outcome.

Life can be beautiful; it's a matter of perspective

Dan's mother, Sally, has many long-range hopes about his future functioning, but he is only two and one half, so she does not allow her long-range expectations to cause arguments, confrontations, or tugs-of-war. **For this reason she has wisely placed most of the things she would like Dan to do into the category of "desirable."** This allows her to let Dan know her thoughts about appropriate behavior. She shows satisfaction when he is successful but is fully prepared for the failures, which are much more common. Her emotional blisters have been quieted by her appreciation and understanding of Dan's actual abilities and her confidence in her long-term success. She is able to avoid the most common trap for parents at this point, getting upset and angry. This is easier to achieve by placing as few things as possible into the category of "necessary." Let's see how this works in several examples.

Common sense avoids hassles

When Dan became mobile, his mother decided it would be easier if she made a number of logistical changes in the house. She removed many of the objects that Dan was beginning to reach and that could be destroyed. There would be plenty of years ahead when she could enjoy having her favorite pottery pieces displayed where they would now be at the mercy of Dan's whims. Sally found that there were many other ways that she could alter the turf to avoid confrontations. For example, she vetoed her husband's suggestion that they take the entire family to an upscale restaurant that she knew was far beyond Dan's abilities.

Today, he has played with his blocks and they are scattered all over the living room floor. Sally has decided that in the future she will confine block play to his bedroom, but that decision does not solve the immediate issue, putting the blocks away. **Based on her assessment of Dan's capabilities she has chosen to place this task into the category of "desirable."** She tells him that it is time to pick up his blocks. Dan flashes his mischievous smile and instead of cooperating, he pushes blocks further into the corners of the room with renewed energy. Sally is on a tight schedule. She and her husband have plans for the evening. Nevertheless she is able to avoid getting caught up in a battle of wills with her three-year-old that will not serve her long-term goals.

She quickly reviews her choices and picks the one that seems most reasonable. She begins picking up the blocks herself, paying little attention to his provocative behavior. She knows that parents can't always get what they want, but they can always be reasonable and loving. She is not allowing Dan to get what he wants. He wants to continue playing and be the one who decides when he will stop. She has combined not giving him what he wants with at attitude that remains calm and loving.

Some parents might object, contending that by not getting him to do what she wants she is "giving in." They don't realize that Sally has chosen the strategy she believes will encourage what she wants most, developmental progress towards mature self-control. This is obviously more important to her than to win a petty battle of wills over a tiny, helpless child. She has remained aware that her primary goal is help him to gradually break the link between getting what he wants and being loved and valued. If instead she had demanded compliance at any cost she would be emulating her son's level of thinking and decision making. She would not be pleased watching a movie of herself in a battle of wills with her son, nor happy knowing the movie will play over and over in Dan's mind for him to emulate.

This time the strategy of placing the task into the "desirable" rather than "necessary" category has paid a rich dividend. In addition to avoiding an ugly nonproductive scene, Dan decides to cooperate. He really does want to please and at this delightful moment this motivation has won out over his need to get his way. Sally immediately notices and says happily, "How nice, you are helping me." Dan beams with pride and puts several more blocks into the container. For a moment she thinks, "Finally, miracles do happen." Hopes for rapid progress are dispelled when she watches him dump the contents of the container back on to the floor. Sally remains unperturbed. She quickly decides that it would be unreasonable to allow him to continue to empty the container. She has placed this in the "necessary" category rather than being merely "desirable," so she gently terminates his behavior by leading him away from the container to another activity.

Later, as Sally reflects upon the day's events, she is glad that she can appreciate how precious and important all these moments are in both of their lives. With the right frame of mind, and some understanding of development, even life with a two-and-one-half-year-old can be beautiful. She has not allowed the pressure of time or not getting her way to knock her off balance. With practice, it has become easier for Sally to avoid being stressed during the many daily encounters that prove so frustrating to many parents. She has become more adept at doing what she hopes Dan will learn to do. She is able to make decisions based on reason rather than having them prodded by her own need to get what she wants.

Placing behavioral expectations into the "desirable" category allows us to praise our children for compliance, and at the same time avoid the tension and anger that would ensue if we demanded compliance. If Sally's strategy towards Dan were put into words it would sound something like this, "I understand my limitations. At this point in your life I cannot expect you to comply with many of my wishes. I will therefore place most of them into the category of 'desirable' rather then 'necessary.' If you do comply, I'll acknowledge that, helping you see the benefits of cooperation."

Sometimes it Is "Necessary"

Question – I understand now that with younger children it is important to keep confrontation to a minimum. But there are many things my child does each day that I can't place into the category of "desirable." Do you have suggestions about handling these?

Dan is a bright little boy who has become very adept at finding ways to thwart his mother's will. There are times that Sally cannot place problematic behavior into the category of "desirable." Preparing him for leaving the house is always difficult, and he seems to be intuitively aware when his mother is pressed for time. This is when his mischievous smile can always be expected to appear and his level of cooperation plummet to zero. Sally realizes that if she placed getting ready in the morning in the category of "desirable" they would never depart. It is entirely reasonable that this action be placed in the category of "necessary."

Instead of saying, "When you get dressed we will leave," a comment that might be appropriate if the destination was one of his favorites, she says, "It's time to get dressed and go in the car." She is fully prepared and unruffled by one of his typical responses, which is to flee. This does not upset Sally, who is fully aware of her son's level of development and realizes that he will use opportunities like this to pit his will against hers.

With just a bit of thought, kids are easy to manage and she is prepared to implement the strategy she believes is the most reasonable alternative.

Without anger, but using as much firmness as needed, she captures Dan, and with his jacket in hand guides him out of the house towards the car. Dan naturally protests vehemently at what he believes is a terrible injustice being perpetuated upon him. His plan for his Escape from Mommy game has been thwarted by a mother who at this moment seems to him to be a replica of the scary dragon in his storybook. Sally disregards his thrashing and screaming as she makes her way to the car. She has combined not giving Dan what he wants with an attitude that has remained loving and calm. She is helping to correct his distorted perceptions of the experience and is getting the job of parenting done effectively.

As they approach the car, Dan turns his attention to the fun of a car ride and his mood brightens. Sally immediately notices that he has begun to cooperate and says, "How nice, now we will be able to have fun together in the car." She belts him into his car seat and off they go. In a year or two, Dan may be receptive to some additional comments she might make to him in a similar incident. As he makes progress at eliminating the influence of distorted perceptions, she might say something such as the following: "Dan, Mommy loves you very much and I know how angry and bad you feel when you don't get what you want. You are old enough now to understand that there will be so many times that you can't get what you want. Perhaps we can talk more about this. I know it's hard, but it would be nice for you not to have to feel so bad at those times." But this is a long way off and there are many adults who are unable to think about not getting their way with even this amount of insight.

In the daily lives of small children there will be numerous times that parents need to insist upon compliance. The same basic principle applies, combining love and reason. Reasonableness does not include arguing, getting angry, or attempting to persuade by discussion. At some point, much later on, there may be a place for a verbal appeal to reason, but even kids five or six years older than Dan can rarely profit from talk when emotions are running high. During this earlier period, that is not possible. But our children are, nevertheless, learning extremely important lessons by the model that we present as well as the other nonverbal messages that are communicated by our actions and attitudes. Sally knows that Dan is continually taking pictures of all this. These are being assimilated and will gradually become part of his personality.

Knowing when and how to use "it is necessary"

Upon deciding that leaving the house was "necessary," Sally was prepared to calmly follow through with the efforts needed to complete the task. She would avoid an "it is necessary" approach if she thinks that the effort and turmoil to bring it to fruition would outweigh the advantage. For example, it would be absurd to believe that it would be possible to enforce "be quiet" without committing child abuse, so she would never place it into the "it is necessary" category. Common categories of behavior that always require an "it is necessary" approach are all those actions that carry some danger of physical harm to the child. If she saw Dan wandering into the street she would move quickly towards him, saying calmly but firmly, "You must come out of the street." She would pay scant attention to his screams of protestation or actual resistance as she escorted him out of danger.

There would be no shouting, admonishments, or holding of grudges after the incident. This would tend to mix emotions and distorted perceptions with the simple necessity of remaining safe. Children will attend to their own safety as soon as they have the understanding and the skills to do so. Naturally, parents must assume the role of guardian of their child's safety for a number of years.

Behavior that may be only "desirable" in one setting may become "necessary" in another. There are patterns of behavior that can effectively be placed in the category of "desirable" at home, but need to be moved to the category of "necessary" in another setting. During a visit to the supermarket Dan has decided that he must have a toy he happens to spot and won't accept a negative reply to his repeated requests. His requests rapidly turn to shrieks of protest. At home, she would usually place temper tantrums in the category of "desirable." Since their persistence in this public setting might be a nuisance to other shoppers, Sally decides that it belongs in the category of "necessary" in this public place. When her attempts to distract him fail, she quietly tells him that they can't remain in the store if he does not stop screaming. At this point she has minimal expectations that he will heed her words and she is prepared to choose the most reasonable alternative – to terminate the shopping and quickly escort him from the store. She cannot get him to stop his shrieks, but she can remove him from the store. If this is a repetitive occurrence she might decide that at this point in his life he does not have the necessary skills for this type of outing. If he asks at another time to accompany his mother on a trip to the store, she is not being punitive when she tells him the truth. She might say, "When you can go with me without needing to cry when you don't get your way we will be able to go again."

SUBSTITUTION AND DISTRACTION – ANOTHER APPROACH FOR YOUNGER CHILDREN

A charging locomotive without brakes cannot be stopped without considerable damage, but it can be diverted. Another way to avoid destructive tugs-of-war, and at the same time nudge our very young children in the direction of mature self-control, is by using substitution and distraction. Sally understands that during Dan's third year of life he will usually not have the internal apparatus needed to comply with a request to immediately change direction. For this reason she has tried to baby-proof the house. In this way she is able to safeguard more expensive items, without constantly remaining one step behind Dan. But this has not prevented him from finding unique ways to do damage.

He loves to listen to CDs and on a previous occasion he was able to get into his father's collection and destroy several of them before his mother could retrieve them from his clutches. This time she is a bit quicker and notices that he is getting into an off-limit areas. Naturally, it is entirely appropriate to immediately stop him. The only question is how. She is bigger and stronger and at times faster than her son, so she has the power to enforce a firm "No!" After a stern "Get away from that!" she could yank him away and escort him to another part of the house. This would produce a painful confrontation. Parents persist in believing that their kids learn something useful by these types of actions. They erroneously reason that no pain means no gain. If the lesson learned by the repetitive pain we inflict is the conviction to make sure that they will be on the giving side of pain rather than the receiving side, the parents will need to anticipate considerable pain coming their way from their kids in the future.

Instead of precipitating an ugly confrontation, Sally wisely chooses to use substitution and distraction. Dan wants to continue playing with these prized objects. He perceives any interference with this activity as an act of cruelty and unfairness. She hopes to dispel this perception, so instead of an angry confrontation she gently bars his access to the CDs and says, "Those are Dad's things. Let's go and play with Mom's pots and pans." She knows that these are Dan's second-favorite playthings, coming right after Daddy's CD collection. She has diverted him from what he wants to do to another activity, enhancing the attraction for the alternative by indicating a willingness to participate with him for a few minutes.

Isn't Sally spoiling him? Doesn't he have to learn to accept no for an answer? Of course he does. At some point, preferably before he takes his own bride, he will need to be able to stop on a dime and change course comfortably. There would be little hope for the world if most people needed a pleasant alternative in order to accept not getting what they want. This more advanced goal cannot be reached quickly. Attempting to accomplish too much too soon creates a clash of wills and heightened emotions that tend to solidify distorted perceptions. This mitigates against the achievement of a favorable outcome for this developmental hurdle. Devising parenting techniques such as substitution and distraction to avoid the endless confrontations and anger makes very good sense.

This technique certainly makes things less rancorous for parents. Its implementation helps preserve the loving involvement of children with their parents, which is the foundation of effective discipline. It is another way for Sally to become her son's ally rather than his adversary as he struggles to cope with not getting his way. Remaining loving, combined with the substitution of another activity that he enjoys for the one he must relinquish, helps to dispel distorted perceptions. It is harder for him to continue to believe he is hated with so much evidence to the contrary. Dan's increasing willingness to accept an alternative in place of his first choice means that he is progressing towards a more mature level of self-control. While it is true he is being offered something in exchange for what he cannot have, he is nevertheless learning to tolerate not getting his first choice. There are many adults in the world who have not accomplished this and who continue to insist that they be pleased on their terms.

"When Then" – A Reasonable Way to Encourage Compliance

Any reasonable parenting technique that encourages appropriate compliance should be considered. Reasonable techniques are those that are based on an understanding of the developmental hurdle that needs to be mastered, take into consideration the tools and skills available to tackle the task, and conform to the principle of a little at a time. The "when then" technique is helpful for tasks that fall into the category of "desirable" rather than "necessary."

Instead of cooperating with the morning exercise of dressing, Dan has decided to play his favorite game of Mommy, Catch Me if You Can. This day Sally has no scheduled appointments, so getting him dressed and on the road is not necessary. In fact the only plan had been to take Dan to the park. Dan enjoys the park very much, so instead of corralling Dan and finding some way to get him dressed and out the door, she uses the "when then" technique and says, **"When** you are dressed, **then** we will be able to go to the park." She then has the luxury of waiting and allowing him to struggle with the decision on his own. Sally is prepared for him to make either choice and will not be disturbed if the hours pass and he is still in his pajamas. Placing the whole thing in his lap makes it harder for him to continue to believe that any suggestion that he comply is based on a power play by his parents, resulting in a winner and a loser.

Children tend to believe that everything they do falls into two categories, things they do for their own pleasure and those they are compelled to do to please others. Unless they are helped to dispel this immature perspective they are not likely to ever appreciate that many activities that don't provide immediate pleasure, such as reading and studying, are sources of enormous satisfaction. Over the years, a number of parents have recounted their dismay when one of their kids has said to them, "You can't make me do my homework, and I don't have to if I don't want to!" My suggested reply is to smile and say, "I am so happy that you are now old enough to realize something you did not understand when you were younger. Of course I can't make you do homework or even learn at school. The reason to do those things, that I value very highly, is because you are now smart enough to appreciate the many advantages that an education will provide for you. As long as you believed that doing schoolwork was to please me at the expense of your pleasure, you would never appreciate that learning can be a source of even more pleasure. I will do whatever I can to help you to know this. If you don't do your homework and refuse to learn, it will only mean that you will miss all the wonderful opportunities afforded by education."

There are many other times that Sally might use the "when then" technique. For example, when Dan is a bit older she might use it to encourage him to cooperate with putting his toys away. In this scene we find out that Sally had mentioned earlier that she would have time to play one of his favorite games with him. She enters his room, finding his toys scattered over the floor and says, "Dan, **when** we get the toys picked up, **then** we will be able to play your game." Or at bedtime when he refuses to get into his pajamas, she might say, "Dan we are in the middle of your favorite story. **When** you are in your pajamas and under the covers, **then** I'll finish reading it." This particular gambit would not be acceptable to parents unless they were willing to place getting into bed into the category of "desirable."

Learning to Do Nothing Constructively – Another Technique to Avoid Confrontations

I would rank doing nothing constructively very high on the list of effective parenting techniques. Parents who have the knack of being able to do nothing will have an enormous advantage over those who lack this skill. This concept has a central importance in parenting. There are many times that there is nothing we can reasonably do to relieve the distress our children may experience when they were not able to get what they want. If there are no better alternatives, reasonable parenting requires that we do nothing. **But doing nothing turns into something very special when it is combined with love.** We often find it very hard to do nothing when our child is fervently demanding that we do something. Emotional blisters prod us to do something to help. This help is usually not very helpful and is motivated by our own need to feel better.

This concept has a central importance in parenting. Parents should never underestimate the importance of being a loving presence in their children's lives. The emotional messages conveyed by parents to their kids during these moments are often a more accurate measure of the quality of their love and parenting than an analysis of the astuteness of their parenting techniques. Again, be reminded that our goal as parents is not merely to influence behavior. It is to influence the development of our children's character.

Doing nothing constructively – A formula for stress-free parenting

Question – Doing nothing still seems so contrary to everything I have believed. Can you clarify how it helps with an example?

Let's see how doing nothing unfolds in real life. Today, Sally has used every skill she had available to gently deter Dan from another attack upon his dad's CD collection. She has tried substitution and distraction without success. She certainly is never going to allow him to get what he wants when that is not reasonable. But this time Dan cannot be diverted. He points a finger at Dad's CDs and his face becomes contorted with a loud shriek. Sally has already acquired the knack of being able to do nothing constructively, so she is not fazed by this turn of events. She is sufficiently immune from emotional blisters to realize that she can't get what she wants. Naturally, she and all parents facing this common dilemma would like their little kids to comply happily, especially after they have made an extra effort to elicit at least a little cooperation. She also knows that punitive actions will probably engender more anger and if escalated to sufficient intensity, might get him to cower in fear and timidly comply. But this would certainly impede progress towards any real mastery of this developmental hurdle.

She remains calm and loving but does not give him what he wants. She does not allow him access to the CDs and Dan has a temper tantrum. She has elected to respond to his display of anger by doing nothing constructively. Many parents object to this suggestion, contending that Dan is not learning that his temper outburst is unacceptable behavior if his mother lets him get away with this kind of nonsense. They are completely in error about this. They don't realize that when kids grow up with behavior problems it is never because they don't know right from wrong, or that they were not punished often enough or harshly enough for "wrong" behavior. It is because they still perceive not getting what they want as they did when they were very young. They are linking it to being treated unfairly, being overlooked, and being unloved. Doing nothing lovingly helps to break that link.

Question – Why are you dwelling so long on doing nothing?

In the face of distress, our own as well as that of our kids, the capacity for clear thinking and a calm demeanor is rapidly lost. Family life often seems an endless series of mini crises. Years later we can look back and wonder why we became so emotionally unhinged about what in retrospect were trivial issues. The problems that loomed so large at the time now appear to be insignificant. But the damage has been done. Emotional chaos is like a communicable disease, it spreads quickly from one to another. During our children's formative years our emotional confusion, anger, and stress, and the distorted messages that are a part of all this, has a dramatic and usually deleterious impact upon their developing minds.

Doing nothing allows us to avoid this common trap and is an essential attribute of good parenting. It is actually an essential attribute of our involvement with all individuals. Given what we know about human nature, we can be certain that the moment there is another person in our lives, we will be facing not getting our way on a daily basis. And most of the time we will discover that there is not one reasonable thing that we can do about it. We doom ourselves to endless stress and frustration with our kids and others if we are not able to learn to do nothing constructively, since that is so often the only reasonable alternative.

Doing nothing sends many constructive messages to our children. It is helping Dan to begin to understand that not getting his way does not mean that he is hated and unloved. There is the evidence before his eyes.

He did not get what he wanted but Sally remained loving and held no grudges following the incident. In addition, Sally has modeled what she hopes Dan will be able to do by remaining at ease and reasonable in the face of not getting what she wants. Her calmness in response to her child's enormous display of emotional pain also shows him that she has confidence in his capacity to learn to handle this kind of frustration. She would not be communicating this to him if she felt compelled to do something to take away his hurt. Attempting to eliminate the pain that our children feel when reality denies them their coveted prize implies that this is a viable solution for the endless frustrations they will later encounter. This is called indulgence.

Being ready to do something when reason demands

Doing nothing is only reasonable when there is no other alternative that is more reasonable. What would Sally have done during her son's display of temper if he made additional attempts to get at the CDs, or, if he decided to engage in destructive behavior elsewhere in the house? Naturally doing nothing would no longer be reasonable. It would need to be abandoned in favor of another action. Guided by reason and love she would gently stop him, and stop him repeatedly, as long as this more violent pattern persisted. Parents have told me that this might go on forever unless it was backed up by an additional punitive response. I have found this to be inaccurate. If parents are calm but firm in their effort to prevent their children from acting destructively, they will relent after two or three tries. This might be followed by a spate of crying, until calmed by our loving presence they pull themselves together and go on with their business.

Children will generally continue their antics as long as they have reason to believe that their action will get them what they want. And they will take what they want in either of two forms. One is actually getting what they want. The other is eliciting rage and helplessness in their parents. When kids and immature adults don't get what they want, they feel helpless, weak, and mistreated. A common channel for relief among immature individuals is to find a victim and make him squirm. Even tiny little kids become adept at this device if their parents allow their efforts to be successful. The best insurance against this is being able to do nothing constructively.

Doing nothing is not the same as ignoring

Question – I have heard about the effectiveness of time-outs. Is this the same as doing nothing constructively?

There is a dramatic difference between doing nothing constructively, which combines reasonable decision making with love, and what most parents mean by ignoring. Ignoring implies not noticing or not paying attention. Its intent is to coerce children into compliance by giving them a dose of what it feels like to be disregarded by their parents. There is no place for this kind of ignoring in the rearing of children.

One of the most commonly held myths among parents, as well as educators, is that ignoring undesirable behavior is an effective method of discipline. It may be transiently successful in achieving compliance, but is not likely to have a positive impact upon children's thinking or on their developmental progress. The message that ignoring conveys might be paraphrased this way, "I disapprove of what you have done and will punish you by removing you from my attention and love." This is a very powerful motivator but is it not effective discipline. Linking a child's sense of being loved and valued to pleasing others confirms the distorted perceptions that we hope to modify. The belief that being valued and loved is dependent upon pleasing others is the definition of low self-esteem.

Many children have told me repeatedly about their experiences with ignoring. One eight-year-old girl described being timed-out. She said, "Mommy makes me go into my room. I think of getting out and I feel real mad. I feel like running away to a friend's house, she has a nicer mother. Then I think she does not do anything for me and everyone is against me. I get very mad. Once I threw my toys at the wall and made a dent in the wall. I felt like punching her. She made me stay longer. Then I get sad. I'm all alone and think that she does not love me anymore, that is why she is being so mean. I cry because my mom does not want me anymore. I think everyone is against me and my father does not want me anymore. I think I should kill myself. I feel like getting run over by a car or stabbing myself. She wouldn't care because she does not want me around anymore."

Ten minutes later this little girl is able to divert her attention to something else and appears compliant and pleasant to her mother, who congratulates herself for using such an effective technique. This mother was completely oblivious of the tenor of her child's thinking and of the possible untoward ramifications that this might have on her developmental progress.

Isolating or ignoring kids because of their undesirable behavior is risky. The parents' expectation is that the child will learn something useful from the experience. Believing this requires a total disregard for the actual thoughts that helpless and vulnerable children are likely to have during these times. If there is any question about this, parents should ask what they, with the full armor of adult intelligence, would most probably think if their employer ignored them or timed them out over a disagreement. I can imagine only one result, a million-dollar legal settlement in favor of the employee. Obviously, many children are not as adversely affected by "ignoring" as the little girl I just described. But does it make sense to take a chance when there are better disciplinary alternatives?

Question – Is ignoring, isolation, or time-outs ever preferred methods of discipline?

The answer depends on the comparison. They are never the best methods, but may be better than some alternatives. For example, if carried out calmly, keeping the threat of rejection to a minimum, they might be a far better technique than an angry spanking. For many parents with a short fuse, the use of ignoring in spite of its risks might literally save their kids' lives, emotionally as well as physically. But we should be clear that it is only the more desirable of two less-desirable approaches. Parents sometimes say that they only have two choices. They can "tan his backside" or "isolate him until they both cool down." Which is better? This would be analogous to asking which I would prefer, a punch in my nose or a punch in my arm. I might prefer one to the other, but neither would be my first choice.

Some parents will do perfectly well with this technique. This usually means that their brand of ignoring is closer to doing nothing constructively than it is to actual ignoring. In these instances the love that is communicated outweighs the message of rejection incorporated into the isolation. As a general rule, isolating young children by putting them alone in a room or a small space is not an effective method of discipline. They will inevitably interpret this as a personal, hurtful rejection of them. Children treated in this way may eventually display surface conformity. But so did political prisoners when they were subjected to similar treatments. Parents need to continually remind themselves of their long-range goals. Children who comply because of the superior strength of their parents or by the very compelling fear of rejection are extremely unlikely to develop the attributes needed for mature self-control.

A good safety measure for parents as they assess the appropriateness of their interventions is simply to ask each other about the probable effect of the method upon their children's thinking. If they are unsure, they should consider how they might feel subjected to the same treatment by people who had sufficient power to easily impose their will upon them. It is sad that we so often respond to our children with little thought about how they or even we might feel being on the receiving end.

The Difference Between Removal and Isolation

The removal of a child from a setting may be completely appropriate. This needs to be differentiated from isolation, which is never the best alternative.

Dan is now age four and is making it impossible for his father to watch his favorite sporting event. His father, Bob, asks him several times to stop playing in front of the television, but these and other attempts to divert him fail. At other times he might choose to use the time to interact with his son, but it is entirely reasonable for Bob to have some time for himself and Dan must learn to get along when he does not get his way. He addresses Dan saying, "Dan, you can't play in this room unless you stay away from the television set." Dan still retains his mischievous smile and persists in being a nuisance. From his point of view it is unfair that

Dad gets what he wants and his own desires can be vetoed. His father says calmly, "It is necessary for you to leave this room now," and he firmly but pleasantly removes him if he does not cooperate on his own. He does not isolate him since he is aware that would cause an escalation of his son's anger and confirm the distorted perception that he is being mistreated.

Bob is perfectly prepared for Dan to return to the television area and is willing to remove him again and again if that is necessary. This is rarely needed. The message communicated by Bob's action is, "I know that you want me to play with you and that you are angry that I am not willing to oblige. Gradually you will learn to cope with these kinds of disappointments, but now your capacity to do this is limited, so I'll provide some external assistance. But I will do this in a manner that will help you to know that my intent is not to reject you, overpower you, or treat you meanly. You will see my continuing love for you, and this will help you to break the link in your mind between getting what you want and being loved. I am helping you realize that my love remains undiminished during the entire time that I am implementing my decision to not give you what you want."

Dan's father may modify how he uses this parenting technique. If he senses that his son may need a bit more reassurance that he is loved, he might get Dan started on another play project before returning to his television program. Other times, especially as the years pass, he might communicate his message verbally saying, "Dan, Daddy loves you very much and I know how you feel when I have decided that I can't play with you now because I am watching the game. Let's find something else for you to do that you like. Or, if you want to come and sit next to me, we can watch together. I would love to teach you about the game."

The words and methods I am describing are not meant as formulas to be copied. My intent is to emphasize the need to understand the developmental level of each unique child and to respond flexibly. I have found that there is nothing, absolutely nothing, that young kids do that is difficult to understand or difficult to handle. This only requires a bit of thought, patience, and an understanding of long-term goals.

What about Spanking?

Many children are spanked and do quite well, and there are many kids who are never spanked and do poorly. The reason is simple. Parents who are basically loving and reasonable can convey constructive messages to their children, regardless of their style of parenting. While it is true that many children who are spanked do well, it is nevertheless an extremely ineffective method that carries the risk of later problems. In families that tilt towards more frequent displays of anger and are less loving, that risk increases dramatically.

The danger inherent in spanking is the same as for ignoring. Both pose an unnecessary additional risk for children. Spanking is risky even when used by loving, mature parents in ideal circumstances. It nearly always intensifies anger, communicates rejection, and precipitates feelings of being overwhelmed and helpless. In addition, it carries the danger of eroding the bonds of love between parents and children that comprise the foundation for effective discipline. Finally, it sends a powerful message to children at a time in their lives when they are most impressionable.

Nearly all children who are spanked feel humiliated, enraged, and helpless. Many children have told me about their actual feelings after being spanked. Generally these are feelings of being powerless, rejected, and worthless, and are accompanied by thoughts of revenge. Adults feel the same way when they are "spanked." It is a rare adult who does not feel demeaned and enraged when his wrist is slapped, even verbally, by an authority figure. Employers understand this very well. They have learned that workers are far more productive when treated with dignity and respect than subjected to intimidation or humiliation.

Even if spanking were less risky, there would be another persuasive argument for its elimination as a form of discipline – there is always a better way. There is nothing a child can do or say that parents cannot handle by using more constructive methods than spanking. It merely entails a willingness to expend as much energy and thought about our children as we devote to most other parts of our lives. Most parents have the ability to do this. The businessman who spanks his kids would not spank his employees, and most of us try to carefully weigh the impact that our actions and words may have on friends. We even try to be civil and polite with strangers, yet with those who are most dear to us we are willing to blurt out whatever comes to mind, sometimes accompanied by a swat on the rear.

The guideline about spanking can be easily spelled out – Don't

During recent years there has been much debate about the causes of violence in our society. Many have indicted the media, television, the movies, and the prevalence of guns as contributing factors. While these may play a peripheral role, they are not the primary causes. Adults prone to violence have a definite set of personality characteristics. These are elevated anger, a sense of being mistreated when they don't get what they want, and a tendency to blame others for their distress. They hate easily and intensely, have inadequate tools to control and manage frustration, and feel little remorse for their deeds. If these sound familiar, they should. I have been addressing them repeatedly in the present chapter. These are the characteristics of young children who have not mastered the developmental hurdles leading to mature self-control. Children who are fortunate enough to have received loving and reasonable parenting during this early period rarely become violent adults.

Better schools, less violence in the movies, and the elimination of all handguns, if that were possible, would not substantially reduce violence. As long as very young children continue to be violated emotionally as well as physically we will be plagued by significant violence in the world. The violence that created violent adults is the violence that surrounded them during the first five years of their lives. This is a formative time when their parents were the sole influence on their thinking.

Question – But why do we so often hear about violent people who seem to have come from "good homes?"

The violence done to children is often not of the physical variety and can be easily overlooked when it is happening and then forgotten with the passage of years. We all tend to have, at best, only hazy memories of our own childhoods, and the same process of forgetting seems to govern our memories of that period our children's early lives. A closer look at the early lives of out-of-control adolescents will invariably reveal homes devoid of the essential ingredient for the mastery of the developmental hurdle leading to mature self-control – loving and reasonable parents.

The story of a mother who was sure she had done the right thing

Mary's mother never read anything about child development, but she supplied Mary with favorable amounts of love and attention during her child's first year of life. When Mary reached one-and-one-half years of age she was her mother's pride and joy. Mary bubbled with laughter and contentment and made her mother proud and happy.

Something began to change as Mary reached her second birthday. Mary had become more willful at the same time her mother had begun to demand more compliance. Mary was a high-spirited child who protested vociferously when she did not get her way. This trend of behavior is an expected part of normal development. But it was confusing and disturbing to her mother. She felt frustrated when Mary responded angrily or refused to comply with her simple requests. Mary no longer made her mother feel so happy.

Instead, Mary's mother often felt personally hurt and angry as she might if a trusted friend had let her down. Without giving it a great deal of thought, she felt that she wanted to find some way to stifle this new streak of defiant, irritable behavior that was so unsettling to her. A campaign to accomplish this was begun, which brought her into harsh conflict with Mary during most of the child's waking hours. Arguments, shouting, sending her to her room, and spankings became the order of the day.

At times there seemed to be temporary gains, but overall the situation did not improve. In addition to Mary's anger and noncompliance, other forms of unsettling behavior became apparent. Mary became whiny and more demanding and her enthusiasm for play diminished. Worst of all, as far as her mother was concerned, she began to do something her mother had not seen since she was a little baby. At bedtime she was cranky and difficult to get to bed and her baby pattern of awakening and crying in the middle of the night returned. During the day she had become fearful of new situations and would protest strenuously if her mother left her with a babysitter.

Nothing seemed to work for long. Mary's mother became bewildered and increasingly irritable at her child's unwillingness to be the kind of little girl that had been so dear to her. The encouragement of her husband and of his mother reinforced her own conviction that it would be a mistake to allow Mary to believe that she "could get away with her behavior." She escalated her campaign to "make Mary good."

The days were painful for both of them. Attempts to discipline Mary became emotionally charged power struggles. Mary began to suck her thumb during the day and before going to sleep at night. At times she remained quietly by herself, rocking back and forth.

Mary's mother also became unhappy and she was having more disagreements with her husband. Her friends encouraged her to get out of the house, saying that she needed to be among adults more of the time so that she would feel better about herself. "It would do you a world of good to feel that you are accomplishing something."

Mary was put into daycare. After several weeks her mother inquired about her daughter's adjustment. She was told that Mary was not a problem to anyone. She was a well-behaved little girl who seemed content to play by herself most of the time. They were happy to have her.

Mary's mother held Mary's hand as they left the daycare center that day. She smiled to herself thinking, "I have done the right thing, and Mary is now doing fine."

Many children like Mary do seem to do "fine." That is, until they reach adolescence. Then the problems that arise are inexplicable to the parents. They may have no recollection of any past difficulties. From their point of view, things suddenly went all wrong. "It must be the influence of peers or something they saw on television." The seeds of problems planted during their early years may sprout later in the form of substance abuse, school problems, or depression. In boys these seeds may later bloom into behavior much more disturbing to society – violence against others.

Points to Remember

Keeping Confrontations to a Minimum

- Repeated confrontations have a deleterious effect upon young children and are stressful to parents.
- Keep confrontations to a minimum.
- There are simple ways to significantly reduce confrontations.

Sometimes it Is "Necessary"

- When confrontations cannot be avoided, parents need to impose their will and insist upon compliance.
- At these times, parents need to remain calm and loving. This helps to dispel their children's belief that their parents hate them and are being mean.
- Parents' anger during confrontations confirms children's distorted perceptions and is a model the children will take in and make their own.

Substitution and Distraction

- For younger children, substitution and distraction are useful methods for avoiding confrontations.
- It's easier for children to take the first steps towards leaning to accommodate frustration if a second-best alternative is provided.

"When Then"

- Use the when-then strategy in situations that fall into the category of desirable, rather than necessary. For example, say, "When your toys are picked up we will finish the game."

Learning to Do Nothing Constructively

- In some situations, there is nothing constructive that parents can do. For example, when a two-year-old is having a screaming tantrum.

- At these times, any attempt to intervene is likely to escalate the already high level of turmoil.
- Parents have only one option: to do nothing well. A calm loving presence when children are in turmoil is reassuring to them and in presents a model of maturity that they will emulate.

The Difference Between Removal and Isolation

- Parents should never forget that their goal is to influence thinking, not merely to obtain compliance.
- It is crucial for children to learn that frustrations they experience in response to their parents' actions don't mean that they are unloved, are hated, or in danger of being abandoned.
- Unfortunately, this is exactly the message conveyed by parents when they ignore or isolate their children.
- Parents must understand the difference between not responding to undesirable behavior or removing a child from a particular location, and ignoring or isolating them.

What about Spanking?

- Although many kids who are spanked turn out well, there is never a reason to resort to this ploy.
- Children turn out well in spite of spankings, not because of them.
- Spankings engender anger and increase the strength of distorted perceptions, both of which act as impediments to developmental progress.
- There are always better methods than spanking. If in doubt, reread this chapter.

CHAPTER 12

SUMMARY

LEARNING TO GET ALONG WHEN YOU
DON'T GET YOUR WAY – SELF-CONTROL

Dan is nearly four and is a happy, very active little boy. He is still a handful for his parents, but with each passing month becomes more adept at conforming to the rules of acceptable behavior. His temper outbursts when he does not get what he wants are infrequent occurrences. Many times he is able to accept frustration with negligible distress.

Sally is happy with the progress he has made but understands and accepts that his control mechanisms are still very wobbly. Many times each day, especially when he is tired or irritable, his behavior deteriorates. He is able to entertain himself for longer periods but still needs some intermittent emotional refueling from his mother to remain on an even keel.

Transformations are occurring within Dan's mind that are as important as the ones that are evident in his surface behavior. The distorted perceptions that dominated his thoughts earlier are being replaced by ones that are more in accord with reality. Not always, but much more of the time, he knows that the frustrations imposed upon him do not mean that he is unloved, devalued, or being horribly mistreated.

PART FIVE

BECOMING AN AUTONOMOUSLY FUNCTIONING PERSON

ONE-AND-ONE-HALF YEARS TO FOUR YEARS

PART FIVE

SECTION ONE

BECOMING AN AUTONOMOUSLY FUNCTIONING PERSON – THE TASK AND ITS IMPORTANCE

Chapter 1

A BATTLE OF WILLS

Dan was in his third year. The knowledge Dan's mother has acquired about developmental hurdles has provided her with a level of comfort and skill that few of her friends possess in dealing with Dan's daily antics. There have even been many times when she could smile and inwardly chuckle during episodes that proved chaotic and stressful to other parents. She has become very familiar with the underlying distorted perceptions that fuel his behavior. They became easy for her to spot once she learned what to look for. Knowing reasonable ways to respond has also helped. But today her attention has been drawn to behavior she has noticed before and is a bit more difficult to understand.

Dan got angry and stubbornly resisted a request to engage in an endeavor that he had favored in the past. He was refusing to eat one of his favorite foods, mashed potatoes. Dan had always enjoyed his meals, so Sally was surprised at his irritable fussing over one of the foods that he liked best. The fussing turned into a stubborn refusal to eat when Sally suggested that he have a bite or two. He had been happy and active until he sat down at the table, so he was obviously not sick. With a smile, Sally resorted to a maneuver they had both enjoyed earlier in his life. She put some of the potatoes on a spoon and said, "I'll bet you'll like this, I made it just the way you like." She then moved the spoon towards his mouth saying, "The choo, choo train is going into the tunnel." Dan spit out some dribble and turned his face away from the oncoming food and his flailing hand caught the spoon and sent it flying across the room.

Sally had become very adept at maintaining a calm, pleasant demeanor in the face of nearly anything he could dish out, but she was only human. A fleeting picture came to her mind of picking up the spoon, scooping up some of the potatoes that had not splattered on the walls, prying open his clenched jaws and shoving some of the stuff down his gullet. She smiled at this fantasy knowing immediately that it was motivated by one of her emotional blisters knocking at the door of her consciousness.

She was not sure what Dan's behavior meant or what needed to be done. But she had learned enough to know that it is always far better to do nothing constructively than to act precipitously when she was confused. She had decided that during times of confusion or stress an important principle of parenting was to place thinking before actions.

She did feel a bit uneasy about the scene that had just unfolded and recalled her own mother insisting that she try everything on her plate when she was a young child. Her mother reinforced this admonition by telling her about the poor children around the world starving for the food she was prepared to discard. Thinking about this now, she found it curious that her mother had such a preoccupation about making sure that her children consumed enough food. It was now blatantly apparent that the only problem anyone in the family now had with food was one of over nourishment. Sally could not think of any family member who had completely escaped this affliction.

As Sally thought about Dan's behavior at mealtime, she became aware that it was part of a more general pattern of resistance and stubbornness. He used to like the feeling of running water when his mother made a game of washing his hands. Now his squirming made the task an ordeal. After Sally pointed it out to Dan's father, Bob, he recalled that he had also noticed this pattern and commented to Sally that "the kid is getting as stubborn as your side of the family."

Dan had loved to roll a ball back and forth with his father. Bob imagined being Dan's future coach. He was proud of his participation as a second stringer on the basketball team in high school. He liked the way Dan was beginning to handle the ball and was disappointed when this pleasurable activity took an unexpected turn. As usual, Dan would be eager to receive the ball from him, but he became unwilling to throw it back. His father tried everything he could think of to coax his son to resume the old style of play, but to no avail. Dan would hold on to the ball with glee and shake his head "no" when his father asked him one more time to toss it back. Becoming a bit pessimistic about his son's prospects for a career under the hoops, he would finally give up and move away, only to see the ball come bouncing past him.

Numerous other small activities that had been going so smoothly were becoming chores again. Dan was displaying an exaggerated resistance to being dressed, coming when called, and cooperating with the preparation to leave the house, even when the destination was a place he liked. He began to repeat his old game, Escape from Mommy, with renewed enthusiasm. He found this most exciting when he knew that his mother was impatient to leave. Sally was sure that his grin became wider as her level of frustration rose. He was also getting into things more of the time and needed constant surveillance. His mother was spending much more time catching him before he toppled off the edges of tables, chairs, and counters. Whatever was left of her time was occupied by clearing the trail of spilled things and other messes he left in his wake.

Sally's mother-in-law suggested that he might be "hyper" and needed to be drugged. Her own mother thought that he was cute as long as she didn't have to take care of him. Dan's father was a practical man whose ancestors had been ranchers. During evenings at home, he had begun to design a corral that could be custom made for their house.

Chapter 2

BECOMING A SELF – WHAT DOES THIS REALLY MEAN?

Question – Why is my child so stubborn? At times it seems as if he is saying "no" before he hears my suggestion.

Something extremely important and exciting is happening to Dan. It accounts for his increased stubbornness, as well as many other trends of behavior that parents typically find disconcerting during this time in their children's lives.

In the earliest months of his life he was introduced to the world of people and learned about the wonder of love. Later, during his first year, he grappled with the problem of being alone and learning to trust. In his second and third years, he began to cope with daily discrepancies between what he wanted and what was actually supplied.

Now a new idea is evolving in his awareness. This is an extremely illusive concept that we take for granted, yet few can define. It is the concept of self. It is the center of our lives. Our motivations, actions, and thoughts are usually grounded in the self. It is the what "I" think, what "I" want, what "I" feel, and what "I" am doing of our lives. We all know of its presence, but it's difficult to describe in words. Dan is becoming aware that he is a "self." Even before this happened, Dan knew that others could leave and he would experience being alone, but until now he had not really conceptualized that they were leaving him, the self we call him.

It is exhilarating to be a new self and have a will owned by that self, and a body commanded by that self. It is wonderful, but also very frightening. Side by side with the illusion of power derived from this new sense of self is an implicit danger. What if the self seems to be threatened or even in danger of being snuffed out? This concern looms large in the minds of young children. To a variable extent it persists into adulthood, accounting for an array of behavior aimed at obtaining confirmation or assurance that the self is intact and not in danger of being eroded and even annihilated.

This pattern is most pronounced in children Dan's age. This is a time in their lives when their world often appears to them as a battlefield in which the respective strengths of the contestants are completely lopsided. Upon arising and until bedtime, Dan's whims are repeatedly frustrated, leaving him angry and hurt. With the development of a sense of self, the emotional wound associated with frustration has a new dimension. It is increasingly viewed as a personal assault on his budding sense of being a separate person, a "me." Dan's capacity to express himself verbally is progressing rapidly, so it should not be surprising that he uses this vehicle in his power struggles with others.

No wonder his protests are so loud. No wonder he will go to such great lengths to avoid complete defeat. An adult cliché to describe this might sound like, "You have to do what you can to get a little respect." The younger the child, or more immature the adult, the greater the lengths he will go to "get a little respect." It takes considerable maturity for adults to finally understand that they do not need gratification, or even respect from others, to be certain of their intrinsic worth and to feel confident about the status of their "self." It is be difficult for young children and even many adults to understand that the words and actions of others cannot erode the status of the self. We are not, after all, puppets whose importance can be elevated or trivialized by the thoughts, words, or actions of others. Who we are, our "selves," have a significance and value that is completely independent of others and whatever they may think, say, or do. But little children, and sadly many adults, fail to comprehend this. Dan's progress towards that goal will, to a large extent, depend upon his parents' responses to him as this developmental phase unfolds.

There is a general principle that applies to the perceived strength of the self among individuals of all ages. It is the following: An individual, who perceives his "self" as weak, will use more primitive, infantile, and excessive methods for reassurance. On the other side of the spectrum are those whose security is so solid that this concern about the status of the "self" does not even enter into their thinking. Their sense of self is not vulnerable, so there is no need for behavior aimed at obtaining reassurance. They are not easily hurt or offended by the comments, attitudes, or behavior of others. Children of Dan's age always fall on the lowest part of that spectrum, so much of their behavior is motivated by their perception of such threats.

Adults on the favorable side can cooperate with others without fear of surrendering their "power" or losing their sense of autonomy. They go through life with the capacity to respond realistically to people and situations. They are not hampered with the need to continuously monitor the status of their "selves" or use maladaptive methods to ward off perceived threats. Childlike concerns about "being put down," "diminished in value," or "being made less significant" do not complicate their interactions with others. Having mastered this developmental hurdle, they are not saddled with the burden of going through life needing to confirm their autonomy by winning power plays with others.

Young children of Dan's age have not yet mastered this developmental hurdle. As a consequence their budding sense of autonomy is easily threatened and prods them into responses aimed at getting reassurance that they are not powerless. This is entirely normal at age two or three, but if they are not able to strengthen their sense of autonomy they are destined to continue to respond inappropriately into adulthood. Refusing to comply with reasonable requests may be acceptable at age two, but on the job at age twenty-two it is a formula for discord and failure. Many adults have significant problems in their relationships with others for this reason. A similar dynamic often accounts for the thinking and actions of groups of individuals and even of nations. The principle is the same. Groups or nations that are comprised of individuals secure in their autonomy have less need to obtain reassurance by primitive or infantile displays of power. On the world scene, the most primitive method is to destroy the lives of those who disagree.

Normal at two, but a problem at twenty-two

There are two very unpleasant consequences that will follow if developmental hurdles are not successfully negotiated when they are faced for the first time. The basic problem will remain and be played out repeatedly during later years. In addition, the very limited coping methods used by very immature children will continue to be the only ones available. This inevitably leads to impaired adaptation. An understanding of the fourth developmental hurdle clarifies the meaning of Private Joe Smith's behavior.

Private Joe Smith's commanding officer had sent him to see the psychiatrist. He was in danger of being court-marshaled and sent to prison because of his unwillingness to salute his sergeant. Private Smith had a ready answer for his intransigence. He said, "Why should I give in to him? He is not better than I am! I won't salute him! What do you think I am? A nobody? I'd be nothing if I gave in and saluted him."

A careful explanation that saluting was a symbolic ritual needed for military discipline and that it had nothing to do with the relative importance of the individuals, was to no avail. He would not budge from his position, despite his full awareness that the consequence of not making this seemingly trivial gesture would lead to a court-martial and possible prison time.

Points to Remember

- Parents are often bewildered and stressed by children's stubbornness and negativism during this period of development.

- Children's array of frustrating behavior is usually normal and in part caused by their struggle to define their autonomy.

- Young children are just developing a sense of autonomy, but it is still extremely weak and easily threatened, prodding them into responses aimed at reassuring themselves that they are not completely powerless.

PART FIVE

SECTION TWO

UNDERSTANDING THE MEANING OF CHILDREN'S BEHAVIOR DURING THEIR STRUGGLE FOR AUTONOMY AND ITS MANAGEMENT

Everyone is familiar with the typical array of behavior that has been given the label "the terrible twos." Most parents are perplexed and stressed when they encounter their child's litany of "nos." This can emerge in any setting, but many parents feel certain that their child, in Machiavellian fashion, has cunningly conspired to find the avenue that would be most unsettling to them. Some of the main variants of this pattern and its management will be described in the following chapter.

CHAPTER 3

THE DIFFERENCE BETWEEN BEING APPROPRIATELY ASSERTIVE AND BEING "STRONG WILLED"

Question – My three-year-old is very strong willed. He has a mind of his own and uses any available opportunity to let me know it. Does this mean that he is developing a firm sense of autonomy?

It is fairly typical for two-year-olds to be strong willed. Their propensity for saying, "No, no, no!" is well known. Parents sometimes believe that this excessive assertiveness is a sign of secure autonomy. The opposite is true. Most children are overly strong willed precisely because their sense of autonomy is so fragile. The mastery of this developmental hurdle is aimed at helping children to think reasonably about the world and use good judgment about their actions. The capacity to pursue reasonable goals in an adaptive manner is a much better definition of healthy assertiveness. This has nothing in common with being strong willed, which leads to maladaptive patterns of behavior usually in the form of resisting others and an unwillingness to cooperate.

We are not interested in turning our children into petty tyrants who go through life exercising power over others to compensate for their inner feelings of weakness. The two-and-one-half-year-old is only two-and-one-half feet tall and doesn't have a dime to his name. His sense of autonomy is just emerging and is still extremely fragile. His silly battles of wills are feeble attempts to feel more powerful.

Dan's emerging sense that he is an autonomous self coincides with the acquisition of two other skills: the use of words and the ability to be very mobile. These are quickly drawn into the service of protecting his fragile sense of self. Saying, "no," one of his first and favorite words, and running from others and exploring new things have become his preferred pastimes. Understanding this developmental stage affords parents useful information about the meaning of a wide spectrum of behavior that might otherwise be perplexing.

Parents need to understand this developmental hurdle and be on the lookout for it at other times in their kids' lives. Many times during normal development events both external and internal conspire to engender feelings of vulnerability and powerlessness. At these times children, and adults as well, often fall back upon the more primitive methods used when their sense of autonomy first emerged. This is common during adolescence when many youngsters find themselves at a crossroads of life, but unprepared to confidently face what lies ahead. Feeling ill equipped to cope with a bewildering array of new and formidable tasks, they experience feelings of helplessness and may repeat behavior patterns more typical of this much earlier stage of development.

Points to Remember

- Young children are perceived as being strong willed, but their behavior is actually motivated by feelings of powerlessness and vulnerability.
- Parents must avoid being drawn into a battle of wills and instead help their children to become confident about their emerging sense of autonomy.

CHAPTER 4

THE TWO TASKS OF PARENTING – CARING AND LETTING GO

Question – I understand the meaning of so much more of my child's behavior. I realize that his stubbornness represents his struggle to develop a more secure sense of autonomy. I also know what I hope to accomplish. Can you provide additional information that will help me to get the job done?

Dan's struggles for autonomy or for a sense of a self that has a will of its own separate from the will of others will unfold in nearly every facet of his life. Nearly all of these struggles will involve his parents, and the outcomes will depend on their attitudes and behavior. Many of the interactions that will influence these struggles fall into the category of discipline. The principles and guidelines already addressed in Part IV are entirely applicable to the mastery of the fourth developmental hurdle. An additional focus needs to be placed on helping our children develop confidence that they own their own minds and bodies and can feel comfortable with that ownership.

Question – We have sometimes been uncertain about how much we should do for our child. I can now see that leaning too far in the direction of helping and making it easier for him might interfere with his emerging autonomy. Can you clarify this for us?

Newborn babies and infants have virtually no conscious control over their behavior, mobility, thoughts, feelings, or body. Their well-being, even their survival, depends completely upon care provided by others. Nearly all parents intuitively know this and willingly cast themselves into the role of the protectors and supervisors of their infants' bodies and emotional well-being. It would be unusual for them to consider their other role as they attend to this important task. It is certainly true that the immediate focus during this very early period must be on the role of protector and regulator, but it would be extremely useful for them, right from the beginning, to be aware of their ultimate goal: **the gradual transfer of responsibility for these tasks from themselves to their children.**

At some point, sooner rather than later, our children will need to have confidence in their own ability to control their behavior, bodies, thoughts, and feelings. At some point they will need to be able to regulate their lives without having their parents in the background to ensure success. They need to learn to be at ease with their feelings. These should become a source of pleasure for them and a reliable rudder that they can use to direct their lives. Eventually they will need to learn to channel their thoughts productively and creatively. They must learn to feel comfortable with their bodies as their bodies become trustworthy and reliable to them, vehicles through which their feelings, thoughts, and behavior can be constructively expressed. None of this is possible if these facets of our children's lives continue to be extensively monitored, supervised, and controlled by their parents.

During the early months, the parenting role obviously needs to be tipped heavily on the side of functioning as the regulator of the child's body and his protector and buffer against the world. This is required to forge the bonds of love that will become the foundation of a mature personality. The child's actual helplessness leaves no alternative. Yet even during this early time the buds of individuality are sprouting and should be nurtured.

Apart from alerting parents to this side of their parenting duties during the period of infancy, there are few actual guidelines for them to follow. Parents are successful in this endeavor if they are able to accurately read their child's signals instead of imposing their own feelings about what is needed. The nonverbal message communicated by this quality of positive parenting might sound something like this, "I am comfortable with the ebb and flow of your needs for nurturing and can be in harmony with you. The sense of well-being that you experience as a result of my reliable and comfortable care will help you to feel increasing comfort and confidence with your own internal signals. This will help you to build confidence that you can trust and control your body and its feelings."

Love comes in two forms, caring and letting go. During the first year the balance swings dramatically towards the caring side. By the second year it needs to gradually shift towards letting go. Many parents find considerable difficulty making this change. There is a profound closeness and intimacy between infants and their parents during the earliest months that many parents are loath to relinquish.

Points to Remember

- In addition to their roles as caretakers, many parents overlook an equally important task: letting go.

- During the second year, parents should think about providing more opportunities for their children to express themselves.

Chapter 5

SURRENDERING OWNERSHIP OF OUR CHILD'S MOBILITY

The development of autonomy is best served when parents adhere to the principle of surrendering ownership of as many parts of their children's lives as soon as possible. Parents neglect this rule if they attempt to function as guardians of their children's mobility in a manner that conflicts with the children's emerging sense of autonomy. The well-intentioned desire by parents to be protective may prod them to excessively interfere with this important developmental trend. Parents must remember that mobility is the vehicle through which their children learn about and master the physical world.

Question – Now that my child is walking he is constantly getting into trouble, knocking things over, and putting himself in places where he might get hurt. Can you help me to understand the best ways to handle this? Some of my friends are keeping their kids in playpens.

Making Sense of the Mobility of the Two-Year-Old

Understanding the meaning of our children's behavior is the essential starting point for the elaboration of reasonable parenting strategies. Between ages one and three, our little ones seem to be in constant motion. They get into things and out of things on top of things and under things. Things are pushed and pulled, they topple and fall, and are mashed and banged. And how our little ones love to squirm, fuss, and flee. There is little time for parents to rest. The typical day with kids this age seems like an endless round of supervision, "No, no," cleaning and picking up leading to another round of "No, no," and running after them with more "No, no." Uppermost on the minds of these harried parents is containment, with relief and some rest for themselves, and the assurance of safety for their kids.

Understanding the meaning of this behavior can reduce parental stress and provide useful insight about their objectives during this period of development. Uninformed observers of the incessant movements of two-year-olds would label this as random movements or just "blowing off steam." These activities and movements actually serve a significant purpose. They are part of a learning experience that plays an important role in the development of autonomy.

The experience of being able to function with autonomy is intricately entwined with bodily control and movement. The typical endless activity of two-year-olds is the vehicle through which they are learning about the movement and control of their bodies. They are beginning to make sense of a world of bewildering visual stimuli. A map of the home and then the neighborhood is being drawn in their minds. Their movements through rooms, down halls, and around corners are all explorations of new territories providing information about their body's ability to assert itself in the world of space and objects. Moving towards and away from things allows them to define their relationship to the objects that inhabit their world. An increasing ability to negotiate over, around, and under objects and to pull and to push them away is tied to the emerging image of themselves as active and independent individuals. They resist their parents and then cooperate. **They are discovering what they can will their bodies to do in a world with expanding horizons.** These activities, so often perplexing and frustrating to parents, are important learning experiences for little children.

This important process comes into conflict with the natural inclinations of many parents whose primary goal with their active two-year-olds is containment. If the harried parents of children of this age are asked about their fondest wish, many might say, "Rest for me and out of trouble for him." Interesting insights derived from the observations of the development of blind children might broaden their perspective.

Observations of the development of blind children – A lesson about the importance of understanding developmental hurdles

The physical and emotional development of blind children is similar to normally sighted ones until the age of six to eight months. At that point, sighted children are able to take a developmental step that blind ones cannot negotiate without help. Sighted children reach out and explore the things they see. Blind children cannot do this. They hear but have no way of knowing that the sounds signify things that can be touched, manipulated, and used for play. For this reason blind children don't easily begin to explore their surrounding world and, as a consequence, miss this tremendously rich and important learning experience that accounts for much of the behavior of toddlers.

This period of exploration is linked to children's increasing ability to control their bodies, understand the world around them, and establish the foundation for a stable sense of autonomy. Bereft of this experience, blind children's visual disability extends into other important facets of their development.. Their hands become blind because they do not spend hours touching, feeling, and exploring objects. Their bodies become blind because they cannot observe the effects of pushing, pulling, running, and falling. And ultimately their development of independence, control, and autonomy may become damaged.

Blind children can be easily helped to negotiate this extra hurdle, but this requires parents who understand the importance of the normal activities of very young children. Motivated by a desire to touch and explore the objects about them, normally sighted children spontaneously begin to crawl and explore their surroundings. In order for blind children to take this first step towards control of their bodies, they need to be helped by their parents to link the sounds of things to their shapes, sizes, and textures. Without this linkage there is no incentive for them to begin the process of exploration.

To accomplish this, blind children are given as many opportunities as possible to reach for and grasp things that are heard. If blind children master this concept, the sounds of things will act as stimuli for them to explore their world. This initiates their mobility and leads to an increasing control and ownership of their bodies. As a consequence, blind children remain sightless but their hands and bodies learn to see. Of even greater importance, their increasing confidence in their bodies plays an integral part in the development of their sense of autonomy. They cannot see with their eyes, but they are beginning to see themselves as autonomous selves with the capacity to use their bodies effectively.

There is a startling difference between blind children who have been helped to make this transition and those who have not. As the months pass, those who have mastered this learning experience appear similar in their movements and activities to sighted children. They are mobile, reaching for things, playing with objects, and continually moving about and exploring their worlds. Those who have not been helped, appear passive and immobile. Now their hands and bodies as well as their eyes have become blind. Observations of these kids often find them standing or sitting, passively waving their arms back and forth and moving their hands aimlessly. Their exploration of the world, their control of their bodies, and the foundation of autonomy has been blocked.

This information highlights an important principle. Many parents are unaware of the developmental implications of the normal exploratory behavior of young children. As a consequence they may find this behavior disturbing and inadvertently take actions that impede rather than facilitate the mastery of this developmental hurdle.

PROTECTIVE FACILITATION VERSUS CONSTRUCTIVE PROTECTION

Question – I am concerned about my child's safety. Is there a balance that will encourage the development of autonomy without risk to life and limb?

Few parents neglect their role as protectors of their child's body. The extreme fragility and utter helplessness of infants and very young children are compelling. Precautions taken to safeguard this precious newcomer are a continuing focus of concern. This emphasis, however, may stand in the way of another goal of parenting, their children's facilitation of bodily skills and mobility. Missing opportunities to help our children master these tasks may diminish their budding autonomy, leading to less spontaneity and inquisitiveness. Children are not best served if they mistrust their body's ability to manipulate objects and negotiate space.

The guideline needed to help children master this developmental hurdle is clear. **Protection must be combined with facilitation.** It should not be at the expense of facilitation. Given the high activity level of most toddlers and their propensity for overlooking their own safety, this is a full-time and taxing job. Fatigued parents may be tempted to search for some type of mechanism or disciplinary approach (constrictive protection) to curtail their child's mobility and provide relief from the necessity for endless supervision. For the most part the answer is, "Sorry there is none. Children this age require nearly continuous supervision." While protection is essential, it must be incorporated into strategies that develop confidence in the use of their bodies.

Most of the methods already described in the section about parenting strategies to avoid confrontations are applicable. Baby proofing the house, placing behavior into the category of "desirable" rather than "necessary," and the use of substitution and distraction are all useful in the implementation of parenting based on protective facilitation rather than constrictive protection. The most important adjunct to the successful implementation of this goal, however, entails a shift in how parents think about their children's activities and play.

Whose Play? The Child's or the Parents'?

Question – Are there forms of play that I should encourage?

Play is an arena in which children are assimilating huge amounts of vital information needed for emotional and cognitive growth. Recently there has been an emphasis on the importance of parents playing with their children, but there has been little clarification about the types of play that should be supported. Since most of us generally assume that others, especially our own kids, should share our beliefs, well-intentioned parents tend to impose their own ideas about constructive play upon their kids. They may even believe, encouraged by the media and advertised products, that their brand of play will help to instill creativity or advance their children's intellectual skills. Any pleasant time spent together is beneficial. But parents would be better advised to act as facilitators of the play their children choose spontaneously rather than imposing their own.

Children are exercising their minds much more effectively when they are devising the play. In addition, their play is not chosen randomly. It is nearly always linked fairly directly to a task or problem that they are attempting to master. We are functioning optimally if we participate with our children by combining our facilitation of their choice of play with our role as protectors. When well-intentioned parents too energetically impose their form of entertainment upon their kids, they may inadvertently communicate, "I lack confidence in your ability to do things on your own. You need me to direct your thinking and activities. You are not able to learn on your own or be happy without my help." This is not the type of message that encourages the development of autonomy.

This relatively recent trend of parental involvement into the domain of children's play now often extends far into later childhood and even adolescence. Older children profit from the social skills derived from play organized and conducted without adult supervision. Now, in many communities, the play of older children has been taken over by adults, eliminating so many important opportunities for developmental progress.

Facilitation should not be confused with indulgence. It is not the role of parents to keep their children happily entertained. When kids are busily engaged on their own, they usually need nothing more than a watchful eye. It's possible for motivated parents to keep a two-year-old at a game or task by making it a pleasing or exciting interaction. When this is done excessively, the child is deprived of opportunities to use play to work out solutions to many of the developmental issues he is attempting to master.

Autonomy means knowing the capabilities of one's body. This is acquired by initiating activities and exploring their possibilities. Autonomy also entails the capacity to assert oneself and exercise some control over things and people. The child achieves this by making choices, pushing things, pulling things, pulling people, and pushing against people.

Unfortunately, these are the types of activities and movements that disturb many parents who pat themselves on the back when they have directed their kids into what they assume are more appropriate endeavors.

CONSTRUCTIVE SUPERVISION

Question – I understand how the concept of facilitative protection applies to play, but I am still uncertain about what I can do about the daily tugs of war. I seem to be continually reining in his behavior. Are there any guidelines that might be helpful?

Parents are completely responsible for their children's protection and supervision. In order to ensure their safety, children need fairly constant supervision. Parents need to remember their other task, helping in their child's development of autonomy. With a bit of thought they will discover many times each day that they can safely allow their kids to make their own choices. Naturally there will also be countless times that parents must act as a traffic cop, stopping potentially dangerous behavior, and attending to the many other tasks that are necessary but children may find disagreeable.

Parental attitude

My emphasis is on the manner in which this is done. Sometimes the distinction may be unclear, but we are usually aware of the dramatic difference in the ways directions are communicated to us by others. We can appreciate the experience of our very helpless children by recalling our own reactions to people who push us around. Regardless of the level of our maturity, it is hard to resist feeling degraded and the temptation to resist. Attention should be given to our tone and wording when we are supervising our children. Most parents seem to be more willing to make the effort needed to acknowledge the dignity and value of others in the business world, or with casual acquaintances, than with the ones who are most dear to them. There is no reason for us to overlook the importance of kindness, thoughtfulness, and understanding with our own children. These are important ingredients for the nourishment of our children's spirits and souls.

There will be many times that we must tell our little ones what to do. We are helping to strengthen their sense of autonomy if we add love and understanding to our actions and comments at these times. This, as much as anything else we can do during this stage of development, will help them to learn that compliance and cooperation does not need to be equated with surrender and loss of autonomy. This is a crucial lesson for their successful entry into school just a few short years ahead.

Other ways to facilitate the children's mastery of their mobility

Question – I now understand the importance of the development of autonomy. Are there other opportunities for me to help my child with this part of the developmental hurdle? An example would be helpful.

Dan's mother is aware that she will have many opportunities each day to actively facilitate her son's development of autonomy. She is always on the lookout for safe arenas in which she can allow him to explore the world with less need for external, physical restraint. She often finds ways to act as a catalyst for Dan as he is acquiring new skills. For example, at fifteen months Dan discovered the stairs. When he was out of her sight for more than a few moments, she knew where to find him. She tried using substitution and distraction and repeatedly took him to another area to play. She soon realized that he would spend the entire day at this game. She was considering placing a gate across the stairway but thought of a better plan, one that would allow her to act as his facilitator rather than protector.

She remembered how she had helped him to climb on to the sofa as he was struggling to master that task many months earlier. He had made a number of attempts but was not quite able to accomplish the task on his own. She helped him to place a foot in a position allowing him to complete the activity. Following his success, he beamed with pleasure. Sally realized that she had helped him master a small learning experience, a far better alternative than either directing him to another activity, or lifting him onto the sofa to eliminate his mounting frustration. She decided to try to do the same with his attempts to get the best of the stairs.

Sally watched carefully as Dan approached the stairway. She realized that he did not have the capacity to successfully negotiate the stairs and would stumble if he attempted to step down while moving forward. She encouraged him to turn around and move down from a backward crawl position, one step at a time. As soon as Dan got the knack of it, he happily repeated this new maneuver under his mother's watchful eye. Sally quickly became convinced that he could tackle the stairs on his own and she no longer needed to restrict this activity. She could have chosen to err on the side of safety and continue to bar him from access to the stairs, but knew that the trade-off, both in terms of increased confidence and autonomy, outweighed the small risk.

The behavior of toddlers seems less random when observations are combined with the knowledge of our kids' struggles to gain mastery over their physical environment. Their incessant activity represents their continuing efforts to accomplish this task. Keeping this in mind allows parents to replace the typical pattern of a repetitive "no, no," with, "Yes, I understand and will help you successfully complete the behavioral sequences that will give you increasing confidence in your control of your body. As soon as your skills permit, I will eagerly transfer ownership of another facet of your mobility to you."

Points to Remember

- Parents often perceive their children's seemingly ceaseless activity as a nuisance.

- What often seems like random movement serves a purpose: It helps children develop mastery over their bodies, an important facet of their emerging sense of autonomy.

- Parents need to function as catalysts in this process, not impediments.

Chapter 6

SURRENDERING OWNERSHIP OF OUR CHILDREN'S BODIES

Question – I understand the concept of autonomy and how it applies to my child's play and mobility. Does it also apply to other parts of his body?

Who owns our children's bodies? This depends on their age and, more important, on their capacity to assume this role for themselves. Our children's emerging sense of autonomy will be impeded if we attempt to maintain that role when it is reasonable to have transferred it to them.

The general guideline for this is once again very simple: **Sooner rather than later, more rather than less.**

In the following discussion, I will be addressing eating and toilet training in more detail, but the concepts apply to many other facets of our children's lives. During many moments of each day, parents are involved with the care and supervision of their children's bodies. The information and principles formulated about eating and toileting apply equally to dressing and undressing, washing, tooth brushing, and decisions about using the proper clothing for the weather conditions. It is important that parents are prepared to find appropriate ways to transfer these responsibilities safely to their children.

BATTLE FOR THE OWNERSHIP OF OUR CHILD'S TUMMY

Question – I have always believed that one of my most important roles as a parent is to ensure that my kids eat a proper diet. I now realize that I will need to gradually relinquish this role and that my failure to do so may impede their development of autonomy. Can you provide information that will help me to pursue a successful path?

It is the rare family that has negotiated childhood without some conflict over eating. Among the wide array of childhood behaviors that parents tend to place in the category of problematic, this is actually the easiest to resolve. Any perceived difficulties are solely due to parental baggage. Parents tend to measure their success by their children's eating habits. From the start, eating gets wrapped up in a web of mixed-up emotions. In our culture, providing food is generally perceived as an act of giving and loving and the rejection of food an act of hostility. Children are told before their visit to Grandma, "Mind your manners and eat a little of everything or you will hurt your grandma's feelings." Even some ardent vegetarians have been known to allow a fatty piece of steak to pass down their gullet to avoid upsetting their host.

The link between food and love, perhaps understandable during infancy, usually continues into the second and third years. That link makes it difficult for parents to forego their desire to continue to own their children's mouths and tummies. Every parent I have spoken with about eating problems have strongly voiced their contention that it is essential for them to remain guardians of this part of their children's bodies. They quickly provide elaborate justifications to support this belief. Some of the ones I hear repeatedly include, "He will become undernourished . . . not get enough calcium . . . eat too much sugar; He is irritable if he doesn't get a good breakfast; He would live on deserts if we let him;" and so on.

None of these concerns have any merit. In fact, children as young as age one or two will consume an appropriate diet, even when their parents eliminate all prodding and coaxing. Parental concerns that their children's diet will suffer if they cease to supervise the eating process is entirely unfounded. The opposite is the case. If children develop hang-ups about eating, these can nearly always be traced back to excessive parent-child conflicts about food.

Therefore, it is appropriate for parents to surrender ownership of their children's mouths and tummies as soon as possible. This can usually begin during the early part of the second year of life.

This does not mean that parents cease to use common sense about their children's food choices. It does mean that they place the entire feeding process into the category of "desirable" rather than the "necessary."

There is never, absolutely never, any reason for confrontations about the consumption of food.

The guideline is straightforward. At the birth of their child, each parent should take the following oath: "I do hereby resolve that from this time on I will never be frustrated, angry, or unhappy about any aspect of my child's food consumption." The corollary to this is that by the beginning of the second year of the child's life, "I will surrender the role of supervisor of my child's food intake to its rightful owner."

Question – But what do I do when he won't eat?

Dan is age two. His mother understands the guideline and is completely at her ease as she faces another episode of negativity at mealtime. This time Dan has pushed away his plate after taking a few bites and, with a scowl, indicates that he has finished. Sally has rehearsed in her mind how she will handle this. She knows that, whenever possible, it is best to avoid getting into a battle of wills with Dan, especially over food. These have no winners, tend to intensify distorted perceptions, and impede his development of autonomy. She is therefore relieved to be able to place eating into the category of "desirable" and avoid tugs of war over food. Knowledge, combined with a small dose of common sense, makes life so much easier. With a note of calm and love in her voice, Sally says to Dan, "This is what I am serving; you decide how much of it you want to eat."

Many parents are shocked when I have suggested this type of response to their young child's intransigence over food. Parents, who might have few reservations about their kids spending long hours in front of the television set, are disturbed that I might be suggesting that they allow them to get away with an act as outrageous as refusing their food. They may be tremendously impressed with the sparks of genius they see in their progeny, but they are certain that when it comes to decisions about eating, these otherwise brilliant kids are very stupid and will remain stupid.

The thought of giving up their role as supervisors of their children's tummies conjures visions of them growing up nourished exclusively on soda pop and Twinkies. They have it backward. Food fads and eating problems of all kinds are nearly always the result of parent-child conflicts around eating and these are generated by the parents' need to control this part of their children's lives. When conflicts of this kind are kept to a minimum, kids nearly always consume adequate amounts of appropriate foods. No one ever hears of children who are malnourished because their parents did not push foods. We often hear of an array of eating disorders, overeating being the most common, that are fueled by the parents' need to control their children's tummies.

Question – Won't we be indulging and spoiling our children if we give them the impression that they are in control of their food consumption?

I need to remind parents that the definition of indulgence is love in a form that fosters helplessness and dependency, rather than autonomy and maturity. We are encouraging the development of the opposite – autonomy and independence. By allowing Dan to begin to regulate his food intake, his mother is communicating several very constructive messages. She is separating food intake from interpersonal conflict. This will help Dan to understand that eating has nothing to do with power plays or getting affection. She realizes that most of Dan's resistance is motivated by his need to assert his will against her and she is taking this out of the equation. This frees him to begin to make more reasonable decisions about hunger and food intake.

The idea that eating entails surrendering to the will of another or is a way to garner approval are distorted perceptions common to all young children, and can only be dispelled with the help of their parents. Mastery of this developmental hurdle leads to increasing confidence that they can trust their body's signals and their own judgment about food intake in response to those signals. Without this help, signals about hunger and eating get mixed up by emotions. Many in our culture are saddled with lifelong problems with food. These can often be traced to parental over-involvement with their alimentary tracks when they were young children.

During the earliest months of children's lives, eating and being fed are inextricably linked to being loved and getting attention. Children do better if that link is dissolved as early as possible. Too often, that does not happen and the linkage persists into the second and third years, and even beyond. The function of eating then remains linked with the variety of emotional upheavals that continue to unfold between parents and children. Eating remains a battleground where parents and children struggle for love, power, and control.

A brief story of a child whose parents won the fight for control of her body

Alice's anxiety was so severe that she had to be brought home from her first sleep-away experience. Alice was nine-years-old, but became afraid when she was away from her mom. She spoke about this saying, "I might have gotten sick and I don't know what would have happened to me. At first I felt okay, but then I became scared. I feel safer at home. My mom knows how to take care of me. She knows what I need." Her mother loved Alice but it was a love that fostered helplessness and dependency. Alice had not developed confidence in her own judgment about the care and supervision of her body. Her mother had not sufficiently supported her development of autonomy.

Avoiding the Battle over Toilet Training

There is never any reason for parents to have conflicts with their children about food. These kinds of tugs of war are unnecessary and always counterproductive. The same statements can be made about the other end of our children's anatomy. Yet I have found that it is precisely these two functions that become sources of conflict and confrontations in many families. It is noteworthy that although many kids grow up with an endless array of problems, undernourishment and continued soiling are nearly never among these. All kids can be counted on to consume food and all kids will eventually use modern plumbing. Parental involvement, especially if stressful, only complicates these bodily processes.

Parents' underlying concern during the toilet training period is, "Will he ever get it right?" From their frantic perspective, it feels as if they are neck high in dirty diapers and that this condition will last forever. They talk about it in the evenings and may dwell on it during the daytime hours. A telephone call between the parents during this stage will often begin with the query; "Did he put one in the potty today?" In the midst of this obsession, the high point of any day would be both parents beaming with pride, as they stand before a potty no longer empty. They have the impulse to wave flags, set off fireworks, and broadcast this momentous accomplishment to the world.

The problem with parental obsessions, or for that matter obsessions of any kind, is that they may lead to actions that hurt instead of help. Motivated by powerful feelings, parents tend to fail in their primary mission, the mastery of developmental hurdles. The misguided alarm that parents feel at the future prospect of living with a kid who might continue to smell when he reaches eighteen, prods them to use strategies that escalate tensions and may impede the child's emerging sense of autonomy.

The key element in effective learning is that it rests on sound motivations. In their zeal to obtain compliance, parents often fail to consider the motivations they are instilling. The array of advantages that accrue from using the toilet over pants are so overwhelming that, over the long haul, a favorable outcome is inevitable. Parents are wholly justified in believing that time is on their side and without confrontational and coercive interventions, the outcome will be favorable. Since the outcome is assured, parents should be more interested in the motivations that are instilled during the toilet training process.

A central theme of this book is to emphasize the importance of understanding the nature of our children's thinking that accounts for their behavior. As we interact with our kids around all the issues that fill our daily lives with them, it is crucial to remember that we are influencing how they think, their values, and the motivations that will determine their character. It is this function of parenting, so easily overlooked, that will be the essential factor in determining their future quality of life. Children will become toilet trained. The important question is, "How will our interventions with them during this process influence their perceptions and ultimately their ways of operating in the world?"

Question – I believe that you are saying that my goals during toilet training go far beyond the ones that are obvious. Can you address what these are and how they can be achieved?

My comments refer directly to toilet training but they apply equally to many other facets of parenting. There are a variety of motivations that prod us towards cooperating with others, being productive and useful, and accomplishing tasks. The fortunate among us pursue these types of activities because they are reasonable and afford satisfaction. Others are propelled by entirely different kinds of motivations. Many go through life perceiving their interactions with others as tugs of war with winners and losers, the powerful and the weak, the victorious and the vanquished. This is nearly always a dominant perception of many of the interactions that occur daily in the lives of our little ones since their sense of autonomy is extremely fragile during this period of their lives. Regardless of the appropriateness of our actions with them, they often feel that they are being pushed around and mistreated. This leaves them feeling weak and powerless. Our aim is to help them dispel these types of early childhood motivations and replace them with ones that are more realistic and adaptive. Acquiring the capacity for cooperation and an interest in being useful and productive may hang in the balance. The messages, emotional as well as verbal, that we communicate during parenting need to be carefully considered since they are gradually molding the shape of our child's character.

Question – I understand that my long-term goals during the period of toilet training extend far beyond the immediate one. The parenting techniques I use should be ones that also help instill personality attributes that lead to mature functioning. Can you suggest useful guidelines for toilet training?

A reasonable plan

The disadvantages of confrontations leading to surrender or victory, with anger and loss of autonomy, are obvious. Therefore toilet training needs to be placed into the category of "desirable" rather than "necessary." There is no realistic alternative to this. After all, parents do not have the power to command obedience from this part of their child's anatomy any more than they have the ability to mandate what will enter their alimentary track at the other end. Once this decision is made, the strategy is simple. It consists merely of praising successes and avoiding temptations to resort to more coercive alternatives. Children's desire for our approval and the pleasure of the accomplishment of new skills will always win out over any continued desire to do what comes naturally.

Question – Can you provide some of the details of a reasonable plan?

Toilet training for Dan

Sally could hardly have refrained from thinking about toilet training after Dan turned two. It was a frequent topic of conversation among her friends who had toddlers. Some had already achieved success, but Sally had held off beginning. She wanted Dan to be a partner in the process and that required a certain level of cognitive and speech skills. Now he was two-and-one-half and had both the capacity to understand what was expected and the physical maturity to comply. She was confident of his readiness to tackle this new task because he had made real gains towards the mastery of earlier developmental hurdles. Signs of separation anxiety had not been evident for some time and he was learning to get along when he did not get his way.

Even before she introduced the project to him, she was aware that he was also thinking about it. On a number of occasions she noticed him looking at her knowingly, immediately before or after squatting to have a bowel movement. She decided that he was ready. Her first step was to give words to the process. When she spotted him having a bowel movement, she indicated her interest in this matter by saying, "Oh you are having a bowel movement." Children's lives revolve around their parents. They therefore become interested in anything that interests the parents. Dan was no exception. On several occasions during the following week he called his bowel movements by name after depositing them in his diapers. His mother then did two things. She introduced a potty-chair and in a pleasant manner indicated her preference that he sit on the potty to have his bowel movement. She chose a potty-chair rather than a seat that rests upon the toilet. She thought the task was difficult enough for him to master without the added dimension of being perched on the edge of what might seem to him a huge void emitting ominous sounds as his feet dangled several inches off the floor.

The scene had been set. Dan's parents have done their part. They have explained one of the simple necessities of civilized society and the potty-chair has been positioned in its rightful place in the bathroom. Everyone waits, but little seems to happen. They have a few doubts about the strength of Dan's motivation for the project, but are able to put these aside and remain patient. On two to three occasions during this period their hopes rise when he comes to them at the proper time, points a finger in the direction of the bathroom, and says the particular word he uses for the toileting process. With the appropriate fanfare, he is enthusiastically whisked to his throne. Sally holds her breath thinking, "This is going to be easier than we thought." The excitement dissipates rapidly when, as proud as punch with what he has done, he gets up leaving an empty potty. A few minutes later the bowel movement can be found in it usual place.

These are the times that try men's souls and patience is required. Many parents are tempted to use a variety of coercive devices to encourage their children to comply. Without an understanding of the entire developmental process, they become confused. They find it hard to understand why their child, who is bright enough to work the television set, cannot accomplish such a trivial task. Based upon this type of thinking they may attribute resistance to stubbornness and manipulation, leading to unnecessary conflicts and confrontations.

Children will become trained. They understand their parents' expectations and their desire for approval and the pride of accomplishment will prod them to master the task. The important consideration is the impact that their parents have on their motivations and emerging sense of autonomy, not how quickly they are able to get them to put it in the pot.

The general model being presented for toilet training is applicable to many learning tasks of childhood. It emphasizes that our influence upon character formation should not be overlooked in favor of an obsession with the immediate task. It also prescribes another central tenet of good parenting, the concept of a little at a time. Too much too quickly overwhelms young children and blocks our primary mission, building a stable mature personality structure. Finally, it highlights the importance of monitoring our children's progress as they negotiate these tasks. This allows us to shift our level of expectations and parenting methods as needed.

Dan's parents are pleased as he begins to have success. They avoid making the mistake of assuming that progress will be continuous. Developmental skills are acquired gradually and at first are extremely vulnerable to many influences, both internal and external. Since his parents' presence and approval play an important role in this process, any disruptions, including brief separations or increased conflict within the family, may set Dan back. These episodes of backsliding will usually not be prolonged if parents are able to persevere with patience and understanding.

The story of a little boy whose parents tried too hard

Mark was in the midst of toilet training. His parents had become frustrated when their initial attempts were completely unsuccessful. Prodded by an increasing sense of failure and desperation, they decided to exert additional pressure on him to gain his compliance. They insisted that he sit on the potty for five to ten minutes at a time, and berated him if he did not produce the desired result or when he soiled his clothing. There were some successes, but no real progress. Mark had been a happy toddler, but he became cranky, irritable, and fearful. He had enjoyed shopping trips with his mother and she would have to watch him closely or he would speed away from her. Now he clung tightly to his mother's hand and repeatedly asked to be taken home. Other immature patterns of behavior, not evident for some time, had returned. He began to get up at night, crying and wanting to come into his parents' bed.

I met with Mark's parents who were very receptive to the information that I gave to them. They were able to understand what Mark was communicating by his changed behavior. Children speak to us through their behavior, fears, and play. Mark was saying, "You are asking too much of me too quickly, this makes me afraid. I get afraid when you are angry, and then it gets worse when my own anger becomes so big that I don't know what might happen. You might stop loving me and I would be all alone." Mark's parents eliminated the confrontations that had become part of the daily routine by placing toilet training into the category of "desirable" rather than "necessary." Soon Mark became the happy little boy he had been before and after several months, toilet training was achieved.

Points to Remember

Battle for the Ownership of Our Child's Tummy

- The parents' role as food providers, while appropriate during the first year of life, needs to rapidly diminish after that period.

- Many parents maintain their role of guardians of their child's tummy long after it should have been transferred to the child, which leads to endless unnecessary conflicts and often long-term eating problems.

- The principle is simple: It is appropriate for parents to surrender ownership of their children's tummies and mouths as soon as possible, usually during the early part of the second year of life.

- There is never any justification for tugs-of-war over eating.

Avoiding the Battle over Toilet Training

- The fuss, stress, and upheaval caused by toilet training are entirely unjustified.

- All children become trained; the advantages of modern plumbing over soiling guarantee that outcome.

- Children understand their parents' expectations, and their own desire for approval and the pride of accomplishment will prod them to master this task.

- Keep in mind the deleterious impact that confrontations and angry exchanges may have on children's emerging sense of autonomy.

- Therefore, to avoid confrontations, place the act of getting it into the pot into the category of desirable rather than necessary.

Chapter 7

SURRENDERING OWNERSHIP OF OUR CHILDREN'S THOUGHTS AND FEELINGS

As the third developmental hurdle unfolds, children are learning about their control of their mobility and bodily functions. They are also learning about their feelings and thoughts. Starting very early in life, children begin to acquire the unique ability to think about what they are thinking and feeling. This gives them the capacity to modify their thoughts and the power to decide how these will be expressed. Some people are comfortable with their thoughts and feelings and can express them constructively. Many remain uncomfortable with thoughts and feelings, and these are experienced as something alien and threatening to them. Parental attitudes and parenting styles will have a profound influence upon this emerging component of their children's lives, but this is nearly always completely overlooked by the parents. As a consequence, they miss opportunities to help their children gradually assume ownership of their feelings and thoughts, feel comfortable with these feelings, and be able to express them appropriately.

Question – How do we help our children to feel comfortable with their feelings and thoughts and learn how to express them appropriately?

NAUGHTY LANGUAGE

Sally and Dan were visiting with a neighbor and her three-year-old son. Dan was playing with the little boy when the boy interrupted his mother's conversation with Sally to ask if they could play in the backyard. She replied, "No you can't because it's raining outside." Sally noticed the obvious disappointment in the little boy. His facial expression became angry and he shook a fist at his mother saying, "You're a doo-doo." The little boy's mother was visibly upset and irritated. She answered, "That's a naughty thing to say to your mother; children should not be disrespectful," and she gave him a slap on his backside.

Sally naturally said nothing and realized that what she had heard was a fairly typical response by many good parents who understand that an important part of their job is to teach their children to be respectful to adults. She might have offered some suggestions to her friend about other ways to achieve her goal, but could already hear the expected response. "Children must be taught to respect their elders; if you don't impress this on them when they are young, you will quickly lose control of their minds. God knows what they will be thinking and saying then."

Question – Isn't it important to teach our children to be polite and respectful of others?

Of course it is. Sally would have agreed with her friend's long-term goal. Children do need to learn to be respectful. But she understood that this is less likely to be achieved optimally unless we are aware of how we are influencing our children's thoughts when we interact with them. The effectiveness of our efforts to inculcate politeness will obviously be diminished if the model we are presenting to them is not one we would want them to emulate. In addition, in order for children to express their thoughts and feelings properly, they will need to feel at ease with them. Sally knew that using intimidation to teach respect might run counter to that goal.

Question – I have sometimes resorted to more drastic measures when I have found that other efforts to impress him with the importance of being polite and respectful to others were just not getting through. The importance of being polite seems so simple. Why is it so hard to plant this concept into his mind? How am I to help him to learn to express his feelings appropriately if I am not firm and willing to admonish him for naughty language?

The mature expression of feelings requires the mastery of early developmental hurdles. Little children and immature adults who never mastered those early hurdles are not able to get along when they don't get their way. They distort the meaning of not getting their way, believing that they are justified in feeling that they have been devalued, mistreated, and pushed around. Their angry responses are predicated upon these flawed patterns of thinking. Children cannot become authentically polite until these developmental problems have been resolved. If the earlier developmental hurdles are not mastered, children will become adults who spend their lives inappropriately venting the outrage engendered by their perceptions of being dismissed and overlooked. Such children can be taught the concept of good manners and, under the scrutiny of the parents, may be able go through the motions. But later, when the external motivators are removed, the power of feelings still fueled by distorted perceptions will usually win out.

Children at the age of Dan's friend feel small, weak, and helpless. When the little boy's mother told him that he could not go outside to play, this was perceived as a personal slight. He retaliated by becoming angry and spewing nasty words intended to even the score. This was the only way he could show that he would not allow himself to be discounted without some protest. This episode of rudeness was a reflection of the little boy's interpretation of his mother's refusal to comply with his request. Her attempt to modify his behavior by threats was futile. We can't force our children to change how they think, but we can influence such a change – a principle as applicable in our associations with other adults as it is with our kids. I have repeatedly mentioned the importance of helping our children to master developmental hurdles. This process is associated with important shifts in their thinking and comprises the only effective way of encouraging the development of politeness.

Children's thoughts cease to be burdensome to them once they have mastered the appropriate developmental hurdles. The intensity of children's anger becomes muted as they learn to get along when they don't get their way and develop a stable sense of autonomy. Parents need to remember that it is the intensity of the anger, rather than the nasty words, that fuels rude behavior.

The principle is very clear. Children who have acquired a stable sense of autonomy, and the skills to cope more effectively with the endless rounds of daily frustrations, will not be troubled by angry feelings that threaten to get out of control. They will have taken comfortable ownership of an important realm of human life, the expression of feelings and ideas. These kids will have no difficulties learning to be respectful and polite. With good controls and a realistic perspective of events it becomes a simple, even pleasurable, task. The concept of politeness will resonate with these kids when it is encouraged by their parents and they will gradually incorporate it into their personalities.

Not all children are so fortunate. In many children, feelings and thoughts maintain the power to erode functioning and engender emotional discord. Some feel guilty and uneasy about thoughts they consider "bad." Others are frightened by thoughts, believing that these have the power to motivate misdeeds. More vulnerable youngsters are prodded into destructive patterns of behavior by thoughts and feelings that have not been tamed by the mastery of developmental hurdles.

The problem is never the thoughts. Thoughts are no more than fleeting concepts in consciousness that are either accurate or not. They are a source of difficulty only when they reside in individuals who have poor controls and remain under the influence of distorted perceptions.

Question — I understand that my long-term goal is to assist my child in the mastery of developmental hurdles. That is a very gradual process. Are there guidelines that can help me to respond more constructively to inappropriate expressions of anger and other instances of impoliteness before this is accomplished?

Whenever possible, parents should respond using strategies that support rather than impede our primary goal, the mastery of developmental hurdles.

Sally understood this, and as she observed the incident unfold at the neighbor's house, she knew how she would have dealt with the "doo-doo" expletive if it had come from Dan's mouth. She would have combined love with reasonable frustration, the basic principle for helping children to learn to get along when they don't get their way. At Dan's age, she might do this by calmly listening to his angry display. If she thought that it would be constructive, she might have said, "Dan, I guess you are feeling very mad because I am not letting you go out and play. That is why you are using words that are not proper. It is raining out now but, if your friend is here when it's nice outside, you can play with him then." It will probably take several years before Dan can fully appreciate these types of comments, but it may be constructive to begin to sow the seeds of this insight as early as possible. Sally has not given him what he wanted, nor has she responded in a manner that might tend to confirm Dan's belief that he is being pushed around. Parents should be reminded that at these times their kids are looking for an immature victory in one of two ways, either by coercing gratification or upsetting their perceived adversary with a verbal assault. I am proposing that parents not gratify either of these tactics.

Sally is helping Dan in another way. She is showing him how comfortable she is with his anger and the words he used with intent to hurt. She has been a model for him of a person who is not intimidated or disturbed by her son's thoughts or feelings. She certainly will not now, nor will she ever, even subtly, condone disrespectful expressions. But she knows that her son's progress will depend upon his increasing ability to take ownership of his feelings and develop the capacity to express them appropriately. She is building the foundation for this process. There will be a time when she will respond to his inappropriate expression of thought more directly. Dan will always know her position regarding disrespectful language. But at no time will his thoughts or feelings have the power to upset her. Nor will she ever use any coercive method in a futile attempt to stamp them out. She is confident that the inappropriate display of these feelings will gradually diminish as Dan acquires the skills to channel and express them more reasonably. This cannot be accomplished by attempting to erase them from his mind.

The Expression of Anger

I have repeatedly emphasized that cookbook-type parenting techniques often miss the mark. This is because our children are changing with each passing day. Our responses must be geared to the ever-changing developmental issues with which they are struggling, as well as the tools they have available. There is a hierarchy of ways children use to express anger. This extends from the most primitive infantile patterns to the appropriate behavior of mature adults. Understanding this spectrum makes it easier to helpfully guide our children, according to the rule of a little at a time.

Screaming, "I hate you" or, "you are a doo-doo, Mommy" are certainly not mature ways of dealing with anger. If a frustrated adult used these types of expressions, he would be unlikely to win friends, influence people, and live happily ever after. On the other hand, very young children availing themselves of this type of immature verbal assault means that they have already taken significant steps up the developmental ladder. Using words to express angry passions requires better controls and the use of more sophisticated cerebral tools than plain screaming or violent actions. It is far more advanced than the meager mechanisms available to the newborn.

Sally understands the gradual unfolding of this developmental process. She is continually assessing Dan's progress and gears her responses to that level. At this point she is perfectly content to respond by silently listening to her son's outpouring of expletives. Sometimes it is wise to nurture the gains made when our children have taken this important step forward and have begun to use words to describe their feelings. There are many adults who often are not able to do as well and resort to more primitive forms of expression, sometimes in the form of violent behavior.

Moving Up the Developmental Ladder – Encouraging More Mature Methods of Expression

Dan has moved along in his development. He is now age four-and-one-half and his mother heard him using language she had not heard since high school. He was venting his anger because his younger brother had displaced him from one of his favorite places, his daddy's lap. His father was tempted to reprimand him harshly, followed by something that would ensure that this would not be repeated. Sally had heard the whole thing and had a fleeting picture in her mind of a bar of soap in Dan's mouth blocking the ugly words. Both were thankful that they were able to resist this initial impulse. Instead, after Dan seemed to run out of words, his father quietly said, "I know that you are angry when I play with your brother or when he sits on my lap. I guess it makes you feel left out. That is why you used such rude language. Maybe we can work together to help you to express your feelings more politely."

It would have been nice if Dan had brightened up after such a comment, and this pleasant outcome may eventually occur. More usually, this type of understanding and insightful comment has a negligible discernible effect upon kids of Dan's age. Although it does not often elicit a favorable response, it is helpful and does begin to accomplish several important things. It communicates his father's disapproval of his choice of language, but accomplishes this without making him feel terribly uncomfortable about his feelings or thoughts. Dan may sometimes be uncomfortable about the thoughts that run through his mind when he is angry, but at this point in his life he is stuck with them. His parents' goal is to help him to develop the necessary skills to express his feelings more appropriately. This is less likely to be accomplished if his feelings are magnified in intensity or become a source of greater discomfort to him.

Making children frightened of their feelings or thoughts are not constructive ways of helping them to develop better methods of expression. Many adults suffer because of their continuing fear of the power of their "bad" thoughts. They have been programmed by their parents to believe that their anger and associated thoughts represent an evil, ugly, destructive part of themselves. Others are prodded by these thoughts into maladaptive types of behavior.

Children can't be given free rein to act as they like. Many times each day we have to curtail our children's actions. Children can, however, be given nearly complete control over their thoughts, feelings, and words. Parents guided by this principle are not being permissive. Surrendering ownership of this facet of their functioning to our children carries no risk to their psychological health. The contrary is true. There is little that parents can do, or need to do, in response to feelings and words. They can be confident that, as their children master developmental hurdles and acquire a variety of new skills, they will incorporate their parents' values about politeness, including the appropriate use of words. This cannot be mandated or successfully inculcated by intimidation.

Question – My child is in his fourth year. Are there better ways to respond to episodes of naughty language or rudeness?

During this period of development, understanding, silent listening, and the verbalization of our children's feelings work best. This does not mean that we are condoning their words. By our own example and the tenor of our comments we are making it clear that we value respectfulness and the appropriate use of language. We need to remember that a series of important tasks need to be mastered in order for children to express their thoughts and feelings appropriately. In addition to the negotiation of developmental hurdles, they must be helped to feel comfortable with their thoughts and to develop the variety of skills that will be needed for their appropriate expression.

I have repeatedly emphasized that I never advocate permitting children to do whatever they want. Parents are in charge, and should always be willing to curtail unreasonable behavior. But actions are not the same as words and obviously need to be handled differently.

Sally noticed that Dan's play had taken a turn for the worse and he was trying to knock over his little brother. She stopped him immediately saying, "Sometimes you are very angry at David and feel like pushing him. That's something you can't do. No hitting or pushing will be allowed." Dan's mother is not critical of his angry feelings but has made it clear that she disapproves of hitting and will do everything in her power to never permit acts of violence. She is prepared to provide external controls for his actions until he develops his own controls.

A large step up the developmental ladder

The important distinction between altruistic disappointment and immature anger

I have found that many parents are confused about the significant difference between disapproval that is constructive and another variety that is unhelpful. Generally most of them would have little difficulty making this distinction when observing other parents with their kids. The difference is immediately evident for a simple reason. The underlying intent of each response is apparent. **It is easy to discern the difference between disapproval based on anger and that based on a loving desire to help.**

There is another important element of the difference that is even less understood. An inappropriate expression of anger is motivated by distorted perceptions of events and people. In other words, this brand of anger is rarely justified by the actual events that bring it to the surface. The anger spills out because of the exaggerated and flawed interpretations that are given to everyday life events. There is a common theme to these distorted perceptions. This immature brand of anger is ignited by common everyday events that engender feelings of denigration, devaluation, or personal rejection. We can see this in our kids, other adults, and can read about it in our newspapers. Among adolescents today the term used to describe it, and often used as justification for violence, is "I was dissed." Parents are never justified in responding angrily because they believed that they are being "dissed" by their little children.

The degree of inappropriateness of an angry response correlates with two elements: the level of misinterpretation and the sophistication of the control mechanism. The two-year-old is sure that he is unloved and has suffered a tremendous humiliation if his parents gently guide him away from playing with their very expensive sound system and he responds with inappropriate anger. An adult is enraged and violent because his wife was on the phone and he was kept waiting for his meal. In both cases, perceptions were extremely distorted and control mechanisms meager. Much of the endless conflicts fueling angry confrontations between adults can be attributed to the persistent influence of distorted perceptions. When very poor controls are added to the distorted perceptions, the outcome may be violence.

It is important to understand the central role played by distorted perceptions in much of the behavioral mischief that occurs in the lives of children and adults. There is a great deal of concern among parents, educators, and society about the inappropriate expression of anger, and this has generated a wide variety of speculations about its cause and remedy. Unfortunately, many recommendations are made with little understanding of the nature of the thinking that motivates these maladaptive expressions of anger. Earlier in this chapter I pointed out that bad thoughts and the behavior these elicit cannot be punished away. These undesirable patterns will gradually be replaced by appropriate behavior only as children are helped to master developmental hurdles. As a consequence, anger becomes muted and the influence of distorted perceptions is diminished. Coercive efforts by parents intended to accomplish this are always counterproductive.

In contrast to the immature expression of anger, the appropriate expression of disapproval is a constructive response aimed at finding a solution to a real problem. Its goal is altruistic rather than self-serving. It is based on an accurate evaluation of the real issues. It is not contaminated by distorted perceptions. The gradual elimination of the influence of distorted perceptions is the crucial step up the developmental ladder towards a capacity for the mature expression of disapproval.

Question – Is there ever a place for a less mature expression of anger in parenting? I have been told that children need to learn to face and cope with this in the outside world, so they should learn to handle it in the home.

Parents have sometimes been told that they should express their angry feelings to their children more openly. This is supported by the explanation that these feelings can't be hidden and that their expression will help children learn to cope with anger. It is certainly true that parents don't have the ability to legislate their anger out of existence. But that does not mean that a freer expression of their anger with their kids makes good sense. The model of an angry parent who nevertheless has sufficient maturity to control and express his feelings more appropriately is far more constructive than one making no effort to do the same. Overt manifestations of anger are far more disturbing to children than more modulated responses, and tend to lend credence to their distorted perceptions.

Parents always have some control over the ways they channel their feelings towards their children. They should do what they often do in other parts of their lives. They should shift their responses away from immature expressions of anger and towards ones that are closer to the ideal, closer to the model that we hope our children will emulate. A parent's angry temper display in response to his child's temper display obviously represents an immature and very inappropriate expression of anger and is, unfortunately, a very common occurrence.

There is actually nothing our little children can do that is difficult or stressful to handle. Parents like to justify their angry outbursts, but it is hard to imagine any situation that anger would remedy. The introduction of anger always compounds problems. Anger invariably represents an immature response to not getting what was wanted. It may have had some survival value in primitive times, when our ancestors roamed the plains and a roar of anger may have scared away predators or allowed for more rapid flight. But it has no constructive use in modern times. Even in an emergency or an adversarial situation, when flight or fight may be essential for survival, anger interferes with the clear thinking that is the best defense in our present society.

An old saying points out the folly of anger at these times, "Getting angry at our enemies gives them power over us." The reduction of stress as well as anger in parenting requires acknowledging a simple but unequivocal bit of reality. Based on everything we know about young children, it is obvious that they will often not do what we want. If we can't learn to get along when we are not getting what we want from our kids, we should not be optimistic about helping them to achieve that same goal.

Children are continuously assimilating our values and using them as a map to guide them towards what will eventually be their worldview. Overt expressions of anger and acts of selfishness and cruelty that are elaborated by many parents present an ugly picture that their children will copy and make their own. Let's hope that parents realize the folly of exposing their children to that brand of feelings.

Perhaps the most significant thing we do in our lives is helping our kids to become well-functioning individuals. As this process unfolds, we have the opportunity to reassess our own lives and make growth-producing changes. Having a child is "the second time around." It rekindles many of the feelings from our own childhood. This second time around provides opportunities for parents to rework old problems and to find better solutions than the ones their parents were able to help them to achieve during their own childhood. Making this effort also pays off in significant dividends for our kids who are helped to do better during their first time around.

Points to Remember

Naughty Language

- Parents often overlook their children's needs to master and feel comfortable with their feelings and thoughts.

- The array of skills that children acquire to express feelings and thoughts will significantly define their personalities.

- The messages that parents communicate to their children, together with their own attitudes and styles of expression, will have a profound impact upon this emerging component of their children's lives.

Encouraging More Mature Methods of Expression

- The spectrum of ways in which children as well as adults express anger runs from the most primitive to the mature.

- Parents need to know what to expect at each age and to encourage continued progress.

- Children tend to emulate their parents' behavior, both good and bad.

Chapter 8

SUMMARY – THE DEVELOPMENT OF AUTONOMY

A little effort each day pays rich dividends

Dan has a friend with him for the afternoon. After about ten minutes of acceptable play, the other little boy comes to Sally crying because, "Dan won't let me play with any of his toys." Sally is disappointed in her son because she knows how important it will be for him to learn to socialize. She is aware of the importance of expressing her values and thoughts constructively, so she prevents the bit of irritation she feels from contaminating her demeanor. Instead of being angry and critical by telling him that he is a bad boy and that she is displeased with him, she expresses her feelings more helpfully. She says, "It's sometimes hard for you to share your things with your friends. Let's see if we can find something for the two of you to play together." Dan understands very well that his mother values cooperation and sharing. Her approach helps to unravel the distorted perceptions that feed his selfishness. This intervention is one tiny step that helps Dan know that sharing is being encouraged because it fosters reasonable and pleasant interplay with others. An angry, critical response would have sent a very different message, one that would confirm that the only reason to give up the desire for selfish gratification is the fear of the power of others.

Much later, after Dan has finally gone to sleep, Sally is able to reflect upon the day's events and can obtain sufficient distance to see more clearly the overall pattern that has been unfolding. Dan's personality is evolving right before her eyes and she is grateful to be able to play such a crucial role in the process. During his earliest months, bonds of love were forged and Dan became a human being who loved and needed love in return. In his second year, a new element emerged – his sense of being separate from others and the development of trust. Now another building block is being laid into place. He is becoming an autonomously functioning person who can exert his will and express feelings that he can claim as his own. Sally looks at him and thinks about what has already happened during so very few years. She smiles contentedly, knowing how well he is doing and eager for the next day and the delightful surprises it will bring.

PART SIX

**LEARNING TO BE A PERSON IN THE
OUTSIDE WORLD OF PEOPLE – ACQUIRING
A SOCIAL IDENTITY**

THREE YEARS TO FIVE YEARS

PART SIX

SECTION ONE

ACQUIRING A SOCIAL IDENTITY – NEW RULES – THE TASK AND ITS IMPORTANCE

Question – My child has made good developmental progress and he is now nearly four years old. He is a loving child who can handle separations and is learning to get along when he does not get his way. What is the next step for him to take?

Chapter 1

ENTRY INTO THE WORLD OUTSIDE THE HOME

The development of our children's personalities is continuously evolving. Each developmental step was accompanied by the acquisition of new skills. If satisfactory progress has been made, our children will be prepared to negotiate the next developmental hurdle. This will entail facing and coping with a dramatic shift that takes place in their lives at this time. Until now their world has revolved around their parents and their home. Within a very short time their lives will increasingly extend beyond the home into the outside world. They have already made many developmental strides that will help them to make that transition successfully. But there are new roles that they will need to assume, and new skills they will need to function smoothly in those roles.

New roles for Dan

If Dan, at three months of age, could have asked his parents, "Who am I?," he might have heard this reply, "You are our little baby learning to know that you are loved by us." At a year, if he asked the same question, his parents might have replied, "You are our little boy and we have a love for you that you can trust even during those moments that we are apart." At two-and-one-half, their response would be, "You are our little boy learning what it means to have a body, feelings, and thoughts that you can control. You are also adjusting to an external world that does not always give you what you want."

Dan is nearly four years old. Now the answer to the same question would be a bit more complicated. He is becoming aware of the complex social fabric in which he lives and has begun to ferret out his role. An endless array of new observations are being assimilated by Dan and used to mold the shape of his emerging personality. He has begun to compare himself to others, engendering feelings of competition and jealousy, longings to be admired, and fears of humiliation. Other elements of his world have gained his attention, bringing with them a new set of uncomfortable emotions. He is grappling with concepts such as illnesses, bodily injuries, disagreements and quarrels among loved ones, and the prospects of growing up. His time sense has moved from being set exclusively in the present to an awareness of the future.

All this and much more compel him to search for new answers to the question, "Who am I?" He is beginning to think about his social identity, with an emphasis on the variety of roles he will need to assume with increasing numbers of people. All of this is being influenced by his experiences with and observations of the people and events that make up his daily life, mainly his parents. The contour and shape of his personality will depend on this emotional interplay. Many modifications can and will occur, but its basic structure will have been set into place.

This process is evolving continuously, but usually passes unnoticed by the major participants. This is why the typical methods used by parents hoping to teach values to their kids and mold their personalities often fall short. They focus almost exclusively on what they want to inculcate into their kids and overlook the child's perceptions of them and their behavior and attitudes.

His parents' fears and aspirations, their unhappiness with themselves and their roles, their feelings about their relationship with each other, as well as their perceptions of Dan, some correct but many not, are all taken in and processed. The quality of his parents' commitment to each other, their capacity for kindness and honesty, and the quality of love they have for each other all become part of the equation. The sum total of these influences, communicated both directly and subtly, gradually scripts Dan's social identity.

I am not in any way negating the importance of communicating values to our children. I am pointing out the obvious. Young children will be most influenced by the tenor of the emotional messages that are transmitted by their parents, usually without their awareness. Understanding the importance of this process allows parents to be more adept at responding constructively.

A mother who said one thing but communicated another

Linda was seven years old but still had many fears and was not adapting well at school. She demanded that her mother accompany her when she went upstairs. She indicated her fear that "something scary might get her" if she was alone. In addition, she felt uneasy each morning when it was time to go to school. Her mother could not understand the basis of her daughter's fear since she had always encouraged her to "be assertive and independent." The message actually transmitted was not the one intended. Linda was able to tell me the following, "Ever since I was very little, I knew that my mother did not like it when I was alone. She always seemed nervous about it and liked to know where I was." Linda's mother later confirmed the validity of her daughter's impression. She recalled that when she was Linda's age she had similar fears, and admitted that she still "feels a bit queasy when she is by herself." The mother's own fears motivated her to encourage Linda to be independent, but she was not able to disguise the hidden message that had a far greater impact upon her daughter.

Points to Remember

- Between ages four and five, children must become prepared to adapt in the world outside the family.

- An array of skills is needed that can only be acquired with their parents' help.

PART SIX

SECTION TWO

UNDERSTANDING THE MEANING OF CHILDREN'S BEHAVIOR DURING THIS PERIOD

BOUNDARIES – LEARNING TO THING ABOUT OTHERS AND ABOUT WHAT OTHERS THINK OF US

To a large extent, patterns of behavior evident during this period are based upon how well the earlier developmental hurdles were successfully negotiated. Residual problems from these phases usually persist and affect current behavior. New issues enter into the equation and influence both the behavior and the special ways past themes are manifested. Learning and conforming to the expectations required by new social roles is not easily achieved and many adults continue to feel uncomfortable accepting the many requirements of the real world.

Question – Can you review the basic skills my child will need to learn in order to adjust to the variety of roles he will be expected to assume as he moves into the world outside our home?

We all tend to fall into the trap of assuming that others think as we do. This tendency completely dominates the lives of very young children. (I will use the word *boundary* to designate the capacity to be aware of and take into consideration the point of view of others.) Young children have no concept of the wide variety of boundaries existing between people. They will be severely disappointed if they count on others to read their minds and play the roles they would prefer. This is true for all of us. There will be many times when others in our lives, even the ones who are most dear to us, will not be thinking of us. There will be many times when they will exclude us from their lives, sometimes for moments, at other times for much longer. These are the boundaries that define human existence. Children need to find ways of accepting and integrating these truths into their everyday functioning. If they have mastered early developmental hurdles, by age four they will have already made considerable progress towards this goal.

Chapter 2

A REVIEW OF EARLIER BOUNDARIES

Each developmental hurdle presents children with new boundaries that must be faced, accepted, and mastered. During the earliest months of infancy it is unlikely that children have any awareness of the distinctions between themselves and others. They are gradually able to appreciate that there are others in their world, people who are in some way associated with their pleasure and pain. In the second phase they learn to accept their separateness from others and the many implications that accrue from this. Later in their second year they need to learn to cope with discrepancies between what they want and what they get. By age four they should be taking ownership of many facets of their lives, including their bodies, feelings, and thoughts. One by one, illusions of omnipotence are replaced by more accurate perceptions of the real world and their limited ability to have it conform to their fantasies of how things should be. Their worldview has been considerably expanded, but is still dominated by a sense of their parents being at its center and their needing fairly rapid access to their parents for their gratification and well-being.

Dan has mastered earlier boundaries and is beginning too learn about the newer boundaries to which he must conform as he moves into the world outside of his home. Within families there is always some flexibility about the expectations of boundary setting. That flexibility disappears in the outside world of social interaction where more rigid demands for conformity are imposed. Between ages three and five he will need to make considerable progress in accepting new boundaries as a normal part of life. Many of the expectations he had about his parents will not apply to teachers, schoolmates, and friends.

If parents have already helped their child to master the previous developmental hurdles, the transition will not be hard to manage. Parents should remind themselves of this important principle as the years fly by. Growing up for kids will be considerably easier if they have been helped to master early developmental hurdles. A recurrent theme with the parents of young children is their fear of adolescence. It is commonly perceived as a time when much of what is unfolding in their children's lives will be beyond their control. They are right and wrong. It is true that in our society there is very little that parents can effectively do to reign in a rebellious teenager. But they have no cause to be concerned if they have laid a secure foundation during the early stages. There is very little that parents need to do if their child has these basic building blocks and, sadly, very little they can do if the basics are lacking.

Points to Remember

- To adapt in the world outside of the home, children need to relinquish many of the early expectations they had for immediate gratification, intimacy, and stimulation.

Chapter 3

NEW BOUNDARIES – WHEN AND HOW

Question – I understand the concept of boundaries and their importance. Can you be more specific and provide information about what needs to be done in the home to prepare our child for what lies ahead?

Boundaries come in many forms, are an integral part of human interactions, and are often communicated by words. Children will need to learn the various implications that words can have and be able to respond flexibly and appropriately, depending upon their meaning. Comments from parents such as, "I'm tired now," or "I need to work," sends a message that differs dramatically from a slammed door signifying, "Get out of my life forever." The mature adult can accurately interpret, adjust, and respond properly to the whole spectrum of boundaries with skills and strengths that are absent in very young children. Early in life, closed doors or parents busy with other activities are viewed as hostile acts of rejection, independent of the actual circumstances or motivations of their parents. Children need to learn to more accurately interpret the meanings of the different types of boundaries and obtain the ability to adjust appropriately.

Many adults fail to achieve this and adapt poorly to the normal and necessary boundaries of everyday life. They expend endless hours attempting to batter down many of the boundaries that are an inevitable part of life to obtain some assurance that they will not be barred from the access they believe they need to others. They naturally fail in their efforts since this desire flies in the face of the realities of the human condition, leaving them feeling isolated and mistreated.

Boundaries come in many forms. I have found that once parents have been introduced to the concept, and the general principles of parenting that are applicable, they become adept at detecting and helping their children deal with boundaries. Guidelines for their mastery will be addressed, using as an illustration one of the most common manifestation of boundaries – the literal closing of doors.

Dan began this journey when he was much younger. One of the things his parent did, months before he began to struggle with separation fears, was to remove him from their room to a nearby room of his own. Even when he became mobile and might have come to their room at night, the door would be closed and they would come out to gently tuck him back into bed rather than allow him to come in with them. They were finding the right balance of gratification and frustration for him to progress.

As progress was made, additional doors could be closed. By the time he was two-and-one-half, his parents decided that he was ready to remain safely outside the bathroom when they were using it. Showering and bathing gradually became activities that his parents engaged in behind closed doors. In our society it is rarely necessary for children to shower or bathe with their parents. After toilet training, Dan was encouraged to take full responsibility for the endeavor. By age four he was competent to do this behind a closed door. His parents made it a rule to close the door when they were in their bedroom dressing or undressing or when they were in bed. If Dan wanted access to them at those times he was taught to knock and wait. By age three he was no longer permitted to romp around unclothed, and the same guideline regarding nudity was practiced by his parents.

The motivation for these changes was not shame or blame. There is nothing wrong with the human body or any of its functions, and we will rarely bar our kids from having access to knowledge about this subject or any other subject. The gradual closing of doors is not because any of this is "naughty." Entry into the outside world of people requires acceptance of the many boundaries necessary for successful functioning. Earlier in their lives it is very natural for kids to have a very close and intimate involvement with their parents and other family members. This is the appropriate way that love is elaborated and it serves to forge strong bonds and an inner sense of belonging.

The necessity for adjustments in this arrangement before entry into school is very straightforward. The favorable progression of development will be stalled if the link between physical access and emotional well-being persists into later childhood. This is a requirement for living in our society and is one more of the many tools and strengths that our children must develop to adapt successfully. The sooner these transitions can be negotiated the better. Long before a child reaches age twenty-one he will need to be able to get along without coming into his parents' bed or having his mommy accompany him when he does his doo doo.

These skills are especially important in our society, which puts a premium on autonomy, independence, and self-sufficiency. Although the requirements for more rapid mastery are greater in our culture, we provide less formalized avenues and guidelines for this to occur. In some societies the progression is formalized, and the steps leading to adult roles much more clearly demarcated. Life in our society is much more complex. Societal expectations are less clear, as are the steps leading to the acquisition of the skills required for effective adult functioning. The burden falls upon parents, who are well advised to think about the skills their child will need rather than allowing themselves to be guided by what others do or by their emotional whims.

Postponing this process serves only to make its successful resolution more difficult. By age five, a child will be entering into many arenas of living that require a higher level of social sophistication. In the classroom he will be literally submerged into a sea of boundaries that would have been beyond his capabilities a year or two earlier. He must accept that he does not have immediate access to his parents, the teacher, or the other kids. And he needs to be able to work when he might prefer to play. These accommodations cannot be put off forever. At some point our kid's free access to us must end and the doors must close. If this does not begin at age three, what age would be better, four, five, fifteen, twenty-one?

The best remedy for uncertainty about parenting is reliance upon the principles and guidelines formulated earlier. Good parenting begins by understanding the meaning of behavior and developmental goals. With this knowledge parents can function as catalysts in a process leading to the achievement of those goals. This is best done in accord with the rule of a little at a time, another key guideline. It entails balancing love and frustration so that gains are made as rapidly as possible without imposing burdens upon the children that are too much for them to manage.

Parents often suggest that the acquisition of the social skills needed for a successful transition into the outside world might be encouraged by putting their younger children into settings with other kids earlier in their lives. If this is done very gradually and monitored closely, it may certainly be useful. But it carries with it a danger that an extremely important principle of parenting may be ignored. There are a series of developmental hurdles that must be successfully negotiated. If children are exposed to new problems before earlier ones are mastered, the outcome may be unfavorable. Entry into a new social arena should never be at the expense of the mastery of earlier hurdles. During the first four years a sound foundation needs to be erected. This cannot occur successfully if parents are not the major participants in the process. If parents have done their job during the first four years, their children will be ready to take the next step.

Chapter 4

ACCEPTING THE CHANGING PACKAGING OF LOVE

Another Boundary

Question – Now that I understand the concept of boundaries, I have some questions about how we have tended to display affection with our child. Since he was very little, my son liked to be cuddled and held. He is now five and we have continued this practice. You have made it clear that love is the most essential ingredient of good parenting, but are there any guidelines about how it is shown?

My response to a parent asking how to supply a newborn with love would sound something like this: The more the better, this is not the time to worry about indulgence or spoiling. Infants thrive on attention given in the form of physical closeness. Cuddling, rocking, and other forms of soothing provide the stuff that forges strong bonds and these are the first building blocks of personality formation. My answer to the same question posed by a parent of a three- to four-year-old would be quite different: Children still thrive on love and the more the better guideline still holds. **But there are two facets of our love that must gradually change as our children progress, its packaging and timing.**

Before a child enters school, he must have the tools to cope with love that is not at his beck and call. In addition, the form of the love required must be modified. The pampering, cuddling, and soothing that infants crave and need should be gradually replaced by the elaboration of affection that will be more acceptable in civil society. Even hugs and kisses become problematic if they continue to be a requirement for emotional stability rather than a pleasant and acceptable manifestation of love. Remaining dependent upon demonstrations of affection, or even assurances of affection, is a harbinger of interpersonal problems and a great deal of unhappiness.

As we can see, the bottle is not the only source of pleasure from which children need to be weaned. Children need to know that they are loved and valued when hugs and kisses are not supplied on demand. Many more adults are addicted to reassurances that they are loved by hugs, kisses, or words than they are to drugs or alcohol. This may sound as if I am the grinch who wants to steal affection from children. The contrary is true. Love is the primary requirement of good parenting. The guideline that I am advocating for parents at each phase of development is the more love the better. But it must be packaged appropriately. Love must be combined with reason and wisdom. Otherwise it may be called love, but it is not love at all. For example, love motivated solely by the desire to give or receive pleasure usually falls into this category. It would be more appropriate to call it indulgence. So often the lament of parents whose brand of care has wrecked havoc with their child's life is, "But I loved him so much, everything I did was done for love." There is a significant difference between wise love and dumb love, but many parents neglect to make the distinction. Wise love leads to the development of a stable, content, and well-functioning person.

Boundaries everywhere

Dan had come bounding into his parents' bedroom with high hopes that his mother would be enthusiastic about allowing him to join her and read his favorite storybook to him. Dan liked to have his mother read to him and knew that she shared this pleasure. As he entered the room early Sunday morning he found his parents in bed talking to one another. Dan interrupted his parents' conversation asking, "Mommy, will you read to me?"

Even before Dan spoke, his mother had guessed what he wanted. She saw the book in Dan's hand and knew how much he enjoyed this activity. Reading was certainly an activity that she wanted to encourage. Sally also knew how important it was that Dan learned to accept boundaries. Dan was a secure, happy child and his parents had decided he was ready to have them gradually prod him onto higher rungs of the ladder of development. They were doing this by gently changing the packaging of their love to those that fostered the acceptance of boundaries. This entailed gradually weaning him from some of the less mature ways they had provided love in the past.

Sally responded to Dan by saying, "Dan I know that you like me to read to you and I think that is wonderful, but right now I'm speaking to Daddy. Please read by yourself for a few minutes until we are through. When we finish I will be able to read with you. Please close the door after you leave." Sally has combined reasonable decision making with love. She will continue to be calm and loving if Dan balks at her suggestion and she has to escort him out of the room. If this adjustment is difficult for him to negotiate, she might, in this instance, shorten the amount of time she keeps him waiting.

The next day, Dan found his dad leaning back in his favorite chair as he watched television. He remembered how much fun they had when they romped on the floor together and tickled each other. Prodded into excitement by thoughts about engaging in some boisterous frolicking fun, he took a leaping jump, landing onto his dad's lap. His father gave him a hug and, holding him on his lap, suggested they watch television together. Dan obliged for a few moments, but soon pursued his primary objective, more exciting fun. He began to tickle his father and giggle. His father also remembered the fun they had wrestling and playing the tickling game. Although he knew that there would always be room for some of that kind of wild play, it was time for him to encourage Dan to learn to handle its absence and enjoy the many more mature alternatives.

Dan was not a very willing partner in this well-intended endeavor, and continued to tickle and squirm, trying to elicit a playful response from his dad. It was not so easy to give up the wonderful baby pleasures that linked these games with feeling loved and valued. Dan's father quietly resisted and did not reciprocate the invitation to engage in this delightful and exciting game. He gave Dan another hug and said, "You're a big boy now. Let's sit and watch television. After the game is over we can read or play ball outside." His father is preparing him for the tasks that lay ahead. Very soon Dan will be entering regular school and needs to be able to sit and pay attention to activities that usually do not provide immediate pleasure and fun. His father was, therefore, resolute and willing to handle any additional protest that Dan might mount.

It was the evening of the next day and Dan had just finished his bath. A year earlier, his mother would have remained with him during the entire time. She helped him to wash, and the splashing and laughing together was glorious fun. During the past year she has gradually encouraged him to take charge of as much of the process as he could. At first she remained close by, giving him needed assistance, but now she often left him alone for a minute or two, and then came by to check. He had no problem drying and putting on the pajamas his mother left out for him. This evening, instead of putting on his pajamas, he darted out of the bathroom with nothing on at all.

When Dan was much younger, he often obtained considerable pleasure by running about in the nude. His mother would corral him, give him a hug, and carry him into his room to get dressed. Every part of this was enjoyable to Dan, and made him feel very loved and special. Sally has been discouraging this more babyish activity. She spotted him immediately and said, "I know how much fun it is for you to run around without clothing but you are a bigger boy now, let's go to your room so that you can get into your pajamas. We may have time to play a game before bedtime."

Dan's parents are aware that there are countless opportunities every day to nudge him gently forward on the path towards mature functioning. They try not to miss these opportunities for growth.

POINTS TO REMEMBER

- Children need their parents' continuous love; this never changes. It's the packaging of that love that needs to change.

- Children need to learn that they are loved during the many moments that they are apart from their parents.

- A confidence of being loved and valued that children can carry with them must replace the love that previously was derived by the immediacy of physical intimacy and verbal reassurance.

Chapter 5

BOUNDARIES, STRUCTURE, AND SELF-CONTROL

Question – I have noticed that when the kids get giggly and excited they find it harder to calm down and behave appropriately when the situation changes and better controls are necessary. How might I understand this and what can I do to encourage the acquisition of better skills?

Boundaries provide needed structure in the daily lives of children and make it easier for them to learn to control and channel their unruly feelings. The progress towards more mature self-control is slowed in children living in homes with inadequate boundaries and structure, and these kids often encounter problems in their transition to school.

Early in life children are at the mercy of their feelings. Tensions, stress, excitement, and frustration very quickly reach levels of intensity beyond the child's capacity to manage. These heightened feelings tend to disrupt clear thinking and interfere with functional behavior. Learning to control and channel unruly feelings are attributes essential for adaptation in school and many forms of age-appropriate play. High levels of tension and excitement impede the acquisition of these controls. In order to lower these levels parents need to gradually curtail activities that might inadvertently elevate tensions.

Activities that were completely appropriate at a younger age were often ones that were accompanied by high levels of excitement and pleasure. While these types of activities are enjoyed immensely, they don't create the frame of mind necessary in older kids for goal-directed thinking and planned behavior. There continues to be a place for these types of exciting outlets in later childhood and beyond. But if they are the order of the day rather than the exception, the resultant heightened tensions will impede the development of the types of skills essential for a successful entry into school. Even many well functioning adults find that it takes some time and considerable motivation to get back to hard work after a period of frivolous activities or in overly stimulating settings. The magnitude of this task is dramatically greater for young children. Every parent is familiar with the expression, "It's time to settle down now," and is aware that this is not easily or quickly accomplished.

Parents should aim at moderating tension levels in the home. Therefore as children move closer to school age, the gradual imposition of boundaries and structure into their daily lives is appropriate. There are many activities completely acceptable for younger children that, if continued into the fourth year, may impede the acquisition of skills necessary for school. These include most forms of wild play, tickling, wrestling, bathing together, excessive cuddling, nudity in the home, and other forms of over stimulation. I am not implying that there is anything wrong with these activities or that parents should ever be angry or punitive in response to them. I am pointing out a requirement for developmental progress, and suggesting that parents can be helpful by giving some thought to the activities they decide to encourage or discourage at each step in their children's development. Children still desperately need and thrive on our love, but the form in which we supply it needs to be modified to foster developmental progress.

Many parents go to great lengths to eliminate sugar or other ingredients from their child's diet because of their alleged link to disruptive behavior. They are overlooking an obvious cause of disruptive behavior in favor of those that have never been supported by research. Parents intuitively know that certain activities invite regression. Even the anticipation of a birthday or Christmas celebration may precipitate wildness and less age-appropriate behavior. Most parents have experienced some dismay when they have planned a special treat for their four-year-old, only to find it ruined when their child's initial excitement turns to crankiness, irritability, and more babyish forms of behavior.

The buildup of tension, especially the pleasurable variety, can quickly overwhelm the meager coping mechanisms of young children and then it is downhill all the way. As children mature they can acquire the tools needed to maintain their emotional equilibrium independent of their external environment. Neglecting to provide sufficient boundaries and structure may preclude the development of those essential tools.

Question – What types of behavior may indicate the need for firmer boundary setting?

Children living in homes with inadequate boundaries often remain easily distracted and find it hard to focus and apply themselves to tasks requiring concentration. Their behavior often emulates patterns more typical of kids a year or two their juniors. They don't have what it takes to be successful at five or six years of age when there is a premium on being able to sit quietly in class, accept instructions from the teacher, acquire reading skills, and learn to play cooperatively with their peers.

I have found that many children who have been labeled as hyperactive and needing medication proved to be quite capable of functioning adaptively when their parents imposed appropriate boundaries, thereby reducing the level of stimulation in the home. Parents often resist this easily implemented suggestion and protest that I am being prudish and old-fashioned. Others accuse me of wanting to interfere with their child's right to freely express his feelings or his right to have fun.

Obviously there is nothing wrong or bad about the activities that elevate tension and excitement. Eventually we want our children to be able to avail themselves of any appropriate form of pleasurable activity. But there is a time and place for all things. This is not the time for activities that create prolonged periods of elevated tension and feelings of excitement. The type of learning required for school is not easily acquired in this type of household. Between ages three and five is the time for kids to learn to adapt in a variety of social roles. Feelings kept in check by appropriate structure, predictability, and boundaries are a prerequisite for this to be achieved

Parents are sometimes uncomfortable about interfering with their children's freedom to express their feelings. They suggest that doing so may stifle their emerging individuality. Their argument has merit only if individuality is defined as the free elaboration of feelings and passions in a primitive infantile form, rather than each person's ability to make decisions and take actions based on his own mature reasoning.

Creative endeavors may require passion and considerable individual expression, but it is always a passion channeled by wisdom and the facility to discern lofty ideals. There is a prevailing myth these days that the free expression of feelings is a source of liberation and is associated with greater happiness. Actually, the unchecked elaboration of feeling leads to a great deal of unhappiness, poor functioning, and less real freedom. The often-heard comment, "If it feels good do it," is a formula for misery, our own as well as those left in our wake. The expression of feelings unmodified by reason is a slippery slope, leading to ever more primitive and immature forms of behavior. This is obviously not very adaptive. It doesn't even accomplish its primary aim, the enhancement of pleasure. And it certainly is not liberating. The infant, freely expressing his feelings, is completely in bondage to those feeling. It would be extremely disconcerting to be owned by another. It is no better to be owned by a need for a fix, or the power of our infantile feelings. Children, who have been helped to adjust to the demands of reality and are capable of modifying their feelings appropriately, will fare far better than those who continue to expect and need gratification of their whims and desires.

The word that creates the most problems for us in life is not one of the naughty expletives. It is a word more usually implied than verbalized by young children as they interact with their parents. That word is *should*. "I should get want I want; I should be allowed to do what I like; I should go first; I should be the most favored one; I should never fail;" the list of "shoulds" could go on and on. So few of us are entirely able to escape the contaminating influence of "should" thinking and be free to more consistently pursue goals based on reason and wisdom. The cherished fantasy that the achievement of what "should be" will be associated with any more than a fleeting high is illusory.

Dan had a thoroughly enjoyable evening. There were presents, surprises, and a merry time playing with his cousins. Their play included episodes of running wildly around the house. His parents interrupted this play many times when they observed that the children's level of excitement had got the best of them and they had become wild and out of control. It did not surprise them that it was difficult for Dan to settle down after the company left. Getting him to sleep would be a bit of an ordeal. He was still a little edgy and irritable the next day, a carryover of the excessive excitement from the night before. His parents understood this, so they were patient and avoided adding to the fires of his already heated emotions by responding angrily. Instead, they supplied more structure to his life by playing quiet games with him. This helped Dan to quickly regain his previous level of functioning. Many other children are not as fortunate. Their homes are devoid of the structure and boundary setting that kids this age need. The persistence of higher levels of tension in these overly stimulating settings tends to abet regressive trends and lead to persistent infantile patterns of behavior.

Points to Remember

- To adapt in school or other social arenas, children must learn to channel their feelings more maturely than they did earlier in life.

- This task is more difficult in homes that are overstimulating or in those that condone or even encourage wildness and other behaviors that escalate tension.

- Children need periods of fun, but also a home setting that provides appropriate structure and predictability.

PART SIX

SECTION THREE

GETTING THE JOB DONE

This section is divided into a number of chapters. Each describes one of the important developmental tasks children must negotiate as they progress towards higher levels of social adaptation.

CHAPTER 6

BECOMING LITTLE BOYS AND GIRLS – SEXUAL IDENTITY

Question – I have heard so much about the molding of children's sexual identity that I no longer know what to think; can you clarify the issue? What does sexual identity really mean?

Most kids at age four will give a simple answer to the following question, "What are you?" or "Who are you?" They will first give their name and next respond by saying, "I am a boy" or, "I am a girl." This conviction about who they are, that requires no supporting data and does not change, is their sexual identity. Gradually, an ever-enlarging web of attributes and attitudes are built on this core knowledge, but the core remains as solid as their sense of self that emerged earlier. Sexual identity is the conviction that we are male or female, combined with the whole spectrum of meanings that become attached to these designations.

Question – How is this knowing embedded into our children's minds?

Some experts say that this knowing may be influenced genetically. Genes and hormones certainly have far-reaching effects upon our lives, since they define our physical attributes, intellectual ability, and a variety of other inborn features. But they can't account for the variety of thoughts children carry in their minds about their gender, and the many special meanings that become linked to it, that gradually become elaborated into their sexual roles. This knowing is learned, but not taught. It is incorporated into the young child's developing mind by a process completely independent of any efforts by others to teach it. It is not learned as we might learn to read. The learning occurs very early and is significantly influenced by the perceptions, many of them distorted, that very young children have about themselves, their bodies, and their parents.

Question – When and how does this happen?

It is unlikely that children are able to observe and think about sexual differences before the age of two. Then gradually their worldview begins to include observations of their bodies and the bodies of others. By age three their bodies, its parts, and its functions have become an increasing focus of their attention and interest. Physical sensations that arise from various parts of their bodies have become a source of their interest. Their earliest words usually include those designating the parts of the body. Many things influence the thoughts that they are having about their bodies. These include observations and comparisons, messages transmitted by others, and the influence of distorted perceptions. It takes considerable training for even intelligent adults to be capable of making objective observations and drawing appropriate conclusions from them. Our thinking is contaminated by our emotional bias. Obviously this tendency is much more pronounced in very young children.

In order to appreciate the tenor of our children's observations that affect their image of themselves, we need to remain aware of the emotional issues that are dominating their lives during this early period in their development. They are struggling with a series of developmental hurdles and at the center of these are their parents. They are watching and thinking about their parents' attitudes, as well as their behavior. Their whole world is dominated by their parents who are continuously transmitting cues about what they think of themselves, and of others.

Our children's emerging identities as little girls or little boys don't need to be formally taught. It could never be taught as effectively and comprehensively as it is being lived out each day with their parents. This data, viewed through the distorting lens of their immature perceptions, mold the attitudes, attributes, and behavioral patterns that will become their sexual identity. There is nothing very complicated about this. Children learn about what it means to be man or a woman from watching how their parents relate to them and to each other. Genetic influences, especially those that determine hormonal and anatomical attributes, play an important part but they cannot account for the constellation of values, motivations, and attitudes that will shape their image of themselves as boys and girls who will become men and women.

Question – What is a favorable outcome?

There should be no ambiguity about what we mean by a favorable outcome in this facet of our children's lives. It includes contentment with their bodies and how they function, combined with the variety of attributes, values, and attitudes that will allow them to live successfully in their respective adult roles as men and women. These were described in the first chapter and have been alluded to repeatedly. Some of the characteristics more directly linked to this process are the capacity to love; a healthy self-esteem; and the ability to express compassion, kindness, respectfulness, honesty, commitment, usefulness, appreciation, and gratitude. It is important to note that most of what we mean by a favorable sexual identity consists of the characteristics that follow from the successful mastery of developmental hurdles. These attributes are ones that motivate a wide array of behaviors. They are only peripherally associated with the functioning of the sex organs.

Many parents have expressed concerns over their child's emerging sexuality. I have always responded with the same answer. I have never heard of, or encountered, an individual with a problem in the sexual arena of their lives that had anything to do with sex. Problems in this role, as well as any other, are always attributable to the attitudes and attributes that comprise character. In giving this answer I have not ignored actual physical problems manifested by some impairment of sexual functioning. Freed from the burdens of distorted perceptions, and armed with good values and mature personality attributes, these impairments don't erode the quality of life. In contrast, a person possessing the world's best functioning sex organs won't lead to a happy life without those values and character attributes.

Question – How can I achieve a favorable outcome?

The answer once again is simple; its implementation more difficult. If you want your children to acquire sound sexual identities, and by this I mean the capacity to function well in their respective roles as men and women, there is basically only one requirement that you must meet. This is to do the same in your own life.

We all know good fathers and mothers when we see them. If a little boy or little girl has good parents of both sexes who have helped him or her to master developmental hurdles, the outcome will be fine. No additional instruction is necessary, nor is it really possible.

Question – What about single-parent families, divorced parents, and other parental arrangements?

None of these arrangements is as ideal as a traditional two-parent family. There is an increasing amount of data that confirms this. Certainly there are many kids from divorced and nontraditional families who do fine and others from stable two-parent families who do poorly. There are multitudes of factors that come into play. This does not negate the conclusion that nontraditional family arrangements present a variety of additional impediments to a favorable outcome. Often, advocates for one alternative or another suggest that the outcome will depend upon the quality of care independent of the actual composition of parents. It is certainly true that quality of care is vital, and if provided it will stack the cards in favor of a better outcome. But this overlooks another important factor in the equation – the child's perspective as this process unfolds.

When I addressed divorce I emphasized its impact upon the children's perceptions and the effects that this is likely to have on their unfolding development. It is important that we understand parental arrangements from the child's point of view, one that is extremely influenced by the distorting lens of their immaturity. A little boy or girl without a father or mother is making observations and often drawing many very inaccurate conclusions about the implications of this arrangement, in addition to any of the emotional or verbal messages communicated by the parents that also play a crucial role. What is the little girl to think when she discovers that she has no father to love her, or that her father was incapable of a committed involvement with her mother? The ramifications and problems that accrue from each of these alternative arrangements could be addressed at length. I do not believe that there is any need to do this. The common sense of parents should suffice if they have an open mind. If they do not, because of their political or emotional agenda, supporting data will serve no purpose.

This book is written from the developmental perspective of children. Using that framework, the ideal setting is the traditional two-parent family. I am not overlooking the real world and the many situations that may preclude making the most favorable choices for our children. And I am certainly not suggesting blame for those choices. My purpose is solely to provide information that can help parents to understand children and, as much as possible, gear their parenting accordingly.

Sex Education

Question – Many of my friends have encouraged us to talk to our preschooler about sex. What should I say?

There are many important things happening during the first five years that will influence our children's sexual identity. Discussions about sexual matters are not some of these. It is extremely unusual for children to introduce this issue during the first five years. I would not have included it in a book about the first years of life if questions about the need for sex education were not asked so frequently by parents of preschool-age kids.

Many adolescents and adults elaborate their sexual impulses irresponsibly. It is extremely unlikely that the main reason for this is ever the lack of knowledge or education about sex. Information about sex or the lack of adequate information rarely has anything to do with immature sexual behavior. The irresponsible sexual behavior of teenagers is always a symptom of a more basic problem. I have never encountered nor heard about anyone who got into trouble because they were not provided with enough information about sex. In fact, I would venture the guess that in our present society, the likelihood of anyone reaching age twelve and not yet having all the facts he needs is fairly remote. I only wish that by that time kids would have acquired comparably accurate data about the many other types of information they will need as adults, starting with reading, writing, and arithmetic.

Inappropriate sexual behavior is due to immaturity, not to a lack of enough information. The underlying principle that applies, once again, is very clear. If parents are concerned about later sexual standards, attitudes, and behavior, they should diligently attend to the developmental process that unfolds early and leads to personality strengths and character. If they have neglected this task, all the best sexual information in the world won't save the day. And if children are helped to master the sequence of developmental hurdles, they will function reasonably and obtain whatever information is needed, even if their parents never mention one word of this subject to them as they are growing up.

There is a multiplicity of ways that parents communicate appropriate or inappropriate sexual roles to their children as their development unfolds. Their own capacity for commitment, and the elaboration of altruistic love, kindness, understanding, and compassion are just a few. We need to be reminded that the final outcome hinges upon the quality of the person rather than on the hows and dos of the sexual organs. Ultimately it is the combination of values and the levels of maturity that will play the central role.

There has been considerable emphasis on the use of information about sex, drugs, and other matters of concern as a vehicle to steer vulnerable youths towards more responsible behavior. In an effort to do something, educators exaggerate the power of information to change deeper rooted personality tendencies. Others exaggerate the possible deleterious effects of sexual education. Both groups are in error.

It would be very nice if it were that easy to alter styles of behavior. If information could so easily modify human nature, the world might quickly be transformed into a place where peace, harmony, and reason would prevail. Child rearing would be very simple. Parents would only be required to give the proper information at the right times and their kids would turn out fine.

This flies in the face of our daily experience. Distorted perceptions and immature coping mechanisms fuel inappropriate behavior in children and, if these are not modified, will continue to do so when the children reach adulthood. Everyone knows that violence, war, and drugs make no sense, but this knowledge rarely deters repeated manifestations of these types of human folly. Human nature does not just happen. It is forged during the early years of development. Any hope to influence our own children, or society at large, rests upon the quality of our parenting, especially during the first five years.

Knowledge has wrought wonderful advances to our lives. It has helped us to cure diseases, design computers, and send men into space. The higher standards of living we have achieved based upon our greater productivity can be attributed to knowledge and reason. There is a brand of knowledge that can also be a vital tool in helping us to raise our children with confidence. This is the body of knowledge that can help parents successfully address their children's early developmental problems. Trying to use education later, in the hope of reversing a poor job done earlier, is rarely helpful. We can improve the design of a computer program at any time, but we cannot significantly change the design of a human personality once the early wiring is in place. Some gains can always be made, but they are difficult to accomplish and usually quite meager in their scope. Parents, educators, and others often tend to focus on education as an approach to children's problems. Doing this is much easier than confronting the much more complicated emotional factors underlying irresponsible behavior in all spheres of human functioning, including sexual behavior.

All children need to learn how the sex organs work. In our present society, they will find out. They will learn the facts, even if they are not lucky enough to have parents who provide the information or attend sex education classes in school. It will be their level of maturity, however, and not education that will mainly influence their thinking and behavior later in life. When parents ask, "What can I do to help my children to express their sexuality appropriately later in life?" The answer is simple. "Help them to be mature, stable, well-adjusted adults. The most important work to accomplish that occurs during the first five years of life.

TALKING TO OUR CHILDREN

Question – I am still unclear about what I should actually say to my pre-school-age children about sexual matters? What do I say if they bring up the topic? Are there general principles regarding communication with kids that you can address?

The most important lessons parents teach their children about the expression of sexual feelings, as well as their attitudes about sex and the roles they will adopt, are imparted indirectly. This is done by the examples of maturity presented by the parents and the multitude of other parent-child interactions that influence their emerging personality. During the first five years of life it is hard to imagine a circumstance requiring the introduction of the topic by a parent, except in response to an inquiry from the child or some other sexually implicit incident involving the child. I have found this to be extremely unusual. The following are some useful principles that apply to all communication with young children and would be applicable for those rare times that the topic of sex needs to be addressed.

Principles of good communication with children

Good communication must be based on an understanding of the perceptions and thoughts of the child. Most of us get this reversed. There is a flawed but prevailing notion that good parents are ones who tell their kids what they think. But so often what we think does not coincide with our child's needs. Good communication must begin with some understanding of the mind that will receive and interpret our words. In addition, the tone and attitude and other emotional messages we transmit as we speak are central to the outcome. Words that are not accompanied by a tone of acceptance and love are unlikely to be heard by little children who are extremely vulnerable to the nuances of our emotional status. Too often parents are diverted from this path because of their own preconceived ideas of what their children need to know.

When parents are in doubt about what they should say to young children it is nearly always best to wait, listen, think, and ask questions rather than jump to conclusions and blurt out words.

Dan's mother described her initial feelings of anxiety and confusion when Dan, age four, announced, "I know where human beings come from." Sally's thoughts ran rapidly through her mind. "He is only four and it's beginning. What has he heard and from whom? Does he need some explanation of the facts of life? So soon!" What would she say? She had heard that it is important for parents to talk to their children and impart accurate information about sex, and she was tempted to launch into this topic. But she had the presence of mind to slow down long enough to catch her breath and ask, "Oh, tell me about it Dan; where do human beings come from?" Dan looked up at his mother, beamed happily, and said, "You plant human beans; that's where human beings come from."

The moral of this story is simple. We all have a variety of preconceived notions about what we believe our loved ones need from us. These should not be allowed to divert us from our primary task of helping our children with the issues that are on their minds. These are the ones with which they are struggling and need help. We cannot do this unless we free ourselves long enough from our own cherished beliefs about what we believe they need so that we can find out what they actually think and need. When we are not certain about what a loved one is thinking, and this is nearly always the case, it is time for further listening and asking few questions rather than initiating a knee-jerk intervention

The simple inquiry, "Where do babies come from?" can reflect a variety of issues. It may represent a child's concern that his mother will disappear into a strange place called a hospital, like the mother of the kid down the street. Or it may be elicited by concerns about the birth of a competitor who might strip him of his coveted role as sole possessor of his parents' attention. Since we don't know, it behooves us to find out. In response to a direct inquiry about the origins of babies, we might say, "Oh, you have been thinking about where babies come from. Good, tell me some more. What have you heard? What do you think?" Our child may mumble something unintelligible and quickly turn his attention to another pursuit. We can confidently let the issue drop with assurance that the door for good communication has been opened, and there will be ample opportunities to pursue this topic again in the future. Sometimes listening and asking a few questions will clarify the special issue that prompted the question, and allow us to formulate a reply that dovetails with our child's real concerns.

This type of approach also conveys our willingness to comfortably listen and accept our children's feelings and thoughts, whatever they reveal. **Acceptance and understanding are the foundations of good communication.** Elaborations of our own feelings, concerns, or beliefs are not. Listening and understanding during this early period lays the framework for good communication. This will serve us well in the future, providing a channel for the exchange of important information during subsequent stages of development.

An important goal of good communication with children is the correction of distorted and flawed perceptions. A setting in which our children know that they will be heard rather than lectured makes it easier for them to share their thoughts with us. Armed with this data we are much better equipped to respond helpfully.

A time will come when it may be appropriate to provide our children with actual information about sexuality. This rarely occurs before the age of five. If we are listening, our kids will nearly always let us know when this time has arrived. Another important guideline is that this information, as well as most other important issues, can't be broached all at one time. It must be elaborated piecemeal, a little at a time, at a rate and in a manner commensurate with our child's capacity to assimilate it. The most important part of this process will generally entail filling in gaps and the correction of distorted perceptions rather than a litany of facts.

When Dan was four he wanted to know if a neighbor's large tummy really meant that there was a baby inside. Three years later, he needed help with the problem of how the baby got out. Only much later was he interested and ready to tackle the question of how the baby got started and the role of the parents. Information given when children are not ready may be misused or discarded.

During the first five years of life many things are unfolding that will have a direct impact upon children's later expression of their sexuality.

While it is important to listen carefully and respond appropriately to children's rare questions and concerns about sex, this type of information is probably the least significant of the various factors that will influence this part of their personalities. The most important will be those that help to forge a mature personality. If good progress is made, their judgment will be sound, their controls adequate, their self-esteem stable, and they will have the capacity for loving relationships with others.

Sexual Behavior – Its Meaning and Management

Question – What should I think and do about actual manifestations of sexuality in this age category? How should I respond to the more common varieties of inappropriate activities and play? One that has repeatedly come to my attention is "doctor play," but there are many others.

The general approach combines a calm, loving demeanor with a firm delineation of appropriate boundaries. Parents must be reminded that very young children have no understanding of the distinction between appropriate and inappropriate behavior. As they master developmental hurdles and acquire an array of new skills they need to learn the expectations of society. The assimilation of this is essential for them to make the transition from baby status to the more complicated roles they will soon be required to assume.

When Dan was much younger, he loved to dash around the house in the nude after being bathed, enjoying the attention and hugs he received. Dan was three-and-one-half and it was a very hot summer afternoon. Dan was wearing only bottoms that he decided to remove. His mother spotted him and calmly imposed an age-appropriate boundary by saying, "Dan I know that it's fun to run around without any clothing. You are too big now for that, let's go to your room and get you dressed."

Dan is now age five and watching television with his mother. She is aware that his hand is inside his pants and he is openly masturbating, something she recalls happening several times before when other people were present. She is accepting and noncritical of his feelings, but is also aware of her responsibility to help him learn to channel these feelings appropriately. In a gentle tone she says, "Dan, I know that all boys like to touch their penises because it feels good. But you're getting to be a big boy now and will be starting school. That's something you can do in private, in your own room."

It was a rainy afternoon and Dan was playing in his room with a friend he met in kindergarten. His mother had not heard anything from them for a number of minutes and decided to check to see what they were doing. Upon opening the door she discovered that they were playing doctor, and were partially unclothed. Pleasantly she commented, "I know that kids are curious about their bodies. If there is ever anything that you want to know we can talk or read about it. But we will need to find some other kind of play for the two of you."

Sally is eager for Dan to acquire any information that he has the mental skills to assimilate. Although she knows that it is very common for kids at this age to be curious about their bodies and to play "show me" games, she is aware that this is not the best arena in which to acquire that knowledge. These types of activities are a problem only if they occur repeatedly. They tend to be overly stimulating and heighten tensions and feelings at a time in children's lives when there is a premium placed on the ability to sit still and concentrate for longer periods of time. Sally is gently encouraging Dan to favor play activities that will help him develop those skills. Without being critical she is discouraging ones that may impede that progress.

Question – What needs to be done if sexual play persists in spite of our efforts to gently discourage this form of behavior, or if it more closely emulates adult manifestations of sexuality?

I have nearly always found that children's overt display of sexual behavior could be traced to an overstimulating home setting. In households devoid of boundaries, children often experience excessive excitation, feelings run high, and it is more difficult for them to channel their behavior appropriately. The guidelines regarding boundaries, spelled out previously, are applicable. Nudity and other forms of overstimulating behavior should be discouraged. It should be obvious that children should never be exposed to the sexual behavior of adults. Parents need to think carefully about how their young children may be affected by the variety of ways that they display their affection to one another. It is important for children to see manifestations of their parents' love, but it is not very constructive for them to witness actual sexual contacts or other behavior that may be overstimulating.

Points to Remember

Becoming Little Boys and Girls – Sexual Identity

- Sexual identity is complex and includes the multiplicity of attributes, motivations, and behavioral patterns that make up an individual's personality.

- Two requirements will help ensure success: the satisfactory negotiation of the developmental issues previously addressed, and parents who themselves embody those attributes.

- Children will function well in their respective roles as men and woman if their mothers and fathers have been appropriate models.

- We all know good fathers and mothers when we see them: If a little boy or little girl has good parents of both sexes who have helped him or her to master developmental hurdles, the outcome will be successful.

Sex Education – Talking to Our Children

- Listening and understanding in an atmosphere of acceptance and love are the essential ingredients of good communication.

Chapter 7

RESPONSIBILITIES – NEW ROLES TO LEARN

Question – I realize how important it is for children approaching school age to be able to apply themselves to tasks that may be difficult or unpleasant for them. I have been told that they will become more adept at this if we ask them to do chores and give them other responsibilities around the house. What do you think?

All parents want their children to grow up to be responsible adults. Adults who are responsible display a number of very desirable personality characteristics. They are well disciplined, able to cooperate with others, and are motivated to fulfill commitments. Parents often assume that insisting that their children take on responsibilities will give them a head start in the achievement of these goals. If it were this easy, there would be few irresponsible adults in the world. Parents and many educators have it backwards. Responsible adults are ones whose parents have helped them to have solid, stable personality characteristics. They have mastered early developmental hurdles. Children who have these building blocks in place will accept and profit from assuming increasing responsibilities as they advance in age. The efforts by parents to paste responsibility on a child without this stable core are never entirely successful.

There is a danger in an early emphasis on doing chores to teach responsibility. In their eagerness for their children to be responsible, parents may embark upon campaigns that impede the acquisition of the skills they hoped to achieve. Parents are bigger, stronger, and much smarter than their three- to five-year-olds. They have the power to coerce their helpless little kids to comply with their expectations. This may seem to reap awards if the aim is superficial compliance, but it overlooks the developmental process unfolding within the children. The goal of parenting is to influence the development of mature values. This is seldom achieved by coercion.

Adherence to parental expectations based mainly upon coercion usually persists only as long as parents have the external power to enforce it. Getting kids to go through the right motions does not mold good character. I am not implying that it is inappropriate for parents to do whatever they can to encourage their children even at this early age to assume responsibilities. But they must realize that there is another goal that takes precedence.

Question – I understand the link between the mastery of developmental hurdles and our long-term goals. Is there, in addition, a place for the introduction of responsibilities in the home and how might this be best introduced?

During this period of development there are a number of ways that parents can help their kids to appreciate the importance of responsible behavior. First, they should never underestimate the impact that their own modeling of this trait will have upon young minds. Children's most effective learning occurs by incorporating the attributes and attitudes of their parents. This nearly always far outweighs in importance the words parents mouth or the demands they make.

Parents also need to show how highly they value manifestations of responsible behavior. Between ages three and five, this is best accomplished by placing their expectations for responsible behavior in the category of "desirable" rather than "necessary." This means that parents simply indicate the desirable behavior and praise successes.

The parents' goal is to encourage responsible behavior and at the same time avoid linking it to a struggle of wills between parents and child.

This approach was addressed fully in the chapter on discipline. As children move up the developmental ladder it is reasonable for parents to gradually increase their expectations. This should proceed in accordance with the rule of a little at a time. Parents are reminded that most children place all activities into two categories, those done to please others, called *work*, and those done to please themselves, called *play*. Work, which unhappily soon includes school lessons as well as chores, is resisted or done with limited motivation since children assume that the efforts required are to please others at the expense of their own pleasure. Many children carry this perception into adulthood and are never able to obtain fulfillment from work. Tugs-of-war over chores reinforce the belief that adherence to the expectations of parents is at the expense of their own desires.

We are after bigger game than rote compliance, especially when it is motivated by fear. We will not be able to continue to stand behind our children as they grow older, using our will to ensure that they act responsibly. At some point they will need to be self-motivated. This requires that they have learned that the reason to act responsibly and to cooperate with others is its own reward and that those individuals who have incorporated these values live more fulfilling, happier lives. This is less likely to occur if the emphasis in a family is on power and control rather than on cooperation, compromise, and harmony. The picture of the surly adolescent begrudgingly going through the motions of compliance paints a good picture of how this is played out during later years. There will come a time when parents might constructively require that their kids take on certain responsibilities. Between the ages of three and five is not yet that time. I am not suggesting that there are not many times that behavior will fall into the category of "necessary" and that parents will enforce their expectations, but chores and duties are not part of that list at this stage.

There is something else of importance that we are beginning to teach our children by the parenting techniques and model we are presenting to them: Helping others and gratitude for their help can be a meaningful and potentially satisfying part their lives. There are so many times each day when parents are compelled by reality to exercise control over their children's behavior. Since our goal is to help our kids appreciate more altruistic motivations, it is best during this period that the issues of chores and helping others remain apart from that struggle. A case can be made that the lives lived best are those motivated by an authentic interest in helping others.

Parents have no confidence in this. They are skeptical that their children can learn to be motivated by reason and love. They believe that in the internal struggle between actions based on getting their way and those motivated by a desire to cooperate, the power of greed and selfishness will always be the winner. They are entirely wrong and have based their assumption on observations of a world in which most of us rarely saw or were helped to learn another way. We are hoping that our children can reach a higher rung on the developmental ladder, one on which responsible behavior becomes motivated by the fulfillment derived from cooperation rather than through the pursuit of rewards or avoidance of punishment. The use of power to demand compliance is not compatible with the achievement of this goal.

Points to Remember

- A sense of responsibility resonates in and will be assimilated by children who have mastered the early developmental hurdles.

- A sense of responsibility can't be pasted on to children devoid of this foundation since they will have acquired the array of personality skills and strengths needed for this to happen.

- Parents must not be diverted from their primary mission by a desire for rapid results.

- Parents should encourage their children to take on responsibilities during the first five years, without creating the conflicts and tugs-of-war that run counter to their primary mission.

Chapter 8

THE MANAGEMENT OF FIGHTING AND WILD PLAY

Even kids this age who are making good progress will revert to wild and out-of-control play when unsupervised with siblings or friends. If this trend persists they will encounter problems in school and other arenas that demand better self-control.

Question – My little ones seem to love bickering, fighting, and wild play. I have found that there is little I can do to deter these activities. Do you have any suggestions?

Here come the judge

Bickering, fighting, and wild play between brothers and sisters is often one of the categories of their children's behavior that parents find most exasperating. We long for a bit of relief from the pressures of life, and hope that sanctuary can be found in our homes. Our fantasies of a place of peace, harmony, and love are fractured, and it is as if our own flesh and blood are conspiring against us when our homes seem like continual battlegrounds.

Interventions at these times are especially difficult, as parents find themselves torn by a variety of conflicting motivations. Being fair, punishing, teaching a lesson, and often just ending the turmoil are a few of these. Most parents would agree that this is generally a time of high stress. The feelings that come to the surface at these times interfere with the application of one of the basic principles of parenting, mentioned repeatedly, the rule of comfort. We do well when we feel comfortable and understand the task at hand

Understanding what can and cannot be done

An appreciation of what we can accomplish requires understanding and accepting what we can't accomplish. We are rarely able, with our children or in life, to achieve our fondest fantasies of making others conform to our expectations. Attempts to do this fly in the face of reality and create a tremendous amount of mischief for us and for others. When our children's passions are running high and they have become wild, parents may be frustrated and disappointed if they are unable to accept their children's limitations and their ability to influence their children's behavior.

What parents can't do

Parents who attempt to "get the facts" so that they will be fair, nearly always encounter a dead end. This can't be done. Each child's point of view is based on his emotional hurt. Any hope that an attempt to be fair will quell emotions and reestablish harmony is an illusion, as is the expectation that it is possible to find out what actually happened in the middle of the kitchen at 5:00 P.M.

Helping their kids to understand the inappropriateness of their altercations during these episodes also falls into the category of "can't be done." Sadly, in this, children are not dissimilar from most adults, often including our world leaders.

Nor is there any action that parents can take to please the participants. Each child wants to be the sole winner and during these heated moments would emphatically declare that the only acceptable compromise is the summary execution of the other.

There is a delightful story, *I'll Fix Anthony* by Judith Viorst, in which Alexander is complaining about his older brother Anthony:

> Mother says, deep down in his heart Anthony loves you. Anthony says, deep down in his heart he thinks I stink. Mother says, deep, deep down in his heart where he doesn't even know it Anthony loves me. Anthony says, deep, deep down in his heart he still thinks I stink.

Deep, deep, deep, deep down inside of warring kids they may have some benign feelings. If they are there, they are sure hard to find in the midst of turmoil.

Parents often think that they can use punishments, including spanking, time outs, and other penalties to deter this type of behavior. This gives parents the satisfaction of believing that they are "doing something," but it rarely helps with the real problem, the mastery of developmental hurdles. An angry child who is sure that he has been wronged is not very likely to learn to be more cooperative and flexible by being punished. Parents who assume that the hurt they inflict upon their children will help them learn a useful lesson and motivate them to be more reasonable might ponder what they might be thinking if they were similarly treated. Most children have told me that their prevailing thoughts are of revenge. And it is just a matter of time until they are big enough and smart enough to begin implementing their fantasies.

What parents can do – Making an accurate assessment

Take a deep breath, step back, observe, and be willing to think. All good parenting strategies should begin with some objective assessment of the child's current level of functioning and the meaning of the behavior that is being addressed. Children are on emotional roller coasters. Few, if any, children in this age category can play with others constructively for more than brief periods without parental supervision and frequent interventions to keep them on track. This is par for the course.

A downward swing in this capacity with a marked increase in wild, out-of-control behavior requires that parents monitor their child more closely. If more persistent backsliding becomes evident, it is usually not difficult to spot the cause. Often this is a new problem the child is facing, or an additional stress encountered in his life. A parent returning to work, marital problems, depression in a parent, or parents who have become less attentive for other reasons are a few of the situations that may elevate emotional turmoil and account for increased fighting and other forms of disruptive behavior. These and other issues that have tipped their child's emotions in the direction of more immature patterns need to be detected and addressed. Failure to attend to this may convert a transient problem into one that is permanent.

Sam was unmerciful in his attacks on his little brother. He teased him, ignored him, took away his playthings, and would push him to the ground whenever his parents were not watching. Sam's parents were having marital problems. His mother was unhappy and had become much less available to Sam. This was extremely disturbing to Sam since it represented a dramatic shift in her responsiveness. He had been the apple of her eye, and now it was as if she did not even see him. The discrepancy between the love and attention he had received and the closed emotional doors between them now were too much for Sam to handle and he felt excluded and mistreated. He was very angry but tried very hard to bottle this up when he was with this mother. Instead, his anger was aimed at his little brother. Sam's power to make his brother miserable provided a bit of compensation for his own helplessness and misery.

Question – I do appreciate the importance of understanding the meaning of my child's behavior before intervening. But these are situations that ultimately require intervention. Do you have any suggestions? How might I intervene when the kids are at one another?

Being a good traffic officer rather than judge, jury, and executioner

When children are wild or fighting, parents may be tempted to act as judge, jury, and executioner. These interventions, at best, accomplish very little and often escalate the turmoil. Parents would do better if they emulated a good traffic officer. Traffic, if left to the whims of individuals, may bog down to a standstill and need a traffic officer to get the flow moving more smoothly. Children require similar intervention when they have lost their ability to get back to appropriate functioning on their own.

Question – I am sometimes confused about when to intervene and when to let them handle it on their own. Are there any guidelines that I can use?

A traffic officer who decides to act each time there is a slight deviation from ideal standards will quickly become part of the problem. Often a bit of wildness and some shouting and pushing will be short lived, and the kids will be able to get back to reasonable play without any parental intervention. Knowing when and how to avoid confrontations is as important as the skills to handle them properly when this is necessary.

A good peace officer knows his area and the people in it. This familiarity helps him to use better judgment in the discharge of his duties. Parents have been slipshod if they are not well aware of their children's capacities and use this insight when interventions are needed. They need to know how their children operate, what it takes to light their fuses, how they react when they lose their emotional balance, and their capacities to regain it on their own.

The general guideline is to provide external structure and control when it is clear that the kids are beyond the point of being able to pull it together without our help.

For example, older and more mature kids might be permitted to flounder on their own for a bit longer than ones less equipped to cope without external help.

Sally was feeling gratified that Dan and his younger brother had been playing so cooperatively with each other when the volume of noise coming from their play area suddenly increased. Sally heard the noise and what sounded like the beginning of a disruptive altercation. She was tempted to intervene but held back a bit longer and listened. Although the noise coming from them was ominous, they were not really out of control. Sally was aware that Dan had been making good strides towards cooperative play, so she decided to wait. This decision was rewarded since the noise level gradually diminished in volume and the play resumed. When Dan was a bit younger, she had to interrupt their bickering or teasing quickly or it would rapidly deteriorate. Sally understands that her main goal is to help her children acquire the skills needed for smooth functioning, not merely to prevent bedlam.

The bearing of a good peace officer

Good peace officers have a certain bearing – friendly, relaxed, even caring, but also strong with clear expectations. We tend to lose respect for peace officers if they are confused or show signs of anger or loss of control. A good parent, like a good peace officer, sets an example of behavior and bearing that others can emulate. In the world of adults, there are times when even exceptionally competent peace officers may be unable to maintain this ideal, for example, when they are in real danger of bodily harm. But there is no reason that this standard cannot be consistently achieved in our own homes, when our focus is on our very small, helpless children desperately dependent on our continuing good will. Can there be any justification for a parent threatening or coming down like a ton of bricks on a child who is only two-and-a-half-feet tall? How would we feel in a similar encounter with a police officer?

Fights and bickering occur because little kids are at the mercy of their feelings and under the influence of distorted perceptions. Hurt feelings lead to anger and a desire for revenge. How can we help our children to be less vulnerable to distorted perceptions if we continue to be propelled into action by our own?

Keeping the peace – getting the job done

Question – I understand the importance of the model I present to my kids and can better appreciate my role. Can you outline an actual parenting technique?

When war breaks out between kids there is usually just one thing parents can do constructively – **keep the peace.** When feelings are running this high in children of this age the parents' efforts should be aimed at only one goal, disentangling the warring participants as quickly as possible. Understanding this simple truth transforms seemingly difficult situations into simple ones.

The volumes of the shrieks are loud enough to be heard by Sally, who is working in the garden. After listening for a few moments, she realizes that the children's behavior has become out of control, and her intervention is necessary. She quickly discovers that Dan is miffed because his younger brother is using one of his new toys. He tried to take it back, and soon they were pushing at each other. The younger brother was crying and Dan was screaming as he continued his attempt to dislodge the coveted toy from his brother's grasp.

Like a good traffic officer trying to get the traffic flowing smoothly, Sally quickly but calmly separated the combatants and got them back on the path to more reasonable play. She does this without reprimanding either one. She decided that it would be reasonable to take possession of the contested toy, and she said, "I know that you are both angry but there will be no fighting. Let's find something else for each of you to do." She makes no attempt to designate blame or implement some form of discipline, knowing that at this point the effort would be completely useless. If they are reluctant to disengage, each demanding a pound of flesh as compensation for perceived hurts, she will remain firm. She is prepared for their typical responses, each claiming with conviction, "It's his fault, and he started it." She knows the futility of responding to any of these noises. Sally understands her one goal, **to end the fighting and help them to reestablish their emotional balance.**

Dan calms down more quickly than his younger brother and is able to get involved in another activity. The younger child continues to cry. He is barely three years old, so Sally elects to make no comment to him about the preceding event or his present state. Instead she uses substitution and distraction, and encourages him to become involved in a different activity in another room.

Ten minutes later, Dan joins his mother in the kitchen and complains angrily about how his little brother always takes his things. Sally listens patiently and then helps him to feel less uncomfortable about his feelings saying, "Dan, I know you get angry when your little brother uses your things without your permission. He certainly should not do that, but it will probably continue to happen until he becomes a bit older. Let's see if we can think of what you might do next time if something like this happens so that it won't upset you so much."

Points to Remember

- Parents often find wild and disruptive play and behavior difficult to manage, and in their attempts to intervene may inadvertently be brought down to their children's level.

- Parents must do what they often are able to do successfully in other taxing arenas of their lives: think reasonably and remain calm.

- Sometimes there is no alternative to coercive parental intervention, but parents need to remember that the model they present during these episodes will be assimilated into their child's emerging personality.

Chapter 9

GETTING READY IN THE MORNING – ADAPTING TO SCHEDULES

The concept of time and the need to adhere to schedules have little meaning during the first years of children's lives. During most of this period, responsibility for appointments and other time considerations rest nearly exclusively upon the parents. This changes as children come closer to their entry into school, when this burden must be increasingly shifted to them.

Question – Do you have any suggestions about getting the kids ready to leave the house? I have always found that this is a terrible time for all of us.

The ordeal of getting their children dressed and ready in the morning in preparation for a busy schedule is a recurring nightmare for many parents. It is very difficult to dress a limp, completely passive child, and virtually impossible to dress one who is activity resisting. The problem is compounded when, in addition, parents are pressed by a variety of other agendas demanding their attention. Breakfast has to be served, other children usually need help, and lurking in the background is the pressure of deadlines. A husband must leave by 7:30 A.M., the little one has to be delivered to preschool, and an older child must catch the school bus at 8:00 A.M. In addition, the employment of many mothers contributes to the pressure to execute this activity efficiently.

The best and hoped for solution of this common nightmare will be the willingness and ability of the children to assume responsibility on their own. Unfortunately, this is a very gradual process and progress during the first five years may not be rapid. Our ultimate goal should nevertheless be kept in mind since there is much that can be done daily to nudge our children farther along the path to that destination. Earlier, parents helped them to gain ownership of their bodies, their mobility, and their feelings and thoughts. Now they are preparing their children to assume responsibility of the many other facets of their lives that are becoming increasingly complex.

It would be a dream come true if Sally found that nothing more was needed apart from pleasantly awakening the kids and reminding them to dress, eat breakfast, get their things together, and be ready for their transportation to school, but that will take considerable time to achieve. Both children are doing well, and their capacity for independent behavior has steadily improved. Food intake has been solely the children's responsibility for several years. With his mother's encouragement, Dan has been dressing and washing on his own for many months. He basks in his mother's approval and takes personal pride in his many new accomplishments. On many mornings, only minimal help from his mother is needed for him to complete most of his morning activities and be ready on time to leave the house. But there is still a streak of more infantile thinking that sometimes comes to the surface in Dan, a trend that remains in all of us in various degrees.

Today is one of those days. Dan is cranky and noncompliant. He has all the skills needed to dress, toilet, eat, and be ready on time without his mother's help. But today, he has a bit more of the "Mommy needs to do everything for me" feeling that was far more common two years earlier. Sally has been pleased with his overall progress, but is also fully prepared for these inevitable regressive episodes. She knows what she needs to do to get the job done and is also aware of her very important long-term goal, the emergence of a self-sufficient, responsible person who no longer needs even occasional doses of baby care and love.

She begins by using a verbal approach that on this day is unlikely to be successful. Helping Dan to develop the capacity to reflect upon his actions will nudge him upwards on the path towards mature functioning, so Sally often verbalizes both his feelings and her expectation. She might say, "Sometimes it is hard to get up in the morning and you would like

Mommy to dress you. Mommy loves you very much and wants you to learn to do these things for yourself. I'll put your clothing out so that you can dress yourself." Sometimes this is all that is needed for Dan to take responsibility for completing the task, but Sally is prepared to deal with continued noncompliance or whining.

If this occurs she has several strategies she can employ, depending upon the situation. On days when there are no deadlines for Sally or Dan, she might place dressing into the category of "desirable" rather than "necessary" and say, "When you get dressed, I'll give you breakfast." Or if Dan is looking forward to playing outdoors, she might say, "When you get dressed, we'll be able to go outside and play." These are not meant to be punitive or manipulative maneuvers, but are the most reasonable, available alternatives. Sally is adhering to the most basic principle of parenting. She is combining love with reasonable decision making. If Sally uses this approach, she must accept the possibility that Dan will remain in his pajamas and forego breakfast for many hours. During this period of prolonged delay she remains loving but does not give him what he wants, his mother's care on his terms.

Obviously this option is not viable on days with deadlines such as school for Dan or an appointment for his mother. For working mothers it is never an option. Today Sally has to leave the house at 8:30 A.M. and Dan has shown no inclination to cooperate. Dan is at his worst. His response to her insightful comment is a grumble accompanied by a scowl. Sally knows that further attempts to reason or cajole him will be exercises in futility, so she calmly tells him that they must leave the house at 8:30 A.M. She returns to his room periodically to check on his progress and remind him of the passing time. She is pleasantly supportive of any efforts he has made. Dan was awakened at 7:30 A.M. At 8:00 A.M. she finds him on his bed playing with his toes. She takes out some of his clothing for him and leaves once again, explaining that they must leave the house at 8:30 A.M.. At 8:15 A.M. he has his top off, but is playing with his favorite toy. His mother says, "Dan, you must be ready to leave the house by eight-thirty." She is communicating the concept of time while avoiding a confrontation. When Sally returns at 8:20 A.M. Dan is only half dressed, unwashed, and has not eaten. Sally calmly tells him that it is time to leave; she selects his clothing, and with friendly firmness escorts him to the front door. She tells him that it is necessary to complete the process of dressing so that they will be able to leave on time. She will listen to what Dan may say but will not argue, reprimand, use the threat of punishment, or an actual punitive action to gain his compliance.

If Dan still resists there are two options. She might elect to dress him, regardless of his efforts to resist. This may prove difficult and often requires physically overpowering a young child, a tactic usually best avoided whenever possible. The other choice is to explain that they must leave and if Dan is not dressed his mother will need to place both him and his clothing in the car, adding that he will have to dress sometime during or after they arrive at their destination. It would be extremely unusual for children this age to elect going out to meet the public half-dressed.

When parents are calm and kind, but firm, I have generally found that children will finally, usually begrudgingly, do the appropriate thing. We should never discount our children's capacity for better judgment as well as their pride in achievement. In the end, the trend towards adaptive behavior will win out, unless parents make the mistake of too frequently entangling these episodes with emotionally charged confrontations.

Chapter 10

GETTING A HEAD START FOR ENTRY INTO SCHOOL

Question – What can I do to help my child to be able to adjust to and profit from school? Of all the roles he will need to assume, this is the most important.

At the present time this issue leads the list of concerns among the American public. We place a premium on education, which is entirely justified. The quality of our children's educational experience does play a central role in determining their success as adults. In most discussions about how this can be achieved, lip service is paid to the importance of the parents but then the focus is shifted towards the educational process itself. Few real gains have been accomplished in spite of the tremendous amounts of time, effort, and money already spent. There has been any number of theories about the underlying problems, and all have a bit of validity. Some correlation can be shown between the educational outcome for children and certain societal and economic conditions, school programs, and the quality of teachers. But many exceptions are always evident. Many kids who seem to have all the educational advantages do poorly, and others fare well in spite of the cards that are stacked against them. The theories themselves are inadequate since they show correlations between a variety of external conditions and educational outcomes, but fail to adequately explain how these conditions actually influence children's acquisition of knowledge. For example, the link between poverty and lower achievement has been pointed out repeatedly, but the actual mechanisms that account for the correlation is never delineated. And why do some children from poor homes do well?

Addressing external factors leads us away from asking the crucial questions. **What is happening in the minds of children who thrive in school, and how does this differ from the process of thinking in children who fail to learn? Or more specifically, how are the minds of children from certain homes or certain types of classrooms influenced, so that one group does well and another does poorly?**

As I have repeatedly emphasized, problem solving must begin by understanding what is happening in children's minds. Any improvement in school readiness entails salutary changes in children's thinking. Unfortunately most parenting techniques, as well as educational policies, tend to jump directly from the recognition of a problem to a solution, leaving out this crucial first step. They neglect to ask the key question: How must we influence a child's thinking to help him improve his performance in school? This simple exercise of thinking before acting usually helps to lift the curtain of ignorance, and leads to solutions that are closer to the target rather than ones whose only merit was that they were well-intended. Just as love must be combined with wisdom for it to be altruistic love, good intentions must also be combined with wisdom for a better educational outcome.

Understanding the mental requirements for a good adjustment in school

Question – What do I need to understand in order to help my children prepare for their school experience?

In order to succeed in school, children need to have a variety of developmental skills. I will list them briefly, but they have been thoroughly detailed in the preceding chapters of this book. Children who have successfully mastered the first four developmental hurdles will do well in school. It's that simple.

1. Good bonding lays the groundwork for an inner core of contentment that is the foundation of self-esteem.
2. Children who reach school age and are still excessively dependent upon their parents cannot function well in a setting that requires hours of separation from loved ones.

3. Learning to get along when they don't get their way is an obvious prerequisite for school. Many children are classified as hyperactive when they enter school. They can't sit still, they talk out of turn, and they are unable to learn. Other kids who can't cope with frustration tune out in class. Giving kids like these labels is not enough. They need to be helped to acquire the skills they should have learned during the earlier years of their development.

4. The development of autonomy is essential for learning. Children who have not acquired confidence in their ownership of their bodies, thoughts, feelings, and actions will not do well in the educational environment.

5. During the years immediately preceding the start of formal education, children are acquiring a variety of skills and personality attributes that will allow them to function well in school. The quality of parenting, the models presented by their parents, as well as the overt and coded messages transmitted to the children by their parents, combine to influence the outcome.

If parents of a newborn voiced a concern about the future educational adjustment of their child, my answer would be simple and encouraging. I would begin by commending them for such foresight and then say that baring the unexpected, they have it completely within their power to guarantee their child the gift of being able to fulfill his academic potential. I would explain that the quality of their parenting and their love will be the key factors in their child's success. Then I would add that there are a series of developmental hurdles that all children encounter. Understanding these and helping their child to negotiate them successfully is the only prescription for a favorable outcome. **The efforts made during this entire formative developmental process are the best guarantees of success upon entry into school.**

All this is straightforward, but is rarely mentioned or given much thought. Our focus is drawn to concerns about the quality of our schools but overlooks the preparation needed for successful entry into school. It does not suffice for the public to be told merely that "parents should be involved." We need to be as specific about the needed developmental skills as we are about the educational ones. This is the real head start that gives kids a boost that lasts. This brand of head start will guarantee that they remain ahead, since it is not a superficial effort pasted on to the surface of a personality lacking a strong foundation. A "village" cannot provide this head start. Only parents can make this contribution to their children and it needs to be given during the first time around, during the formative years of their kid's lives.

Question – I understand the importance of the mastery of early developmental hurdles, but is it sensible to also provide actual assistance?

Many concerned parents work with their children to help them succeed at school. This is entirely appropriate and should be encouraged. But parents must not view this as their primary mission. Children who have mastered the early developmental hurdles will do well in school even if they are raised in homes with parents who have no education of their own and spend little if any time with them on educational pursuits. They will do well even if they seem to be behind when they enter school. Many of our greatest minds and highest achievers have fallen into this category. On the other hand, kids who have fallen behind developmentally will often find the task of learning insurmountable. It is exceedingly difficult to teach reading to an immature youngster who has not learned to get along when he is not being gratified.

In my emphasis on the mastery of developmental hurdles, it was not my intention to negate the usefulness of parents' educational involvement with their children. I was pointing out the importance of keeping priorities clear. The basic tools necessary for success at school cannot be obtained from early tutoring. Frequently, parents who are interested in introducing their children to learning at an early age are the same ones whose kids also develop mature coping skills. These parents accomplish their educational goals precisely because they have helped their children to master developmental hurdles. Reading and tutoring their children was an additional arena for them to provide more of the love, stimulation, and structure that their kids had been receiving since birth.

Other parents who value education but spend little or no time engaged in actual early tutoring are not neglecting their children's preparation for education if they have provided what is needed to build a stable personality. The learning most crucial to later success has been occurring day by day as children are being helped to successfully negotiate developmental hurdles. These precious moments pass quickly and can be easily overlooked. The learning deficiencies that arise as a consequence are usually very hard to reverse.

The two guidelines for successful entry into school

The first guideline is the mastery of early developmental hurdles. The second guideline has been implied but not yet spelled out clearly: Parents need to place a high value on education.

The reader, by now, is clear that the focus of this book is on the importance of developmental hurdles. The success of this gradual process is what leads to the acquisition of the skills and other attributes children must have to profit from and enjoy the formal educational experience that begins upon their entry into school. The following is a brief description of why these skills are so essential.

Dan has begun school

Dan is now age six and has just entered first grade. Sally is gratified that he is happy and enthusiastic when she picks him up at the end of the school day. After several days of school, his class is introduced to reading. Having mastered early developmental hurdles, Dan is well-prepared to learn.

As the teacher begins to articulate reading instructions to the children, Dan has no problem paying attention. We may take this seemingly simple task for granted, but there are many children, as well as adults, who do not fare as well. Considerable maturation is required for its implementation. Children who are deficient at getting along when they are not obtaining external gratification will do poorly. They will be easily distracted, daydream, or move about, often to the point of being a disruptive influence in the class.

Dan has not seen his mother for several hours, but can remain focused on his teacher's words because he is no longer afraid of being alone. Less mature children still experience loneliness, fear, and helplessness that dramatically erodes the level of their attention and, ultimately, their capacity to learn.

As Dan sits quietly in class he is bombarded by all kinds of stimuli, internal as well as external. While he listens to his teacher, Dan has many fleeting thoughts and urges. He has learned to control these and express them appropriately, so he automatically dismisses them from his mind. Other less-mature children are distracted and disturbed. Their poorly controlled thoughts, often distorted ones, impinge upon their awareness and take their attention away from the lesson.

Dan was gradually introduced to boundaries by his parents, so he is well equipped to cope in the classroom. Classroom discipline demands the acquiescence to a large number of boundaries. There are rules to follow that often collide with urges and fantasies. Contacts with others, both verbal and physical, are dramatically restricted. Approval and love are not available and tasks must be undertaken regardless of feelings that might have diverted him in the past.

Dan's mastery of early hurdles allows him to sit quietly, listen, and assimilate his teacher's instructions. We should not underestimate the importance of this attribute and the many small steps taken to reach it.

Dan is also eager to learn. He has learned to appreciate the value, importance, and joy of learning from his parents.

POINTS TO REMEMBER

- Helping children to progress through the earlier stages of development is the best way to guarantee that they will have a successful entry into school. This process begins at birth.

- Parents must also encourage an interest in reading, engage in their own enjoyment and involvement in education, and pursue countless other opportunities to instill in their children the capacity and interest to learn.

- Without a solid personality foundation, these additional efforts may fall short.

CHAPTER 11

THE ROLE OF PLAY

Play has an important role during this period. It helps children to adjust to new demands and learn new roles.

Question – I am surprised to hear that. How is play helpful to children's development? If it is, are there certain types of play we should encourage and other types that are not constructive?

Everyone knows that kids enjoy playing and that they need to be allowed time to play. Most are not aware of the importance of play in their children's development. "All work and no play make Jack a dull boy," has implications far wider than those usually considered. For adults, it is often a coveted period of respite from the more important and often stressful activities in their lives. And for kids it is viewed as the pleasurable but unproductive way they occupy free time, until they have developed the skills to engage in more useful activities.

Children do enjoy play. But play is also an important adjunct to their developmental progress. **At each age, it affords a vehicle that helps them to grapple with and solve developmental problems.** Some of the characteristic forms of early play and their purposes have already been mentioned. Very early in life, games such as peek-a-boo and playing with pull toys help children to master the problem of people coming and then disappearing. The endless activities of two-year-olds, who are pushing and pulling and climbing and falling, help them to develop a sense of autonomy and begin to make sense of and master the external world.

As children move into their fourth year of life, a new and very special dimension is added to their play. If children are developing normally, it is during this period that they acquire the capacity to use symbols to represent the various important components of their world. Up until age three, children's play is uncomplicated and reflects their efforts to cope with and master their world. Usually by age three they are acquiring the capacity to use symbols to represent people and events, as well as their feelings. This is quickly incorporated into their play, which becomes much more imaginative.

The use of symbols is a universal and integral part of our lives. Most forms of art derive their power by conveying themes symbolically that reach us on an emotional level. The meanings of some symbols are obvious. For example, the flag represents our nation and its sight may stir patriotic feelings. The link between object and symbol may be more disguised or totally obscured, for example, a storm representing anger, or a giant the father.

Imaginative play using symbols becomes an important vehicle for children, helping them grapple with and solve new developmental problems. By weaving symbols into imaginative play, children are able to express and gain some mastery over the array of very painful problems they are facing in their real world. Inner struggles, fears, and other hurts can be elaborated in a disguised, and therefore safe, form.

Each day, our very small and helpless children experience events that hurt them deeply. They experience repeated humiliations that crush their fragile self-esteem and anger that threatens to overturn their emotional balance. Playing these incidents out in imaginative play, using symbols, provides an opportunity for relief and mastery. We all feel better about our lives and ourselves when the home team wins, even though we know that the sporting event has no relation to our personal lives. It is not hard to understand the sense of glee and mastery when, in our child's play, the main character acquires super strength and can overwhelm his seemingly invincible adversaries. Or when, at a later age, he discovers an imaginary super laser and can become master of the world.

Having this capacity handy serves children well at a time in their lives that they are on an emotional roller coaster. Before they acquired this symbolizing ability they were easily overwhelmed by the upsetting incidents that were part of their daily lives. As a consequence, their behavior would deteriorate. This is especially problematic for children during a period of their lives when it is essential that they learn a variety of social skills before entry into school. Symbolic play affords them an escape valve to dismantle and discharge their hurts so that their behavior is not so adversely affected.

Question – Are you suggesting that imaginary play is useful and should be encouraged?

Yes, without this knowledge parents may subtly or overtly disapprove, or actually interfere with, their children's imaginary play. In children deprived of this outlet, uncomfortable feelings may quickly mount and sabotage their functioning. **Play allows these tensions to be dismantled and discharged, and supplies a new arena for learning, one that encourages the use of abstract and often creative thinking.**

Dan was four. He generally liked Sundays because he was able to do special things with his father. He was disappointed to discover that this Sunday was not living up to his expectations. His father was busily involved with pressing office work and had no time for him. Hoping to engage his father, he repeatedly interrupted the work, eliciting fairly curt responses. His mother was busy with his little sister, leaving him feeling put down and overlooked. When his father ordered him out of the room one more time, he was really peeved. He was tempted to kick something, preferably something that was important to his father. When he was younger, he might have given vent to his anger, but now he fled to his room and took out his toy figures. In the play that followed his favorite character he called Dinosaur Man battled the evil giants. At first they threatened to get the best of Dinosaur Man, but his superior strength won out in the end and the evil giants were systematically defeated.

Had we observed his play, we might have noted that at this point in his life he was fascinated with large creatures, such as sharks, whales, and dinosaurs. We would also have discovered that he enjoyed making up stories of how they roam the world, conquering all competitors.

During Dan's play he was completely unaware of the link between the figures in the play and real people and actual experiences. This kind of play was a vehicle that provided relief from the actual hurts and having this outlet made it easier for him to adjust in the real and often difficult world of people. Many adults are able to achieve similar relief from the cares of their every day world through theatre, literature, and other institutions sanctioned by society that serve a similar purpose.

This form of play also helps children to learn to use their imaginations in problem solving and exploring new roles in a safe arena. During imaginary play, they are able to take the role of the make-believe characters. This allows them to test out a variety of roles and solutions to problems without any of the possible untoward real-life consequences. At many later stages in life, children, and later adults, may continue to use this capacity to imagine different roles in preparation for an anticipated change in their lives. This very special skill, the ability to think about an array of solutions often very abstractly combined with the new symbolizing abilities, enhances adaptation and is the source of so much of our creative and innovative efforts. It evolves normally in the minds of three- to five-year-olds and should be nurtured.

Question – Are there some children who fail to develop this symbolizing function?

The ability to play imaginatively constitutes a significant developmental landmark. Children who have not acquired this ability by their fourth or fifth year lack an important tool needed to help them maintain their emotional stability, learn new roles, and develop important educational skills. There are essentially two reasons why some children are not using imaginary play by five years of age.

The capacity for abstract thinking and the use of imagination and symbols are not created out of thin air. They require the mastery of earlier developmental hurdles. For example, learning that a parent exists and that one is loved even when the parent is not actually present is perhaps the first and most important abstraction learned, and may be the prototype for those that follow. I have found that children who have not mastered separation problems, and certainly children who have not bonded adequately, are saddled with deficits in their capacity to use abstract thinking in addition to their other emotional handicaps. Their play is often devoid of the elaborate and rich fabrications of make-believe evident in children whose development has proceeded normally.

Some children have the ability to play imaginatively, but fail to do so. Their symbolizing capacities have been overwhelmed by the intensity of their feelings. As a consequence their ability to play out their problems becomes blocked. Like a deluge of water bursting through a dam, these powerful feelings press for direct expression and emerge in the form of disruptive behavior.

Question – What might I do if my child is not playing imaginatively?

The first step is to check to make sure that you, the parents, are not discouraging this type of play. Parents sometimes wonder why their children love to hear certain stories over and over again, or repeatedly play a make-believe theme. They may sometimes be tempted to censor these stories or patterns of play because of their own biases. Grimm's fairy tales, for example, may seem grim to parents, but children through the centuries have enjoyed them and many other similar stories. The explanation for their importance in the early development of children should now be apparent and they need to be encouraged by parents.

Next, parents should look for possible external factors that might have elevated feelings to a level too high to be successfully channeled through play. In homes with inadequate boundaries, tensions reach such high levels that the kids are not able to use their symbolizing skills. Their safety valve is overwhelmed and cannot work properly. This can be easily remedied by the introduction of appropriate boundaries.

Finally, they might think about their child's overall development, to determine if there are indications of residual problems left over from earlier developmental hurdles. The signs and symptoms pointing to poor mastery of early developmental hurdles are not hard to discern for parents armed with a framework for understanding developmental hurdles. These kids are usually encountering a wide spectrum of difficulties left over from an earlier stage. These should be addressed, the sooner the better.

POINTS TO REMEMBER

- Parents often assume that play is a frivolous activity, but they are entirely wrong about this.

- Play allows children to develop mastery and control of their bodies early in life.

- At each stage, play affords a vehicle that helps children to grapple with and solve developmental problems.

- As children become older, imaginative play allows then to dismantle tensions and supplies a new arena for learning, one that encourages the use of abstract and often creative thinking.

Chapter 12

IMAGINARY FEARS – NEW ROLES ARE OFTEN ACCOMPANIED BY NEW PROBLEMS

Question – My four-year-old has developed imaginary fears that I had not noticed before. What does this mean?

Higher levels of frustration will often overwhelm even normal, well-adjusted children of this age and their behavior will take a turn for the worse. This is what accounts for their typical ups and downs. As long as the downs are not severe, their level of adaptation will remain acceptable. Let's take a closer look at what may happen in children as the buildup of tension reaches higher levels and threatens to overwhelm their defenses and disrupt their functioning. Children who are loved want desperately to behave, so they struggle to control this buildup of frustration. By dint of considerable effort and many new skills, their outward behavior remains acceptable but they are left with a bundle of very unpleasant feelings. These feelings, often angry ones, remain just below the surface. The threat of them erupting creates considerable discomfort in children eager to please. What can kids of this age do to help hold these feelings in check? Children between ages three and five commonly resort to a mechanism not available before. When it works well it is extremely useful and allows children to maintain their emotional equilibrium. But when it is overloaded it may lead to the typical array of fears we find in kids this age.

In the preceding chapter I defined this mechanism, the use of symbols to express feelings, events, and people. I also pointed out its value to children in providing them with an effective way to deal with unwanted feelings. Children learn to dissipate their buildup of feelings through imaginative play. During this play they remove the frustration and anger from themselves and use other people and objects, both real and imaginary, to symbolically represent these disturbing emotions. They are now temporarily freed from the discomfort caused by those feelings; so far so good. This device works smoothly most of the time, but not always. Feelings may become so powerful that this mechanism breaks down. If this happens, some of the original unpleasant feelings that had been successfully disguised in the form of symbols emerge in their original threatening form. Children are able to divest themselves of this burden by pasting it on to animals, other people, noises, or anything else that will serve this purpose.

The child now has a new problem, tainted by unwanted feelings, an entity in his external world that was previously innocuous seems ominous and threatening. The child no longer feels discomfort because of what was within or of the real people in his world. But he soon discovers a new source of discomfort, the persons and things both real and imaginary that he has designated to be the recipients of those feelings. Instead of being afraid of becoming angry with his mommy, or afraid of her, he now finds that he has become afraid of the things that represent that danger. These could be anything, monsters, ghosts, the boogie man, dogs, noises, darkness, or anything else that is compatible for this exchange.

Old problem, different cause

Sally was sure that she would never again hear Dan say that he needed his mom to be with him at night. He had mastered separation anxiety much earlier, so she was surprised when, at age four, he once again voiced fear about being left alone in his room at night. He begged his mother to stay longer after being tucked in. Sally was willing to linger a bit longer but then left, knowing that remaining would foster helplessness and lend weight to his fears. She also knew that he was fully capable of being by himself. He had been having no problems separating at preschool. In fact, his teacher noted that he was one of the more independent and self-sufficient youngsters in the group.

After his mother left his room Dan pulled the covers tightly around him and murmured, "There really is nothing scary in the closet." But then he heard a noise and was not so sure.

Parenting guidelines for the typical fears of children between ages three and five

Question – I now understand what these types of fears represent. How should they be handled?

Fears, and for that matter problems, generally cannot be tackled reasonably without understanding their cause. Parents need to remind themselves that fears during this period nearly always begin with the presence of disturbing thoughts in their children's minds. Our long-term goal must be to influence how our child learns to handle those thoughts, rather than attempting to provide some kind of external solution. Without this insight parents may lose their patience or attribute the fears to some kind of external stimulus. Under the pressure of wanting to do something, they often detect a recent event that seemed to be excessively upsetting to their child. Trivial events, such as a stranger at the front door, a dog's loud barking, or a scary television program may seem to be associated with the onset or intensification of these fears.

These events may be linked to the fears but are rarely their primary cause. Children use them as symbols to represent something inside that is much more frightening, and from which there is no escape. These are the unwanted feelings and the ideas that are attached to those feelings. Reassurance referenced to the external source, or an attempt to eliminate the source from the child's life, is an exercise in futility since the actual basis of the fear comes from within.

Therefore, the parents' primary objective must once again be aimed at helping their children master the appropriate developmental hurdles. Learning to get along when they don't get their way renders anger more manageable and less apt to be entwined with distorted perceptions. If this progress is impeded, feelings will remain a source of extreme discomfort and may spill over in the form of fears.

Question – You have once again emphasized the long-term goal but have not addressed how I might respond to my very anxious child; are there guidelines for this?

Avoiding catching the crisis

Children who have developed an imaginary fear are already very uncomfortable with their heightened feelings. Anything that parents do that may tend to intensify feelings would be expected to strengthen the fear. The most common trap that parents fall into is responding to their child's fear with anxiety and fear of their own. Many parents find it hard to remain calm and confident in the face of a terrified child. The second trap is losing patience and becoming irritated.

Infectious diseases aren't the only things that are contagious. Emotional unrest and the distorted perceptions that accompany them spread just as easily from one person to the other. And the damage done by this contamination is often longer lasting than the bacterial variety. Children are very disturbed by their fears. Parents become confused and anxious when their efforts to provide relief are to no avail. At this point the parents' responses, prodded by their emotional blisters, may compound their child's dilemma. The best defense, probably the only defense, against becoming part of the problem rather than a catalyst in its remedy is knowledge. Let's see how Dan's mother handles the issue.

Dan had recently begun to complain at bedtime that he was afraid that the thing in the closet will get him. Sally has listened to his concerns calmly in spite the obvious distress he feels at these times. Understanding the meaning of his fear, she is well aware that her loss of patience or irritation would escalate his distress and, in Dan's imagination, make her seem similar to "the scary thing in the closet." She is fully confident that Dan will soon master the struggle he is having with his feelings and knows that her attitude will help to him to progress.

It has been fairly simple for her to decode Dan's fear that the thing will get him. What has actually generated his fear is a scary force within him that he is afraid might come out. This might be the anger he feels towards his parents when he does not get his way and the thoughts that are associated with these feelings. He has made gains in controlling them but they still seem very powerful and intimidating to him. When he was younger, they were too much for him to keep in check and they emerged in the form of disruptive behavior. Now at age four, when feelings are intense, some seep out and he gets rid of them by pasting them on to external objects. This is what accounts for his fears. If his mother lost her patience and became irritated or upset, his own unwieldy feelings would become even more unmanageable and his fear of "the scary thing in the closet" would be strengthened.

The imaginary fears of childhood are benign and represent part of the normal developmental process. They linger on when they are reinforced by misguided parental responses. The impact that childhood fears will have upon later life, like so much of the behavior and struggles of early development, will depend upon the parents and the emotional climate in the home

Question — You are recommending patience and understanding, suggesting that these fears will disappear as the children master developmental hurdles. Is there more that we can do to speed the process?

When their kid develops new fears, parents are well advised to assess the tenor of their recent interactions with their child. They should be on the lookout for any trends of increased confrontations or other recurrent situations that ignited their child's anger. If they review these objectively, they will see how frightening this may have appeared from their child's perspective. Angry, threatening parents loom large and powerful to little kids who feel weak and helpless. It is not hard to account for the fear this engenders in them, or the real identity of the scary thing in the closet that may come out and get them.

Indulgent responses are also contraindicated. For example, it would be a mistake if Sally decided to take Dan into bed with her to quell his fears. This would provide temporary relief for both of them. Dan's mother would no longer be required to contend with a panicked child and Dan, snuggling next to his mother, would feel temporarily protected from the scary thing in the closet. The problem with this solution is obvious. This type of parenting would support Dan's belief that his fears were justified and that he did not have the capacity to master them.

Explaining the difference between the real and the imagined – A very gradual process

This evening, ten minutes after Dan is tucked in for the night, he comes bounding into the his parents' bedroom. He has a look of alarm and he quickly blurts out that he is escaping from "that thing in the closet." She gives him a big hug, and then, after listening to him for a few moments escorts him calmly back to his room. She lingers for a while, talking to him and then says, "Sometimes your scary feelings seem real. If you are very afraid again, come knock on my door and I'll give you another tuck in." Sally has repeatedly discussed the concepts of imagination and exaggeration with him during the day, making it a bit easier for him to understand her present comments. Dan has heard his mother's explanation of the difference between real and make believe many times. This is helpful to him and strengthens his reality testing. During the daylight hours these comments make sense and he is able to see that the interior of his closet contains only familiar possessions. But at night the power of his frightening thoughts and feelings may still get the best of him. We will need to wait a bit longer for the fear to completely evaporate. That will happen as he becomes more comfortable with anger and confident about his ability to express it more appropriately.

With each passing day, Dan is getting closer to this goal. Feelings of helplessness and excessive dependency upon his parents, such a prominent part of his earlier life, are already receding. He is becoming more adept at getting along when he does not get his way. As a consequence his anger is more manageable. With the increasing mastery of developmental hurdles he will soon reach a level of maturity that will obviate his need to use fears to deal with bottled up feelings. His mother is helping to accomplish this. In addition she is strengthening his ability to separate real from make believe.

Points to Remember

- Imaginary fears are common among children between the ages of four and five.

- Although sometimes precipitated by actual events, imaginary fears nearly always represent some underlying thought, usually linked to a problem with which the child is struggling that is much more frightening.

- These underlying problems are often unwanted feelings and the ideas that are attached to these feelings.

- Most fears will gradually evaporate in homes with responsive and loving parents who help their children to successfully negotiate developmental hurdles.

- If fears are intense or persist, parents should reflect upon the tenor of their current responses to ferret out those that may be elevating their children's anger or anxiety.

- The imaginary fears of childhood are nearly always benign, but may linger on when reinforced by misguided parental responses.

Chapter 13

LEARNING VALUES

Lying – Stealing – Cheating

Question – There are so many important values that I want my child to have. What can I do during the time I have available to influence this important part of his character development? Earlier you emphasized that this can't be accomplished successfully unless a strong personality foundation is in place. My child has been doing well. Earlier developmental hurdles have been mastered, but he still lies. Are there guidelines that will be helpful to me?

Character is generally evaluated by behavior. But behavior that appears reasonable superficially may be motivated by a wide variety of impulses. Many of these are not praiseworthy. Since all behavior emanates from underlying motivations, it is the quality of an individual's motivations that defines his character. Motivations are synonymous with values. Parents need to be reminded repeatedly that values can only be built on a foundation of maturity. They cannot be superficially stamped onto children who have not successfully negotiated the early developmental hurdles. The minds of individuals whose parents helped them to acquire a strong basic personality foundation are well suited to appreciate values and incorporate them into their behavior.

This process can usually begin in their fourth and fifth years of life. Before this, these abstract ideas have little real meaning. Right is whatever provides pleasure and wrong anything leading to distress. From the perspective of three-year-olds, right is obtaining the material and emotional supplies they demand. They would lie, steal, cheat, or use violence to get what they want, with hardly the slightest twinge of guilt or remorse. If little kids were suddenly placed into the bodies of adults they would be the scourges of the earth. Until the early developmental hurdles have been mastered, children are like drug addicts obsessed with only one goal, getting their fix. They will often do the right thing to please their parents upon whom they are still very dependent. But this has virtually nothing in common with real values.

None of this means that parents should not be thinking about and working towards helping their children acquire the important values that define good character during these earlier periods of development. Long before their kids will have the ability to assimilate these values, parents should speak about them and, of more importance, model them in their own lives. They must be aware, however, of the many small steps of development that must be taken before their children can be helped to assimilate values. Progress is not rapid and parents must be patient with repeated episodes of backsliding.

Dan, now nearly five years of age, was envious of his little brother's new set of blocks. His brother had just finished building a tower and was beaming with pride. Dan asked if he could also play with the blocks, and was immediately refused. When his brother left the room, Dan could not resist the temptation to pull out one of the supporting blocks. He watched with some satisfaction as the whole tower tumbled. Needless to say, upon returning his brother was anguished and ran squealing to their mother.

Upon entering the scene, Sally knew exactly what had happened. Dan looked squarely at his mother and said, "Mommy I didn't do it, it fell by accident." Many parents, who have little understanding of stages of thinking and developmental steps, are enraged by such acts of blatant lying. They respond by making comments such as, "I might tolerate many things but not lying to me," or, "Young man, you and I will stand right here until you confess and tell the truth." Other parents use a more direct approach, consisting of a swat on the rear and banishment to the child's room for a time out.

Sally does want to teach Dan the importance of honesty, but she knows that this process is gradual and there are many reasons that Dan is not yet ready. His mother understands his motivation for lying. At this point in his life, Dan's need for his mother's approval is a very powerful and he is willing to fabricate in order to avoid incurring his mother's disappointment. Even his mother's repeated reassurances that it will be all right if he tells the truth could not eliminate this concern.

Sally does want to encourage honesty, but also knows that angrily accusing him of lying and demanding a truthful answer would not foster that outcome. She has confidence that he will learn to value honesty for its own sake when the developmental issues that stand in the way have been removed.

Knowing her goals and armed with an understanding of the developmental issues, Dan's mother says, "Dan, you are telling me that you did not knock over the blocks because it makes you feel bad when you think that you have done something that Mommy will not like. You broke the tower because you were angry that your brother had a new toy and would not let you play. Mommy loves you very much and wants to help you to be able to tell the truth."

Sally was able to emphasize the importance she places on honesty, but at the same time is able to unlink it from her approval or love. Too many children reach adulthood believing that honesty has value only when it is likely to garner love or approval or to avoid disapproval. Sadly, we are all aware how often our political leaders fall into this category. Sally was also able to understand and possibly help Dan to appreciate the feelings that prompted his lie. By avoiding making Dan feel even more humiliated and angry, she is helping to make it a bit easier for him to tell the truth the next time.

I am not suggesting that Sally's words are a formula to be used in cookbook style to respond to lying. I am once again emphasizing the importance of using knowledge about developmental issues and skill levels to forge parenting techniques that will lead to higher levels of maturity.

Similar considerations should enter into the strategies that parents use to respond to stealing or cheating. Young children steal or cheat for the same reasons that they lie. They are often not able to get along when they don't get what they want, and at these times their perceptions of people and events are nearly always distorted. They genuinely believe that they have been mistreated and feel justified in obtaining compensation by whatever means available. As children learn to tolerate frustration and to interpret the events that precipitate these feelings more appropriately their capacity to assimilate values becomes enhanced. Parents need to be reminded that their goals extend beyond the confines of compliant behavior. They are attempting to influence thinking and instill values. Punishments that intensify anger and reinforce distorted perceptions of being mistreated are obviously counterproductive.

Dan's little brother accompanied their father to the store, while Dan remained at home. In addition to having the pleasure of being alone with Daddy on this outing, Dan's brother returned with a treat of several balloons. Upon arriving home he made sure Dan would see his new trophies. As expected, Dan was green with envy. When his brother set them down Dan quickly absconded with the red one. His brother protested vociferously when he spotted what had transpired, quickly bringing the incident to his father's attention.

After surveying the scene, his father responded by saying, "Dan, I know that you are unhappy and angry because your brother went out with me and came home with balloons and you did not get any. You know that there will be so many times that you will not get what you want. Next week you will get a turn. But now the balloons belong to your brother and you will have to give the balloon back him. Its wrong to take things that don't belong to you"

If Dan had been lectured or punished, his anger would have escalated and this might have reinforced the distorted perception that fueled his actions – his flawed belief that his brother was favored and that he was justified in believing he had been mistreated.

Guidelines

Parents are the ones responsible for the transmission of values to their children. They need to clarify their own values and elaborate them in their daily lives. Children nearly always emulate what we are, or our character, rather than becoming what we tell them they should be.

Values cannot be assimilated unless the early developmental hurdles have been successfully negotiated.

As children develop the mental ability to understand the concept of values, their importance should be communicated to children by their parents. This should be done in a manner commensurate with their level of mental and emotional development.

Emphasis needs to be placed on helping children to understand the intrinsic importance of values. This is done by gradually unlinking their acquisition from emotional agendas, including approval, love, disapproval, or fear. During their early years of life, nearly everything children do is motivated by their need for love and attention. In order for children to become self-motivated, this equation must gradually change. This was addressed fully in part four. Motivations based on the need for approval, or worse the fear of disapproval, will inevitably become less effective as children begin to negotiate the problems of adolescence and the external influence of parents rapidly wanes.

If the job is done effectively during the formative first five years, parents can be less concerned about the possible deleterious influences of "the peer group" or a "permissive culture." Our older youngsters cannot be protected from either of these. But if they are armed with a solid foundation, neither is likely to do any harm.

Chapter 14

TELEVISION AND LITTLE CHILDREN

Question — I have heard so much about the influences that television may have on children. Can you clarify this issue so we can be more confident about our decisions?

As you will soon see, I am not an advocate of allowing children to watch more than very limited amounts of television. Nevertheless, it is important to begin by stating what common sense makes obvious. Television does not create disturbed kids. The etiology of the array of problems that children acquire has been addressed. These begin early and include factors that interfere with bonding, the acquisition of trust, the ability to control and express feelings, and the acceptance of boundaries. The hardwiring built into the brain before birth certainly plays a role, but the outcome of development is mainly influenced by the daily interplay between parents and child. The impact of any exposure that young children have to violence on television pales in comparison to the manifestations of immature anger, hate, and actual violence displayed by their parents. Television does not produce apathetic, listless children who can't learn. These characteristics emerge in homes of parents disinterested in their kids and who fail to provide adequate amounts of attention and stimulation.

Violence, disruptive behavior, unhappiness, and the inability to learn, all existed long before there was television. And if with the rising sun of the next day, televisions were suddenly eliminated from every home, these problems would not gradually disappear. There are many children who watch a great deal of television and do very well, and many kids who rarely watch television and do poorly. It is doubtful that there was ever a child anywhere whose problems could be attributed to television. This is not to say that watching television plays a constructive role in the education and development of young children; generally it does not. There is a danger, however, in placing it high on the list of evil influences on our youth. Doing this makes it easier to divert attention from the number one category on the list – parental behavior.

The notion that the content of television programs can make deep and lasting impressions on the personality structure of children is naïve. This makes it easier to avoid thinking about the daily events and interactions that do make lasting impressions on children's lives. It is not television that subjects impressionable young children to models of anger and violence that may distort their development. It is the attitudes and behavior of their own parents as they interact with them and with each other. Mothers angry at fathers and getting revenge, fathers angry at mothers and getting revenge, and finally, children getting angry and using whatever pathetic devices they have at their disposal for revenge.

There may be times when children prone to violence will emulate something they see on television, or when television violence may fuel these children into action. The cause of their aggression, however, is their immaturity and poor coping skills, never the television. Those who are violence prone will never lack models to emulate or reasons to justify their actions. Immature, impulse-ridden children and adults usually come from homes that contain parents with similar attributes. The recording apparatus in the minds of young children, who witness and are participants in the anger and violence that surround them at home, has a far more devastating effect than anything they may see on television.

It is certainly not good for young children to be propped in front of a television set for hours each day. But neither is it good for them to be left at a day care center at a young age, to be given pacifiers past their first year to quiet their unpleasant sounds, or to be ignored by parents who are discontent with their own lives. All of the above, including the television when used as a pacifier, are symptoms of a serious malady called parental neglect. Children who are spending many hours with the television acting as a daily babysitter may later manifest disturbed, even violent behavior. Many might claim that the blame should rest on the content of the television that was watched. That would be a description of only one part of what had happened. The other more important part, parental neglect and other forms of emotional and physical abuse, would have been overlooked.

Question – I am now able think about television watching more reasonably. But I am still not sure about the most favorable policy for children, especially younger ones. Are there guidelines that might be helpful?

Television and the programs broadcast have virtually nothing to do with the causes of children's problems. I would have no objection to a parental decision to have a television in the home or to a decision to eliminate it altogether. Nearly all families do elect to have television in their homes. When used appropriately television can, after all, provide a source of relaxation, information, and entertainment. In these homes parents need to formulate appropriate guidelines for its use.

I strongly favor children having minimum exposure during the period of development covered by this book, the first five years. My main objection to television during this period is its common use as a pacifier. The reasonable use of pacifiers during the early part of the first year of life can be justified since infants have few other ways to relieve the buildup of tension. Used after that period, pacifiers substitute for more constructive activities, especially those that entail loving and stimulating interactions with parents. Children soaking up television are generally not exercising their minds and are missing opportunities to acquire new skills. Allowing, and worse encouraging, excessive pacifier use is an indulgence and breeds apathetic, passive children.

There are television programs, although few in number, that may actually be appropriate for under-five-year-olds. The problem is that most families are not able to reasonably monitor television watching. It has an addictive quality for parents as well as kids. If families find this to be true they would be well advised to eliminate the television altogether or to keep it contained in the parents' bedroom and off-limits to the kids.

The guideline for television viewing for this age group is clear, the less the better. This is not because of any great fear of the deleterious content, especially if a modicum of reason is used when selecting programs suitable for very young children. The guideline, the less the better, follows from something that should be obvious to all of us. There are so many better alternatives. It is far more constructive for children to spend their time in activities that engage their minds and help them develop new skills.

There are television sets in the homes of nearly all the children who become mature, well-functioning adults. Sometimes television in these homes may be watched even more than I would ideally recommend. But in these homes, loving parents provide the love and attention their children require. These kids usually make steady progress on the path towards maturity in spite of the presence of the television.

A television tale

Gloria was three-and-one-half and was generally grumpy after getting out of bed in the morning. It was as if she greeted each day with a feeling of discontent and was saying to everyone, "I'm unhappy and it's your fault, no one is giving me what I need to be happy." Gloria's mother was not at all pleased with her daughter's attitude. And she resented this additional burden on top of everything else she had to do.

She directed Gloria to the television set and both were afforded temporary relief.

After breakfast, Gloria was dissatisfied with everything. She made unpleasant whiny sounds and grabbed at her mother's clothing, getting in the way of her mother's tasks.

Gloria's mother directed her to the television set and both were afforded temporary relief.

At lunch Gloria slopped her food, ate slowly, and complained that she did not like her lunch.

Her mother let her watch television during the meals and both were afforded temporary relief.

The late afternoons were terrible times with endless bickering between Gloria and her mother. Gloria refused to comply with even simple requests and made endless demands.

A solution was readily available. She was directed to the television set and both were afforded temporary relief.

After dinner, Gloria's parents decided that they deserved to have some time for themselves. Gloria made this nearly impossible by demanding their attention and creating a ruckus when she was displeased, which was most of the time.

The television was waiting and everyone was afforded temporary relief.

Five years later, Gloria was in school, but she had already fallen far behind. She was always bored and irritable.

There was no television available during the hours she spent in school but she was afforded temporary relief by tuning out and enjoying her fantasies.

CHAPTER 15

SUMMARY – ACQUIRING A SOCIAL IDENTITY – MOVING FORWARD

Mommy looked at Daddy and beamed. Daddy looked at Mommy and beamed. Dan looked at both of them and also felt very pleased. Today had been his first day at regular school and it had turned out very well. That morning was a bit scary for everyone. It was like exploring a new world. There had been so many questions about what it would be like. New demands would be placed on Dan and he would be away from his parents for many hours. What if he became lonely or needed help? A sea of unfamiliar faces would surround him. What if he embarrassed himself or did not fit in? He would have to adjust to a variety of new roles and know what to do in a variety of different situations. He would need to be able to sit still, listen, and follow instructions. He had practiced this before, but everyone knew that it would be harder now.

All this would mean that Dan was no longer the little boy whose world was confined to an orbit that revolved around his parents. He had often ventured out of that secure zone before, but always with the reassurance that he could quickly return. Now the dimensions of his world had dramatically expanded. Growing up required that this happen and they all knew that there was no returning to the world he was leaving.

The new world included the teacher and all the things that she would ask him to do. And there were so many new children. He needed to learn to fit in and be liked. Life was easier before he embarked upon this new experience. But he knew that he would always have a special place in his mommy and daddy's world and this bolstered his confidence.

Dan was moving forward, out of the small world of his home. He was taking his first steps in the direction of becoming a member of society. They all somehow knew this – Sally, Bob, and even Dan. It made them a bit uneasy and sad, but also excited and confident. Dan was prepared to move forward. He had successfully mastered the developmental hurdles of the first five years, and was ready for the ones that lie ahead. A wonderful time in their lives was coming to a close.

They might think about this time later, bringing to the surface of their minds nostalgic pleasant memories. But now they were very proud of what had been accomplished and were happily anticipating the tomorrows. They were ready to go forward.